MW01090204

The Batak

1 One of the *sibayak* of Kabanjahe, "Pa Mbelgah", with the skulls of his
parents and grandparents. Karo plateau, c. 1910

Living with Ancestors

THE BATAK

Peoples of the Island of Sumatra

Achim Sibeth

with contributions by
Uli Kozok and Juara R. Ginting

Thames and Hudson

First published in Great Britain in 1991
by Thames and Hudson Ltd, London

First published in the United States of America in
1991 by Thames and Hudson Inc., 500 Fifth Avenue,
New York · New York 10110

By arrangement with Edition Hansjörg Mayer, Stuttgart/London

Library of Congress Catalog Card Number: 90-71576

Printed and bound in Germany by Staib & Mayer, Stuttgart

Contents

2 Protective figures with holes for the *pupuk* magic mixture needed to make the figures effective. They stood on the gallery of a house. Toba region, c. 1930

Foreword and Acknowledgements

The Batak of northern Sumatra are one of largest and best known minorities in the multi-ethnic state of Indonesia. They number approximately 3 million, making them the fourth largest ethnic group (among the 300 different peoples of Indonesia) after the Javanese, Sundanese and Balinese. It is estimated that the total population of Indonesia is now about 180 million.

The Batak are a very dynamic and self confident people. Over the centuries they have been able to guard their homeland against intrusion by foreigners, and it is only in the last 100 years that their way of life and culture has undergone a great change under the impact of Christianity, Islam and colonialism. This development did not follow a uniform pattern. In different regions and different periods the Batak had very different experience of their neighbours and of foreign intrusion. The various foreign influences served to intensify the cultural variety of the six different Batak groups, and this can still be experienced today.

My Batak acquaintances often ask me what it is that I find so fascinating about them and their homeland, and why I return again and again to North Sumatra and Batakland. In the first place it is the great friendliness, openness and directness I have always found in my dealings with the Batak. In this respect they are very different from the Javanese, who usually show a very polite, almost artificial reserve, making it difficult to gain any real insight into their emotional life. Besides this there is the inner strength and dignity shown especially by the older Batak. On many occasions – not just at traditional ceremonies – one has the sense that the Batak still retain their ethnic and cultural identity, despite the many breaks in their tradition, caused by the irruption of the modern zeitgeist, which has sometimes been destructive. It is to be hoped that they will not allow themselves to be absorbed into a pan-Indonesian, national identity. At present both identities exist side by side with relatively few problems.

This book on the culture of the Batak appeared on the occasion of an exhibition held at the Linden-Museum Stuttgart, and was also shown at the Rijksmuseum voor Volkenkunde, Leiden, and at the Rautenstrauch-Joest-Museum, Cologne. The great majority of the objects illustrated are in the collection of the Linden-Museum and are published here for the first time. I regarded it as very important not to return to the major pieces that have already been published, but instead to concentrate on the collections of West Germany museums, which are still largely unknown but nevertheless of high quality, and of some private collectors.

The grouping of the material is primarily functional and I believe it gives a profound insight into the culture of the people who made and owned the objects. Because of the range of the material presented this grouping gives a better impression of the stylistic and formal variety of Batak art than photographs of individual items based on purely aesthetic considerations. The juxtaposition of historical and contemporary photographs of the country and its people was particularly important, and is intended to show how the life and culture of the Batak had changed since the first contacts with European missionaries.

A publication is always the product of a collaborative effort. In the first place I must mention my co-authors, Uli Kozok and Juara R. Ginting, with whom I have been linked for many years by a shared interest in research into Karo and Toba Batak culture. I give them special thanks for their spontaneous willingness to contribute to this publication.

My thanks also go to the Linden-Museum's photographer, Ursula Didoni, who, together with the photographic technician Karin Paulus, spent weeks taking studio photographs of the objects. I am also grateful to Christine Schreiber, Tübingen; Doris Gröpper, Berlin, and Mr van Rinsum of the photographic archive of the Tropenmuseum, Amsterdam, for making their contemporary and historical field photographs available for the publication.

I would like to offer my warm thanks to the many lenders whose generosity in allowing objects in their private collections to be exhibited and published has contributed considerably to the range of material shown here. I am grateful to G. Gempp (Stuttgart), A. Flick (Cologne), S. Eilenberg (London), F. Wohlgemuth (Leverkusen), and W. Pietsch (Leverkusen). For loans from the collections of various ethnographical museums I must thank Dr. G. Höpfner (Staatliche Museen Preussischer Kulturbesitz, Berlin), Dr. R. Schubert (Staatliches Museum für Völkerkunde, Munich), Dr. J. Agthe (Museum für Völkerkunde, Frankfurt am Main), Prof. G. Völger (Rautenstrauch-Joest-Museum, Cologne), and Drs. W. Kal and Drs. K. van Brakel (Tropenmuseum, Amsterdam).

I thank Prof. P. Thiele and Dr. G. Kreisel (Linden-Museum Stuttgart), Mrs. C. Schreiber (Tübingen) and Mrs. G. Schuster (Frankfurt) for reading the manuscript and making corrections. I am particularly grateful to the revered patriarch of batakology, Dr. Petrus Voorhoeve (Barchem), for his helpful comments, which have resulted in some corrections in this edition. I would like to thank the translator, Sebastian Wormell, for his speedy and conscientious work and outstanding sensitivity for the subject matter and style of the book. To the publisher Hansjörg Mayer (Stuttgart and London) I owe a special debt of thanks for his willingness to accept the high level of risk associated with such publications and for making this book possible.

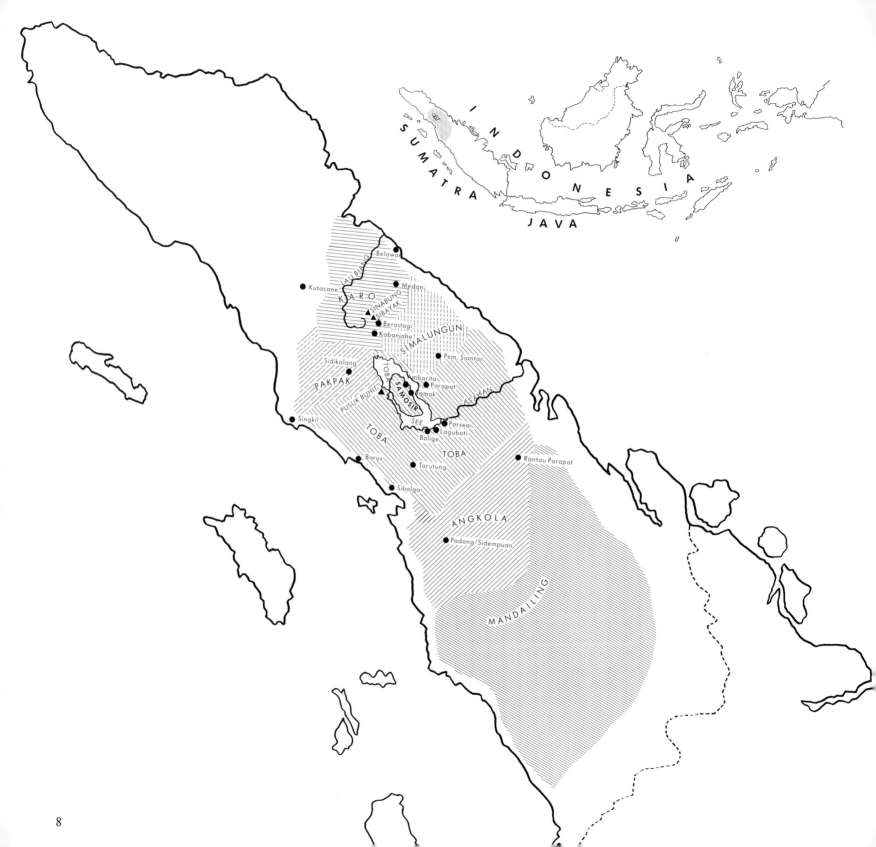

INDONESIA

SUMATRA

JAVA

Belawan

Kutacane

Medan

KARO

SINABUNG
SIBAYAK

Berastagi

Kabanjahe

SIMALUNGUN

Pem. Siantar

KAU BIANG

Sidikalang

PAKPAK

TOBA

SAMOSIR

Ambarita

Parapat

Tomok

ASAHAN

PUSUK BUHIT

SEE

Porsea

Laguboti

Singkil

TOBA

Balige

TOBA

Barus

Tarutung

Rantau Parapat

Sibolga

ANGKOLA

Padang/Sidempuan

MANDAILING

8

The Batak of Northern Sumatra: an Introduction

Travel guides and newspaper articles often give the impression that the Batak of northern Sumatra are a unified people with a common history, culture, language, religion, art etc., but this is an incomplete and misleading picture. True, the various Batak peoples have many features in common, but they have often had very different experiences of the Dutch colonial power and of the Christian or Islamic missionaries, and this has increased the existing differences between their kinship systems, religions and ideas of justice with the result that the features they have in common have become less and less apparent.

The Batak are among the few peoples on earth whose existence has long been known in Europe, but who have only relatively recently "enjoyed" the attention of the West. They were very capable of warding off unwelcome contacts and were protected from alien intrusion by the geography of the region where they lived.

Their homeland is the island of Sumatra at the western end of the modern Republic of Indonesia. It is the fifth largest island in the world, measuring c. 1750 km in length and 400 km across at its widest point. Many other peoples besides the Batak live on the island. Among the best known are the Aceh, the Gayo and Alas in the north; the matrilinear Minangkabau, the Kubu and the Lubu in the centre; and the Abung and the Rejang in the south. The coastal regions have long been settled by coastal Malays who over the centuries have founded flourishing trading centres and even large and influential states, an impressive example of which was the powerful state of Srivijaya (7th century to 13th century AD) whose capital is thought to have been what is now Palembang. Extensive trading links with the Malay peninsula, Java, India, Arabia and China brought a wide variety of cultural influences to the coastal region from the earliest times. During the Dutch colonial period thousands of Chinese and Javanese coolies were brought in as labour for the plantations on the east coast of Sumatra, and in recent times Javanese in particular have settled in East and South Sumatra. A large proportion of these immigrants have been shipped to Sumatra in the last thirty years as part of the great *Transmigrasi* migration project.

The Batak live in the mountainous highlands and in the western and eastern coastal region north of the equator and west of 100 degrees latitude (Map 2). Compared to the coastal strips their homeland is remote. The highlands are part of the Bukit-Barisan range running through the whole length of Sumatra, mostly about 1000 metres above sea level with many deep valleys carved by rivers and streams. These valleys were one

of the main reasons why the Batak region was so inaccessible and impenetrable during the period of scientific, missionary and colonial development.

The narrow coastal region to the west rises steeply to the highlands, where fourteen of the mostly conical volcanic peaks of the Bukit-Barisan range reach a height of more than 2000 m. These highlands are the heart of the Batak region. The slope down to the east coast is not nearly as steep as to the west. For a long time the piedmont zone (i.e. the foothills of the range towards the east coast) which is about 50 km wide, was an area where Batak settled when they could find no new land to cultivate in their mountain home or had left their home villages for some other reason. This area on the edge of the mountains is called *dusun* by the Karo Batak – a term which indicates that the settlements there were once dependent on their home villages up on the high plateau. The eastern coastal region has also long been settled by coastal Malays who have close contact with the Batak because of their proximity and trading connections. In the pre-colonial period few Batak lived there, but since the Republic of Indonesia gained its independence a large part of the population of the city of Medan, once the seat of the Sultans of Deli and centre of the European tobacco and rubber plantations, is now Batak.

Nevertheless, the majority of Batak still live in the mountains. Most villages are situated at an altitude of about 1000 m. Their daily life is determined by a number of factors: the deeply cut valleys, fissured landscapes and high mountains with steep slopes making cultivation impossible; the composition of the various soils, and a distinct mountain climate. Despite its proximity to the equator the climate of Batakland is temperate. The high altitude means that temperatures of c. 28–33 degrees Celsius are usually reached only in the middle of the day; night-time temperatures can sink as low as 10 degrees Celsius depending on situation and altitude. The tropical coastal regions and especially the piedmont zone have very high rainfall (Medan: 2000 mm; the *dusun*: up to more than 4000 mm). Even though much of the rain has already been precipitated on the mountain slopes, the high plateau still has a high rainfall (1500–2000 mm), but there are some areas with comparatively low or irregular rainfall.

Another important reason why Batakland used to be so impenetrable was the thick forest in the piedmont zone and on the slopes of the mountain region. Wide areas of the plateau, too, were still covered in thick primeval forest at the beginning of our

3 Granary (*sopo*) with richly decorated façade. In front is a rice mortar hewn from a large rock. Toba region, c. 1920

century; they had not been cleared in earlier times, because the soil was of poor quality. But here an increase in population and an extensive timber industry have brought far-reaching changes in recent decades. Large areas of primeval forest are still to be found, but there are also broad grassy steppes now covering areas that were once forested.

The Batak consist of six ethnic groups: the Mandailing and Angkola in the south, the Toba in the centre, the Pakpak/Dairi in the north west, the Karo and the Simalungun in the north and north-east (see Map 1). These six peoples can be divided into three main linguistic groups: the Mandailing, Angkola and Toba group in the south; the Pakpak/Dairi and Karo group in the north; and the Simalungun group in the north-east. Within these linguistic groups there are various dialects, but the groups themselves are independent languages with a common origin in the distant past. This means that the various ethnic groups often have to use a language other than their mother tongue, and many Batak will have mastered one or more other Batak dialects, as well as Bahasa Indonesia, the state language of Indonesia, which is based on Malay.

The historical experiences of the various Batak peoples over the centuries and especially in the last 160 years, are as diverse as their languages. At the beginning of the 19th century Islam gained a very strong influence in the Minangkabau region bordering Batakland to the south. In the religious conflicts in that part of Sumatra the dogmatic supporters of the strictly Islamic *Padri* sect conducted a bitter campaign against members of the Minangkabau people who held different or less strict beliefs. The Mandailing and Angkola Batak in the region bordering the Minangkabau were drawn in to these religious wars and by the mid-19th century had been converted to Islam. Islam strengthened the position of the dominant aristocratic class of the Mandailing, which appointed a ruler, the *raja pamusuk*, who was thereafter usually a Moslem. Islam influenced the legal, social and cultural aspects of Mandailing and Angkola Batak life.

The Toba Batak in central Batakland were increasingly Christianized by the German Rheinische Missionsgesellschaft from 1864 onwards, whereas only in very recent times have the Karo Batak turned to Christianity in large numbers, and some of them are Moslems. Even today about 20 per cent of the Karo population still follow the religion of their ancestors and do not belong to any of the "higher religions". Indeed to the Batak to belong to one of the "higher religions" has not meant a complete rejection of their old beliefs. Even the Toba Batak, who are considered the most religious of the Christian Batak, have preserved religious ideas and practices from earlier times. An example is the still widespread notion that the souls of the

ancestors can influence the lives of their descendents long after death.

This book is subtitled "Living with Ancestors", a reference to the fact that many Batak do not regard death as a final departure: their ancestors still play a part in the lives and destinies of children and grandchildren. The spirits of the ancestors (*bégu*) can be put in contact with people; accidents and bad dreams, in particular, are seen as attempts by the ancestors to bring themselves to mind among their descendents.

There are also many differences in the kinship systems of the various Batak peoples. Some of these are due to Islamic influence, but other influences, such as the history of the settlement of various regions or the different mythological ideas concerning the ancestry of the various family groups. The Toba Batak, for instance, trace their ancestry back to a single common ancestor called *Si Raja Batak*, who they believe lived in the village of Sianjur Mulamula at the foot of the Pusuk Buhit volcano on the western shore of Lake Toba, and whose two sons founded the first two families from which all Toba Batak families are descended. Lake Toba, its peninsula Samosir, and the littoral region south and west of the lake are the legendary "primeval homeland" of all the Batak. It was here that the settlement of Batakland began, though we do not know exactly when this occurred. In the course of time the cultural differences of the individual Batak peoples grew stronger as they lost contact with their homeland and developed independently.

Lake Toba – in prehistoric times the vast crater of a volcano of almost incredible size – remained unseen by any European explorer, colonial official or missionary until the middle of the 19th century. Although one of the main goals of explorers in the last century was to discover its exact geographical position, size and origin, it was many years before this was achieved.

4 Street scene in a Mandailing Batak village, c. 1910

Chapter 1   Historical Survey

Prehistory

(Uli Kozok)

In prehistoric times northern Sumatra was not a very hospitable land. We know little about the early inhabitants of what is now Batakland apart from the fact that they were groups of nomadic hunters and gatherers such as were found in many parts of the world during the Palaeolithic age. About 75,000 years ago a massive eruption, the most violent ever known, hurled between 1500 and 2000 cubic km of material from the volcano. This ash now forms the Toba tuff which covers a large part of Batakland. It extended as far as Sri Lanka and the Bay of Bengal. Stone tools found beneath this layer of tuff are evidence of the early presence of humans, but very few of them can have survived this catastrophe. After the eruption the volcanic cone collapsed into itself forming a huge crater – now Lake Toba. About 30,000 years ago the inhabitants of the island were struck by a second great catastrophe. From the bottom of Lake Toba a new volcanic cone arose, which split in two after erupting. The western half formed the Samosir peninsular, and the eastern the tongue of land between Parapat and Porsea.

On the east coast of northern Sumatra large heaps of seashells measuring 30 m in diameter and 5 m in depth have been found. Such shell heaps, or *Kjökkenmöddinger*, are also found in North Vietnam and Malaysia and are evidence of the eating habits of a stone-age population (hunters, gatherers and fishers), whose culture is called Hoabinh Culture after an archaeological site in North Vietnam. They contain stone and bone tools and generally date from the 10th to the 3rd century BC. It is now thought certain that these stone-age people bore little physical resemblance to the present inhabitants of western Indonesia. They belonged to the Australoid race, which now forms a large part of the population of eastern Indonesia, Melanesia and Australia (Aborigines), whereas the inhabitants of western Indonesia are southern Mongolids, who probably originated in southern China and spread through the Philippines, western Indonesia as far as Oceania and Madagascar. It is generally accepted that this Mongolid group spread the Austronesian family of languages to which most of the languages of Indonesia, the Philippines, Melanesia, Micronesia, Polynesia and Madagascar belong. Linguistic and archaeological evidence indicates that the Austronesian-speaking south Mongolids were already agriculturalists when they settled in the Philippines and parts of eastern Indonesia around 2500 BC. The Austronesian expansion to western Indonesia probably did not occur until the first millennium BC. The variety in the appearance of the various Indonesian tribes is probably due to a mixture of Mongolid and Australoid features. In the north and west the Mongolid element predominates, in the south and east the Australoid. Some of the tribes on Sumatra such as the Aceh and the Malays did not arrive in Sumatra until the first or second millenium AD, whereas the ancestors of the Batak seem to have been living in the mountains of northern Sumatra for a long time and hence they show stronger Australoid features.[1]

Archaeological research is not yet far enough advanced for more than a superficial knowledge of the ancestors of today's Indonesians. It is not clear, for example, whether the bearers of the Hoabinh Culture were already agriculturists before the arrival of Mongolid tribes, and we know practically nothing about the presumed expansion of Austronesian-speaking south Mongolid peoples to Sumatra in the course of the next 2000 years.

From about the beginning of the Christian era early Indonesian culture was increasingly influenced from India. According to Chinese sources a state called Ko-Ying, thought to have been situated in south-east Sumatra, imported horses from north-west India. Because Sumatra was on the important trade route between India and China it attracted the interest of Indian and Chinese seafarers. In India the island was known as Suvarnadvipa – the fabulous island of gold. Wolters (1967) makes the bold hypothesis that metallurgy may have come to Sumatra via Koying. It is probable, however, that bronze and iron technology developed independently in South-East Asia. Modern scholarship in general has tended to relativize the former assumption that India played a key role in the cultural and technological development of South-East Asia. Chinese sources show that there was trade with Sumatra before the 6th century. However, the place names in these sources need not refer to Sumatra, so it is uncertain whether and within what framework Sumatra was integrated into the trade relations between India and China. Archaeologists have not found any goods (Chinese ceramics) from the pre-Srivijaya period (before 650 AD), so intensive contacts between Sumatra on the one hand and India and China on the other can only be assumed from the 7th century onwards.

There is sure evidence of relations between Indonesia and India in Sanskrit inscriptions on Java which can be dated to the 5th century. A granite Buddha statue, possibly dating from the 6th century, has been found near Bukit Seguntang in south Sumatra. Five ancient Malayan inscriptions dating from between 683 and 686 mention a state called Srivijaya in south Sumatra. Although more recent research (Bronson 1979) rightly questions whether Srivijaya in fact had a continuous existence as a mighty empire from the 7th to the 13h century, it is certain that Srivijaya was flourishing in the 7th century. This can be seen from the writings of I-Ts'ing, a Buddhist pilgrim who studied Sanskrit for six months in the capital of Srivijaya (which has not yet been located). In his account of his travels I-Ts'ing also mentions that there were more than a thousand Buddhist monks studying in the fortified town. Hall (1976) points out that Srivijaya was able to combine its seafaring and trading skills with the potential of its hinterland. The heartland near the present town of Palembang was linked with the straits of Malacca by semi-nomadic Malay seafarers who had large fleets at their disposal. Srivijaya organized the trade with the hinterland which provided it with such commodities as spices, forest products, camphor and benzoin resin, precious stones and perhaps gold. Batakland with its abundance of camphor and benzoin resin must have been integrated into this network, and Batak culture was thus enriched by contacts with a world influenced by India.

Only the most important of the many influences of the Hindu-Buddhist culture will be mentioned here. There is no doubt that the script of the Batak can be traced back to Indian models, but probably through the medium of other Indonesian scripts (see chapter 5). The Batak language has about 200 loan words from Sanskrit, 60 per cent of which have to do with religion, magic and chronology (Parkin 1978: 132), and it is in these areas that the influences are strongest. From Hindu-Buddhist culture the Batak have taken their trinity of gods, their chronology and astrology. Indian influences can also be found – though to a lesser extent – in the social and political structure, the visual arts, the cult of the dead and many other aspects of the culture. For a long time it was also believed that technological progress, such as metalwork, irrigated rice cultivation, the use of the plough etc., could be traced back to the "superior" Indian culture. This view reflected the way of thinking of European scholars, who sought to legitimize the colonial status quo by giving it a historical precedent. Regarding the "primitive natives" as merely the objects of historical progress, it is also responsible for the long-held idea that the creative reworking of the Indian legacy by the Batak was a degenerative process.

In the last century a stele with a Tamil inscription was found at Labu Tua, near Barus on the west coast of northern Sumatra. The inscription dated from 1088 AD and stated that a Tamil guild of traders numbering 1500 was based there. Intensive archaeological excavations have not been undertaken, but clay potsherds, fragments of jewellery and a granite Bodhisattva torso have been found. The settlement was abandoned in the 12th century. Traders from India sailed with the monsoon winds to Sumatra where they had to stay a few months after carrying out their business so that they could sail back when the monsoon started. This seems to have been the origin of the settlement of Labu Tua. It can be assumed that many people stayed throughout the year and married native (Batak) women, which would certainly have eased contact with their trading partners.

Barus is already mentioned by Ptolemy (150 AD), and later by Chinese, Arab and Portuguese sources. Marco Polo reported that the camphor of Barus was the best in the world and worth its weight in gold.

Direct contact with these Tamil traders was only one means by which Indian culture reached the Batak. Another was through contact at second hand, as the example of Srivijaya demonstrates. Evidence for this is also provided by the many Hindu-Javanese remains in Padang Lawas (southern Batakland).

In 1846 near Gunung Tua in southern Batakland on the sparsely populated steppe of Padang Lawas the geologist Franz Junghuhn discovered a complex of Hindu temples dated by ancient Javanese and Malayan inscriptions to the period between the 12th and 14th centuries. The architecture of these ruins is Hindu-Javanese with south Indian influences. Unfortunately there are no contemporary historical sources which might enable us to connect this temple complex with a particular state.

Parkin (1978: 81) accepts that Hindu-Buddhist culture spread from the south (from Srivijaya via the Hindu-Buddhist states of Melayu in southern Sumatra and Minangkabau in West Sumatra and the Hindu temples of Padang Lawas) into Batakland. This may be true of indirect Hindu influence (i.e. via Minangkabau or Java), but modern archaeological evidence shows that direct contact may have been of greater importance.

In the 1970s excavations were carried out in Kota Cina near Belawan, the port of Medan. The excavators thought that this settlement, dating from the 12th to 14th centuries, was a Tamil trading station. Foundations of three stone buildings with religious functions were uncovered. Some of the inhabitants of Kota Cina were Buddhists and some Hindus of the Sivaitic sects. During the excavations almost a tonne of clay and porcelain sherds came to light. Besides ordinary functional ceramics, some of which were imported from China and some probably produced locally, there were also pieces of Chinese porcelain and Thai ceramics, as well as some sherds of Persian origin. It is notable that some of the Chinese porcelain was not of the usual export quality but of the very highest quality.

Imported goods (porcelain, ceramics and glass), mainly dating from the 14th century, have been found at various other places on the east coast, though no archaeological investigations have yet been undertaken. Finds of sherds of Chinese porcelain and Thai ceramics at Seberaya (Karo plateau) are evidence of trade with the plateau. The highlands provided the trading towns with sought-after wares such as spices, camphor and benzoin resin, receiving in exchange luxury and status goods such as Chinese porcelain, and everyday commodities like salt and iron.

At various places on the east coast of northern Sumatra sherds of Chinese porcelain and fortifications have been found, indicating that Kota Cina was not a unique case. There may possibly have been a number of trading settlements on the east and west coasts by which Hindu-Buddhist culture entered Batakland. We know very little about the dynamics of the cultural contacts between Indian settlers and the Batak of the highlands. The fact that hardly any Tamil words, but almost only Sanskrit words entered the Batak language (Sanskrit was the language of the settlers) and that these refer mainly to religion, magic, astrology and chronology, indicates that the trade contacts seem not to have played an important role. For this reason it seems likely that indirect contacts were more important for the acquisition of Indian ideas. However, there is also the fact that most of the trade items so sought-after in India originated in Batakland, and that the Tamil trading settlements were located close to Batakland. McKinnon (1987) argues for the theory that the exchange of goods took a ritualized form. There is evidence of this form of early trade particularly in the Malay-Oceanic area. If it is assumed that in early times the Batak already had (mainly indirect) contacts with the Indian world, then it is very probable that their culture was strongly influenced, especially in the religious sphere, during the period when there were trading settlements on the west and east coasts and Hindu-Javanese culture was spreading in southern Batakland (Padang Lawas).

One of the five clans (merga) of the Karo Batak calls itself Sembiring, which literally means "the blacks". This clearly refers to the skin colour of the Tamils, as is apparent from the names of the sub-clans. Some of the Sembiring sub-clans are allowed to intermarry, and they also differ in several other respects from the other Karo clans. Their burial customs differed widely (see chapter 4). Among the sub-clans which may be of Tamil origin are the Sembiring sub-clans Pandia, Colia, Meliala, Depari, Pelawi, Berahmana, Tekang and Muham. Pandya, Cola, Maleya and Palawa are names of south Indian dynasties, while the Brahmans are the Hindu priestly caste. It is not improbable that the origins of the Sembiring clan were influenced by the Tamil traders living as middlemen in the coastal towns, who married Karo Batak wives and thus over the centuries assimilated with the Karo. But only future intensive archaeological research will be able to cast light on this question. Archaeologically Batakland is still a closed book. The numerous stone chambers, perhaps used as burial places, which are found on the East Coast and

throughout Batakland, may be of considerable antiquity, but without archaeological excavations it is not possible to determine their age even approximately.

In 1282 the first mention occurs in Chinese sources of a state called Aru. The location of Aru or Haru (a name probably derived from Karo) is known with certainty, and it is highly probable that the centre of the state was near the present-day town of Medan. According to Tomes Pires, a Portuguese writing at the end of the 15th century, Aru was an exporter of camphor, gold, benzoin resin, spices, rattan, honey and slaves. It appears to have lost influence in the 16th century after being defeated several times by the rising state of Aceh at the northern tip of Sumatra, and from the early 17th century it is no longer mentioned in historical sources. It is possible that Kota Cina was the capital of the state in the 13th and 14th centuries.

The 13th century saw the triumphant progress of Islam through the Indonesian archipelago, and it is reported that by the 14th century Aru had adopted the Moslem faith. From the 16th century onwards Aceh, which reached its fullest extent under the Sultan Iskandar Muda (1607–1636), exerted influence over Batakland. The institution of the raja berempat or raja na opat, "the four rulers", originated under the influence of Aceh; the raja received their insignia from the sultan and were, at least nominally, subject to him. But Aceh had greater influence over the Malay coastal states which paid tribute to the sultan and had to provide him with troops in time of war (see Chapter 1, The Northern Batak Lands). In 1509 the Portuguese arrived as the first Europeans in the archipelago. Two years later they succeeded in capturing Malacca on the west coast of the Malay peninsula, at that time the most important port in South-East Asia. The Portuguese were followed in 1594 by the Dutch who soon seized Malacca for themselves. The Portuguese, Dutch and English, who established a settlement in south-west Sumatra (Bengkulu) in the 17th century, were not interested in exercising territorial influence. Their only concern was to gain an extensive monopoly of the profitable spice trade. The Europeans by and large obeyed the rules of trade which had long been customary in the archipelago, and with which they were familiar. Not until the 19th century, when the Dutch began to invest capital on a large scale in their colony, did the age of modern colonialism begin.

---

[1] It should be noted, however, that this is based on as yet unproven hypotheses. In the older literature there is frequent mention of "old or proto-Malays", a term coined by Heine-Geldern. These were thought to have arrived in Indonesia in a putative first wave of immigration, and their descendants to form the present tribes of the Toraja in Sulawesi and the Batak, who were subsequently forced into the mountains by the "new or deutero-Malays", Indonesians who migrated later. This theory was popular for a long time, but modern research does not support it.

The image of the Batak in early travel writings

Our knowledge of the Batak goes back over many centuries. The existence of the island of Sumatra was known in Europe in the early centuries of our era, though there was only a sketchy idea of its location and the culture of its inhabitants. In Chinese sources from the 6th century onwards, and especially in the handbooks of Arab seafarers and in geographical treatises from the 9th century, Sumatra appears under a variety of names. The Venetian Marco Polo, the Arab Ibn Battuta and the Franciscan Odorich of Portenau all visited northern Sumatra in the course of their journeys in the 13th and 14th centuries. Their accounts do not contain much information about the inhabitants, but they all mention the existence of cannabalism and the cultivation of and trade in camphor and benzoin.

The earliest detailed description of the inhabitants of northern Sumatra is by the Venetian Nicolo di Conti (c. 1395–1469) who spent a year on the island in the course of a long trading journey from Damascus to eastern Indonesia (1414–1439). "The men are cruel and have savage customs, men and women have very large ears in which they wear gold earrings set with precious stones. Their clothes are made of linen and woven silk, which they wear knee-length. They practise polygamy, their houses are low to avoid the heat of the sun, they are all idolaters. They have an abundance of camphor, gold and pepper ... In the part of the island called Batech live cannibals who wage continual war on their neighbours. They use the skulls of their slaughtered enemies as coinage in commerce, and the man who possesses the most of these is considered the richest." (Kunstmann 1863: 20). Ever since this account cannibalism in Sumatra has only been mentioned in connection with the Batak.

Scientific study of Sumatra and its inhabitants began in the late 18th century, encouraged by descriptions by colonial officials and merchants. The British and the Dutch competed fiercely on the west coast of northern Sumatra for trade in the natural products of the country, and had already established trading stations in the northern seaports of Singkel, Barus, Tapanuli, Natal and Ayerbangis, and the two trading powers also had bases on the southern part of the west coast, at Tiku, Priaman, Padang and Bengkulu, for instance. The British dominated trade until the second decade of the 19th century when under the terms of the Treaty of Paris they withdrew from Sumatra and shifted their colonial interests to the Malay peninsula.

The History of Sumatra by William Marsden, an Englishman, published in 1783 was the first monograph on Sumatra. Marsden devoted more than thirty pages to the Batak and their culture. His knowledge was mostly confined to the west coast and was based on information provided by English residents in the trading stations as well as on Dutch sources. His ideas about the composition of the Batak peoples and the place names are based more on hearsay than first-hand observation. Nonetheless, his book is an excellent source for the early history of discovery and for the prejudices which existed against the Batak. Many of his descriptions of features of the culture are very precise, and much of what writers in the later 19th century were to describe in more detail is recognizable. His brief but clear accounts of jewellery, clothing, weapons, production of gunpowder, warfare, trading structures, markets, buildings, religious ideas, priesthood and much else are such that we can assume that his informants had intensive contacts with the Batak. Particularly interesting is his description of a magician-priest (guru) "whose limbs are tattowed in the shape of birds and beasts, and painted of different colours, with a large wooden mask on his face" (Marsden, repr. 1975: 388). Tattoos of the type described are not found in the later sources, so it can be assumed that after c. 1800 the magician-priests stopped being tattooed.

Cannibalism naturally occupies a large space in Marsden's book. Even though he himself had not witnessed it – and he frankly admits that his knowledge is second or even third hand – he still thought his informants' stories were trustworthy. He describes the procedure as follows: "The unhappy victim is then delivered into the hands of the injured party ... by whom he is tied to a stake; lances are thrown at him from a certain distance by this person, his relations, and friends; and when mortally wounded, they run up to him, as if in a transport of passion, cut pieces from the body with their knives, dip them in the dish of salt, lemonjuice, and red pepper, slightly broil them over a fire prepared for the purpose, and swallow the morsels with a degree of savage enthusiasm. Sometimes (I presume, according to the degree of their animosity and resentment) the whole is devoured by the bystanders; and instances have been known where, with barbarity still aggravated, they tear the flesh from the carcase with their teeth. To such a depth of depravity may man be plunged, when neither religion nor philosophy enlighten his steps!" (Marsden repr. 1975: 391f)

The German physician and geographer Franz Junghuhn, who travelled through the southern Batak lands in 1840–41 starting from Padang, was the first naturalist to visit the Batak region. In his two-volume book he included descriptions of land and people which give an even clearer picture of the Batak then Marsden. Of course, his characterization of the Batak is not valid today – and it is not my concern to produce a kind of character sketch. Junghuhn's verdict on the Batak is an example of the prejudices of the Euro-centred approach of travellers and colonial officials of that time, whose judgement of people with completely different ideas about the purpose of life and very different values, norms and legal systems, was based on a sense of superiority, arrogance and ignorance. Junghuhn is, however, an exception in that he prefaces his characterization of the Batak with a very modern-sounding justification in which he alludes to the character of the researcher and his attitude to the local population and the variable findings that result from this:

"Someone who had no ex officio demands to make of the inhabitants of the interior, who could expect from them as voluntary assistance what others force from them by commands, who could deal with them on the basis of equality, and whose business and inclination it would be to involve himself in all nuances of the people's life – such a person would, I believe, be in the best position to look at this people more closely and get to know the uncoloured and unclouded truth about them. It is necessary for the understanding of the following to note that this was my position regarding the Battaer." (Junghuhn 1847: vol. 2: 236). In this way he quite rightly attempts to distinguish himself from the colonial officials, missionaries and traders. After this justification there follows a list of thirty characteristics of the Batak at the end of which he sums up the most important points:

"... I have attempted to represent them by their outstanding features as they appeared to me. Their outstanding passions and vices are indicated in Nos. 3, 11 and 12, and their most excellent virtues in Nos. 15, 16 and 19. Their intellectual abilities are underdeveloped, but their understanding is good and their judgement is as a rule correct and circumspect ..." (ibid.: 243)
In the list he describes these qualities as follows:

"3. Addicted to games, with a particularly passionate love of cock-fighting ... 11. Vengeful, but openly without dissimulation and of short duration ... 12. Bloody, cruel, cannibal, especially in wars ... 15. Hospitable: a refugee or victim of persecution who voluntarily puts his trust in the raja of a village will find inviolable asylum there and will be protected from the rest of the world. ... 16. Good-natured, generous to his friends ... 19. Open-hearted, when for political reasons a Battaer has decided to be tight-lipped, it requires only a few trusting words to elicit from him all that he knows." (ibid.: 238f.)
About cannibalism Junghuhn writes in another passage:

"... People do the honest Battaer an injustice when it is said that they sell human flesh in the markets, and that they slaughter their old people as soon as they are unfit for work ... They eat human flesh only in wartime, when they are enraged, and in a few legal instances." (ibid.: 87)

During his one and a half year stay in the Batak region Junghuhn heard of only three cases of cannibalism (ibid.: 161).

Oscar von Kessel, who penetrated as far as the Silindung valley shortly after Junghuhn in 1844, also describes a cannibalistic "ceremony":

"According to the laws of the land certain crimes, especially adultery, are punished by death and the general consumption of the criminal. The same fate is also accorded prisoners of war if they are not redeemed through the good offices of their relatives. The manner is as follows. The prisoner or criminal is tied to a stake; the whole village gathers and after several orators have described in detail the capital offence, the most eminent oft the assembly, or the one who has been injured by the crime, cuts off the tip of the victim's nose, dips it in a vessel with lemon-juice and consumes it like an oyster. Thereupon another cuts oft the cheeks, a third the palms of the hands and they consume these parts before the eyes of the condemned man. Finally everyone falls upon him. The length or brevity of his suffering depends very much on the greatness of the offence and whether persons are present whose hatred has been particularly aroused." (Kessel 1854: 738). Moreover, salt and lemons had to be provided by the relatives of the victim, as a sign that they accepted the verdict of the community and were not thinking of revenge (Willer 1846: 201).

The frequency of cannibalism among the Batak should not be overestimated. It was regarded by the Batak themselves as a judicial act and its application was restricted to very narrowly defined infringements of the law – apart from occasional exceptions. It is also important to bear in mind the social aspect of this ceremonial punishment by the community of a thief, adulterer, spy or traitor. Certain parts of the victim's body were kept as a warning to all. The skull might be buried under the steps of the assembly house (balé) in order to further shame the offender after death – it was considered a great insult that everybody would walk over his head as they entered the balé – or

5 Smoked human hand, Karo Batak

else it would be put on show in a small house in front of the *balé*. Georg Meissner, who formed the large Karo Batak collection of the Linden-Museum in Stuttgart, also donated smoked hands of victims of the Pakpak Batak, described as the cruellest cannibals, to the ethnographical museums of Berlin and Dresden. These are supposed to have been hung up in the *balé* as a sort of trophy. According to Burton and Ward, skulls could also be kept in the *balé* (1827: 494).

After the middle of the 19th century the Toba region as well as the land of the Pakpak situated to the north above the west coast became a focus for European research. In van Rosenberg's description in 1854 of the Singkel district north of Barus the existence of cannibalism seems to stand as an example of the "cruelty and savagery of the Batak" and no future description of Batak culture is complete without it. It was the custom of the magician-priests to seize a boy from a neighbouring village and kill him after he had promised to do what he could for the interests and aims of the village. After he had made this promise his mouth was filled with moulten lead so that his soul could not escape and take back the promise. Out of parts of his body the magician-priests (*datu*) made substances which concealed magic powers. *Pupuk*, the magic mixture thus produced, and the objects in which its was kept will be mentioned frequently in the following pages.

Besides cannibalism and the production of magic mixture there were also particular forms of punishment for wrongdoers, such as slavery and debt bondage, which most European observers regarded as showing contempt for humanity. Criminals and prisoners of war of all ages and both sexes were put "in the block", which meant that their legs were placed between two heavy wooden beams rendering them immobile. They remained in the block until their family had collected the necessary money to release them, and for the duration of their imprisonment they received meagre care. Reports indicate that many such prisoners did not survive their punishment. Slavery mainly applied to prisoners of war and debtors and was not abolished until colonial times. Before that many Batak were kept by their *raja* either in debt bondage until they had worked off their outstanding debts, or else resold. Many Batak slaves passed through the ports on the east coast to the Malayan peninsula where they were forced to work in the British tin mines.

Nearly all the travel descriptions at that time are by officials of the Dutch colonial government, which had its capital in Sumatra at Padang on the west coast. Administrative centres were established in all those parts of the country which had come under the rule of the Dutch colonial power, whether voluntarily or by force. The administrators of the subjugated areas, called Controllers and often the only Europeans living there, made sure that the trading agreements were kept. They made regular tours of inspection in their districts and the reports they wrote about what they found are often rich sources of ethnographical descriptions (e.g. Willer 1846, Godon 1862, Henny 1869, de Haan 1870, van Cats Baron de Raet 1875). From the middle of the century onwards these reports are supplemented by an increasing number of accounts by naturalists and other travellers. Ida Pfeiffer, an Austrian, was the first lady tourist in the Batak region. In July and August 1852 during her second world tour she travelled from Padang into the south Toba region as far as the vicinity of present-day Tarutung. She wrote of the purpose of her trip: "I wished … to visit Mandelling, Ankolla, Great Toba etc. and go as far as the free, savage Battakers among the cannibals." (Pfeiffer 1856, vol. 2: 4); she gives no other reason for her journey. Although her courage and stamina were impressive – at that time such a journey would certainly have been dangerous – she too takes delight in describing a cannibal "ceremony" which she had never actually witnessed (Pfeiffer 1856, vol. 2: 31f).

The descriptions before 1860 were important sources of information for the missionaries, who from 1824 onwards made repeated attempts to civilize the supposedly savage cannibals and convert them to Christianity. In 1824 the British Baptist missionaries, Burton and Ward, set off on foot into the interior from Sibolga, the port on Tapanuli Bay on the west coast. After three days journey they reached the high valley of Silindung and spent about two weeks in the Batak region. Considering the shortness of their stay their account reveals very intensive first-hand observation. In contrast, the journey of Munson and Lyman, two American missionaries, in 1834 was a complete failure; the local people thought they were spies, murdered them and presumably ate them. Herman Neubronner van der Tuuk, employed by the Dutch Bible Society to research the language of the Batak took residence in the port of Barus, north of Tapanuli Bay. He produced a grammar, a dictionary and collections of texts, as well as a translation of parts of the Bible. His pioneering linguistic research enabled the Dutch and German missionaries to undertake the conversion of the Toba and Simalungun Batak which was later so successful.

Van Asselt, a Dutchman, was the first missionary to settle in the Batak region. His area of activity was, however, restricted to the southern parts which were already under colonial control. The situation changed when the German Rheinische Mission entered the Batak missionary field. Ludwig Nommensen, the "Apostle of the Batak", is still revered by them. In 1864 disregarding the colonial government's ban, he settled in the high valley of Silindung which was then still independent. His work began the mission to the Toba Batak. Over the following decades a large number of missionaries and missionary sisters followed him to northern Sumatra to take part in his work. Vast sums of money poured into the Rheinische Mission at Barmen near Wuppertal from the churches in Germany and thence to Batakland. This money was needed to support the extensive missionary work - churches, community houses, hospitals and leper stations, schools and training colleges for teachers and religious leaders. Reports written by the missionaries to their home parishes provided information about the progress of the work and helped to raise more money. It was necessary to impress on the donors at home what a positive effect Christianity was having on the poor heathens thanks to the work of the missionaries and their generous supporters. These reports mostly contain extreme descriptions of Batak customs, including the cannibal ceremonies. One quotation will be sufficient to show how they combined disgust and horror with a fascination for the exotic.

"On his way out of his village a man took a small piece of tree-resin worth perhaps a groschen. Immediately the people of the village, whose property the tree was, fell on him and put his foot in the block. He lay in it for months until his relatives bought his release for a certain sum. But as soon as he gained his freedom and his feet were healed he set in motion his long-hatched plan for revenge. He found some collaborators, who are always available for money among the heathen Battas, and made his way to the environs of the village to lie in wait for the villagers. It was not long before three unarmed persons, two boys and an adult, approached his hiding place. The latter was killed immediately and the two boys were gagged and led off to captivity. The younger was immediately put in the block; the older one, aged thirteen, had a hole bored in his upper lip. Then he was driven into a circle and fury was vented on him in the most horrible way. Then his fingers were cut off and stuck in his mouth. His begging and pleading, his cries of help to his father and mother were of no avail – they did not receive news of their son until he had been eaten except for his head and one arm." (Missionar Freund 1878, quoted in Wegner 1900: 7f).

Of course such tendentious horror stories must be seen against the background of the conditions and spirit of the age. Missionaries – in the past at least – did not have a high opinion of the "heathens" they sought to evangelize, until they had become Christians. Their sense of superiority was so extreme that even Warneck, who had spent ten years among the Toba as a missionary and who later became Nommensen's successor, could write that "the Batak are by nature, like all members of the Malayan race, mendacious, dishonest and deceitful." (Warneck 1922: 317). One has to realize that the most prejudiced descriptions of the Batak come from otherwise honourable missionaries. Their accounts lack the neutrality which the colonial officials and naturalists at least aimed at in their reports.

If one looks at what is offered by modern travel organizations and the descriptions of the Batak and their culture in many travel guides it is clear that even today the Batak are tainted with an image which goes back to the tendentious 19th century accounts. Why the Batak were "man-eaters", how these rare "ceremonies" were rooted in their views of the world and religious ideas, will be discussed later.

In the 19th century the Dutch colonial government banned cannibalism in the regions under their control and any infringement was severely punished. The presence of the missionaries and the increasing success of their missions were also instrumental in putting an end to the practice of cannibalism among the Batak in the last century.

6 Toba Batak Protestant church at Binangalom. Uluan region, 1989

7 Family photograph, c. 1900. A Toba Batak *raja* in full official dress.
   As a sign of their office the *raja* were given white jackets with silver
   buttons and a hat with a silver band by the Dutch colonial government.

The Southern Batak Lands

As we have seen, the various regions of Batakland had contacts with Europeans at different times, and the various Europeans sometimes had very different interests. The experiences of the Batak with the Europeans were often controversial and there were differences between the historical developments in the northern Batak lands (those of the Karo, Pakpak and Simalungun Batak) and the southern Batak lands (the Toba, Angkola and Mandailing Batak).

Because of the nature of the sources, the history of the southern Batak is largely a history of British and Dutch trading relations, the expansion of the Dutch colonial territory, and the history of the Rheinische Mission. Although the Batak had their own script (a fact which distinguishes them from other ancient Indonesian peoples, except for some in southern Sumatra) there are no surviving Batak written sources describing life in the pre-colonial period; the books and bamboo texts in Batak script are mainly religious in content. It is therefore impossible to reconstruct their pre-colonial history. We know from the travel writings of Arabs and Chinese, of Marco Polo, Nicolo di Conti and others, that the Batak had lived in the interior of North Sumatra for many centuries, but when they came to Sumatra from the mainland of South-East Asia remains speculation.

The many remains of Hindu temples in the region of Padang Lawas, all dating from between the 11th and 14th centuries, seem to have no connection with the Batak. There are no inscriptions or sculpture to indicate that the builders were Batak. It can be assumed that the temples were built by Hindu-Buddhist-influenced groups who were living in this area long before the Batak did, though the Batak may have been their neighbours at that time. At any rate, in the few family genealogies orally transmitted by the Batak I know of no information going back that far. In their religion the Batak have preserved many features clearly derived from Hindu-Buddhist influence. The size and number of the temples – there are more than twenty of them – indicate that the country in which their remains can still be seen must have been very fertile when they were built. Archaeologists have related them to the Panei empire, which is supposed to have been under south Indian rule at the beginning of the 11th century (Schnitger 1937). This empire probably had a stratified society with a ruling class and a priestly class for whose use these large brick buildings would have been built. The agricultural production and income from trade in natural products must have been large enough to pay for the extravagant architecture, and there must have been a relatively high density of population. Today the region is a sparsely populated steppe where the scanty grass is mainly used for raising cattle; agriculture is restricted to the areas near the river banks. It is possible that this Hindu-Buddhist centre in Padang Lawas came to an end because of a change in climate following the destruction of the forests in the region, for according to the historical memory of the Batak who lived there in the 19th century, their ancestors found no local population when they arrived. They avoided the area around the temples because they are supposed to have found them uncanny (Willer 1846: 402).

In the 17th century British and Dutch trading companies founded the first trading stations on the west coast. At Bengkulu on the south-west coast the British established one of their first bases in 1633, and in 1668 at Barus the Dutch built an early wooden trading post, which was replaced by a stone one in 1732 (Radermacher 1787: 48f). Barus was already a thriving port where ships from India, Arabia, from Aceh in North Sumatra and other Indonesian islands anchored. The main trade was in camphor and benzoin, which were then much in demand for medication, embalming and incense. Barus had been the main source of these for centuries, as the stone Tamil inscription mentioned above demonstrates (see p. 14).

There was another Dutch settlement at Ayerbangis, south of Natal, but in the 18th century it was the British who were the dominant trading power on the west coast of Sumatra. Around 1760 they had trading bases in almost all the larger ports and it was said that "at least 200 private English ships from all parts of India visited this coast every year, and it overflowed with all kinds of goods" (Eschels-Kroon 1781: 77). Eschels-Kroon, who lived and worked at Ayerbangis from 1766 to 1774 as the Resident of the Dutch United East India Trading Company (VOC), gives a good picture of the goods which were reaching Sumatra at that time, including textiles from Bengal and the Coromandel coast, candy and powered sugar, coffee, arak, wheat, spices, iron, steel and copper. The privately-owned ships brought Chinese products, such as porcelain, lacquerwork and tea, Japanese sake and European manufactured goods. Considering the supposed *isolation* of the Batak region, it seems almost incredible how much was imported into Sumatra from Europe. "All kinds of wines, brandies, pipes, tobacco, bacon, smoked meat, herrings, smoked salmon, cheeses, butter, almonds, raisins, currants, figs, French bottled jams, and fruits in brandy, indeed everything both necessary and superfluous." (ibid.: 39). All these were clearly sent to Sumatra for the European Residents, the representatives of trading companies, to make their stay on the coast more pleasant; they were certainly not intended to be traded with the local population. Nevertheless, the Batak in the ports had an opportunity to get to know such products. Eschels-Kroon also lists the many different commodities brought to Sumatra and Java from the other Indian and East Asian ports. It is fascinating to see what a wide variety of these there was in the period before the French Revolution.

At that time the ports on the west coast were mainly inhabited by coastal Malays who were subjects of the Sultan of Aceh. The Batak villages were not in the coastal region but in the higher hinterland or on the steep slopes above the coast. It was there that the camphor and benzoin trees grew, and the Batak controlled not only the cultivation of these natural products but also their transportation down to the trading centres. There they came into direct contact with the coastal population from whom they received essential salt as well as iron, copper, brass, glass beads and textiles in exchange for their products. The demand for these products was very great, a writer at the end of the last century mentions that 300 to 500 bearers came weekly to Sibolga just to provide the Toba population with salt (Meerwaldt 1894: 527). It must be assumed therefore that trading contacts between the Batak region and the coast were very important even in pre-colonial times.

As we have seen, in the initial period the British were the dominant commercial and economic power on the west coast of Sumatra. The Dutch trading companies had joined together in 1604 to form a large company, the VOC, which had its headquarters at Batavia (now Jakarta) on Java. It main commercial interest was the spice trade with the eastern Indonesian Moluccas, a monopoly which the Dutch kept by military force. In Sumatra they were less successful until the beginning of the 19th century. They had trading settlements in some ports, but their income was hardly greater than their outlay. Their most important base in Sumatra was the port of Padang, in the hinterland of which there were large coal fields which were later important suppliers of fuel for steamships. Wars in Europe against Great Britain and the aftermath of French Revolution resulted in the loss of all Dutch bases in the Indonesian archipelago. At the end of the 18th century the Dutch state took over all the rights in Indonesia of the VOC, which had gone bankrupt through mismanagement. This marked the real beginning of the colonial period in Indonesia.

The Treaty of London in 1814 gave the Dutch back their colonies and a second agreement with the British (the Treaty of London of 1824) laid down a division of spheres of influence: the British withdrew completely from Sumatra and moved their businesses to Singapore, which had been occupied in 1819, and the Malay peninsula, while the Dutch took over the British bases in South Sumatra and from then on controlled most of the trade on Sumatra's coasts. One exception, until the beginning of the

8 Carrier with containers for salt which was carried in large quantities from the coast to the interior. Karo plateau, c. 1910

present century, was the independent sultanate of Aceh on the northern tip of Sumatra.

As they had done on Java, the Dutch corrupted the native ruling elite in the small states of South Sumatra and used military force to place them under direct colonial administration. By the mid-19th century the whole of southern and western Sumatra had come under direct Dutch rule. The *padri* movement, an orthodox Muslem sect among the Minangkabau, caused great unrest in western Sumatra in the early decades, with devastating effects on the southern Batak lands. The aim of the *padri* was to make the orthodox Islamic law of the Minangkabau applicable everywhere. They rejected alcohol, tobacco, opium, cock-fighting and dicing, but above all the matriarchal orientation of Minangkabau kinship relationships and inheritance laws. The British had kept out of the incipient civil war, but the Dutch became involved in the disputes, taking the side of the *adat* party which the *padri* were attacking, and hoped by backing the weaker group to prevent any growth in the power of the *padri*. Only after long drawn out military campaigns did the Dutch succeed in capturing and deporting *Tuangku Imam Bonjol*, the leader of the *padri*, who is now honoured as one of the first anticolonial national heroes and has many streets and squares named after him in Indonesian towns.

The military campaigns of the *padri*, motivated by religion, had assumed the character of wars of annihilation in the southern Batak region. Junghuhn, who had travelled from Padang to the southern Batak lands shortly after the end of the *padri* wars, described the terrible conditions in the homeland of the Mandailing and Angkola Batak: "The invasion of the padries with forced bands from Mandaheling (1830?), who plundered everything and murdered 233,000 people, completed the decline of the poor land. Now the beautiful paradise is a desert; the good-natured, splendidly gifted people is a ruin, and anarchy and collapse are universal." (Junghuhn, vol. 2, 1847: 301) The suppression of the *padri* movement marked a consolidation of Dutch colonial power in western Sumatra and also an extension of the subjugated regions northwards. For a few years broad tracts of land as far as Sibolga and Padang Lawas were occupied by the Dutch. In 1843 they withdrew as far as the Mandailing and Angkola region, which had been under direct Dutch rule since 1835/36. In 1840/41 the Dutch had introduced coffee planting in these two areas, which in the end became a sort of forced labour for the population. Transport routes were laid, bridges built, the supplies and prices established. The local village chiefs were involved in the sales in order to make sure that the agreements were kept. For the individual peasant farmer there was very little profit left after subtracting all the costs of the transport (Godon

1862: 10f). For a time the farmers were forced to carry their harvest to the packing houses without payment (ibid.: 15). Similarly the initial phase of building roads for ox-drawn and horse-drawn carts had to be pushed ahead by the unpaid inhabitants of neighbouring villages. Along these roads the Mandailing and Angkola Batak were grouped together in newly-founded villages. Controllers and inspectors were the representatives of the Dutch colonial power on the spot.

The expansion of coffee-growing led to a demand for clerical workers and native administrators for the packing houses. The first schools were built in 1851 and by 1857 there were four of them in Mandailing and Angkola where besides reading, writing and arithmetic, the Malay language was also taught (ibid.: 22ff). The shortage of European teachers meant that the government had to rely on Malays and Minangkabau, who naturally passed on their Islamic beliefs to their pupils. The spread of Islam through these two regions thus occurred with the toleration of the Dutch. Christian attempts at missionary work beginning after 1859 were largely unsuccessful.

These years saw an increase in opportunities for the Dutch colonial power to get involved in conflicts between individual Batak villages and even between areas, mostly to settle military confrontations. The first expedition into the Padang Lawas county in 1855 ended with a promise of loyalty and obedience to the Dutch government from all the Batak chiefs involved, though the region was not then incorporated into the Dutch possessions. The expansion of the districts under Dutch rule gained a new dimension with the appearance of the German Rheinische Mission in the southern Batak region. Unlike the Dutch missionaries, the Germans penetrated into the independent Toba Batak country and established themselves in the Silindung valley. There they founded mission stations and, in the initial stages at least, even entirely Christian villages. Their courage, stamina and willingness to suffer for the cause of religion opened up Batakland to the influences of the modern world which were to change the culture there with increasing speed. The conflicts between the supporters and opponents of the Christian missionaries repeatedly led to bitter confrontations usually ending in warfare. More than once the missionaries had to call on the Dutch colonial troops to protect Batak converts to Christianity.

The spiritual overlord of the Toba Batak, the *Si Singamangaraja*, was the bitterest enemy of the Christians. His struggle against the missionaries and the Dutch intensified the closer the missionaries came to Lake Toba. The Toba regarded this lake as holy and the Batak were forbidden on pain of death to lead any foreigner to it. The *Si Singamangaraja* had his residence at Bakkara on the south-west shore of the lake, and from there he repeatedly called on the people to resist and threatened the mission stations in the Silindung valley. For a long time the attempts of the Dutch to apprehend him were unsuccessful. The continued resistance gave them the pretext to place the "voluntarily" subjugated villages and areas under the protection of the government and so expand the colonial administration. In 1879 not only the country around Padang Lawas in the border area between the Angkola and Toba Batak but also a large part of Toba Batak land was occupied. By 1890 all southern Toba lands, such as Pahae, Silindung, Hurlang and Humbang, had been annexed. The official annexation usually followed treaties, promises and oaths from the local rulers not to contravene the interests of the colonial government. The success of the Rheinische Mission in this region was an important contributory factor.

Border areas and the less densely populated Toba districts were not brought under missionary influence until a relatively late stage and consequently were not incorporated into the Dutch-ruled areas until later. The Uluan and Si Gaol districts were officially annexed in 1905, Naipospos and the Samosir peninsula in Lake Toba in 1907, and Habinsaran in the east not until 1908. With these last areas the whole of the Mandailing, Angkola and Toba Batak region came under direct Dutch colonial administration (dates in Schadee 1920: 7–16). Connected with this expansion of direct rule was the creation of larger administrative units than had been usual among the various Batak peoples. The size of a residency (a sort of province) and its smaller units (known as departments) depended on the phase of colonial expansion. All the southern Batak lands were in the residency of Tapanuli, which had its capital at the port of Sibolga. This administrative structure created by the Dutch has survived to the present day. Within the present province of North Sumatra there are two districts (now called *Kabupaten*) occupying the former residency of Tapanuli: North and South Tapanuli.

The history of the east coast sultanates is somewhat different. They border the Karo, Simalungun and Toba Batak regions on the east, and are largely inhabited by Malays, though the proportion of Batak in the population of the higher border areas should not be underestimated. These include the sultanate of Asahan, which is just next to the Habinsaran region and extends along the river Asahan as far as the east coast. The Dutch annexed Asahan in 1865 but granted the sultanate the status of a self-governing region within the residency of East Sumatra.

A large part of the Batak population of Asahan came from the Toba region in the distant past. They call themselves Pardemba-nan Batak and since the first half of the 19th century had been under the direct rule of the Sultan of Asahan. Other Batak

groups, above all the Mandailing, migrated there after the Pardembanan (Bartlett 1921: 18f). Under the protection of the colonial administration European plantations were established in the flat coastal region of the sultanate from 1885 onwards. The most important were the tobacco and rubber plantations where many Chinese worked besides the Malays. So in Asahan the Batak population lived in relatively close proximity to the coastal Malays, Chinese and European plantation owners. The Batak were not independent but subjects of an Islamic state which exploited them. This particularly affected the religious ideas and culture of the Pardembanan Batak, many of whom converted to Islam at that time, while the Mandailing brought Islam with them from their homeland.

The crucial difference between these and the Toba Batak in the residency of Tapanuli who had for long been independent, was their direct proximity to and dependence on sections of the population with a different nationality and culture. The Islamized Batak lost their cultural identity and largely assimilated with the culture of their more powerful neighbours. Today only the family names give an indication of the ethnic origins – if the Batak names have not been completely discarded. In the case of the Mandailing such was the rejection of Batak culture and the loss of cultural identity that they denied that they were related to the other Batak and set great store by not being called Batak (Keuning 1952: 162).

After the last independent Batak had been incorporated into the Dutch colonial empire in 1908 the Dutch began to improve the economy and infrastructure in the southern Batak lands. For this it was necessary to improve the coordination and organization of the individual regions, districts and village groups. The sultans of the regions which were still self-governing had their rights severely reduced. Only after they had recognized the supremacy of the Dutch, and committed themselves to make no contacts with other nations without the knowledge of the colonial government, were they accorded the status of autonomous regions. They had the right to raise taxes from their subjects and spend them largely as they thought fit, which often gave rise to irregularities and injustices giving the Dutch an excuse for intervention. To protect the subjects and for the good of individual regions so-called district banks were established for the collection of taxes. These financed the administration of the region and the extension of the infrastructure and schooling. In 1907 the Dutch concluded what are known as the "long treaties" with the sultans on the east coast. Unlike the "short treaties" these defined very precisely the rights and duties of the sultans regarding the colonial government and their people. For the sultans of Deli, Siak, Serdang, Langkat and Asahan these "long treaties" meant a considerable loss of independence and rights, and supplementay treaties in the following years greatly reduced their income.

Not only did the extension of the road network and especially the railways in the province of East Sumatra cost vast sums, it also opened up previously unknown possibilities of earning money to the Batak. European capital invested in the extensive plantations could now flow unhindered into the country, and the system of new dependences made the Batak far more mobile than they had been. The expansion of the area covered by the Rheinische Mission into the Pakpak and Simalungun region gave added incentive to Mandailing and Angkola Batak from South Tapanuli and the large population of Toba Batak from North Tapanuli. In the following decades they migrated in large numbers to the newly established commercial and administrative centres or settled in the less agriculturally developed areas in the neighbouring regions (Cunningham 1958).

The Mandailing and Toba Batak had a great advantage over the inhabitants of the northern Batak lands because of their better school education. The Dutch colonial government and especially the Rheinische Mission had built numerous schools there, establishing a school system which mainly served the purposes of the colonial administration. However, the elementary schools supported by the government were attended only by the children of influential and well-to-do families, whereas the mission schools were open to all regardless of their origins. At that time a school system did not yet exist in the northern Batak lands. The Toba and the Mandailing because of their better opportunities became the intellectual elite, occupying the available posts in government, administration, education and service industries. In the field of agriculture too they outstripped the local population in the immigration areas. In the Simalungun region in particular the government turned the land over to paddy fields. The Simalungun who up to that time had known only slash-and-burn cultivation were simply driven out by the Toba Batak who understood irrigated rice cultivation.

For the inhabitants of the southern Batak lands modern development since 1900 has resulted in closer communications with the economically dominant east coast region. The transport system brought with it not only better and faster possibilities for selling agricultural products, but also unprecedented possibilities of communication. The economic upswing was concentrated primarily in the plantation belt on the east coast, which the Dutch and other Europeans had developed from 1867 with a high expenditure of human and financial resources. There were various reasons why this region was suitable for plantations: the soil was fertile and suitable for tobacco, rubber, oil palms and coffee, and unlike the southern Batak lands it was relatively sparsely populated. The land was nominally owned by a dependent Malay elite, which received a large sum of money for granting concessions and often disregarded the rights and interests of the native population in favour of the plantation owners.

Even though the plantations as a driving force for the local economy remained largely confined to the east coast region, the southern Batak lands also profited from the economic upswing. Because of the development of medical care by the government and the missionaries there was a drop in the mortality rate among new-born babies and a general increase in life expectancy leading to a rapid growth in population. The development of a viable road network resulted in road junctions soon growing into small or middle-sized towns. The age of subsistence cultivation came to an end almost everywhere, and many Mandailing, Angkola and Toba found new supplementary or primary incomes in trade, crafts or service industries. The schools in these small centres had an additional attraction for the Batak, who wanted to give their children the best possible education for life under these new conditions – an attitude that has not changed today.

The increasing population meant that the demand for areas to cultivate also increased in all the Batak lands. The hope of owning land led to a marked pressure of population in areas which had hitherto been very sparsely populated. Many Batak in search of work were also drawn to the plantation region which seemed to promise them a better life.

For the southern Batak the period up to the Second World War was a time of economic consolidation and adjustment to new economic structures. The intrusion of modern life brought with it new ideas. It was not only through the Protestant Church and Islam that the Batak gained new values and norms, but their view of the world was also changed by school education, the flow of information through new media and the freedom from "traditional" economy. Newspapers and radio opened up the previously ethnocentric Batak conception of the world. However, in the years before the Second World War resistence to the colonial government was rare. This was a very successful period for the Christian Church; among the Toba Batak it developed to become the most important religious institution, and it also strengthened its position in the northern Batak lands. When in May 1940 all Germans in the Dutch East Indies were interned in retaliation for the occupation of the Netherlands, the way was open for the Batak Christians to take the leadership and organization of their churches into their own hands.

The Dutch colonial period ended with the Japanese invasion in 1942. Developments since the war will be discussed in the final chapter.

The Northern Batak Lands
(by Uli Kozok)

The activities of the Dutch colonial power in the first half of the 19th century were restricted to the west coast of Sumatra. In the Treaty of London (1824) the colonial powers, Britain and the Netherlands, had divided their spheres of influence in the Malay archipelago and the powerful state of Aceh which bordered the Batak lands on the northern side was given neutral status. The sultan of Aceh regarded the small Malay states on the east coast as his vassals, and hence saw any Dutch involvement as an encroachment into the internal affairs of his state. In 1862 the Dutch went on the offensive for the first time. The Resident of Riau, whose region included the sultanate of Siak, which like Aceh regarded the small states on the east coast as its vassals, visited the east coast and made the rulers there sign treaties by which they recognized Dutch sovereignty. In reaction to this Aceh sent a small armada to the east coast to put pressure on the ruling sultans there. The British governor of Penang also sent gunboats as a sign of disapproval, but did not receive permission from London to become directly involved in events.

A year after the establishment of nominal Dutch rule and a year before the first Dutch colonial official, Controller J. A. M. van Cats Baron de Raet, was sent to supervise the sultanate of Deli, the first planter, Jacobus Nienhuijs, had already settled in Deli and received a concession from the sultan to start a trial plantation of tobacco. The quality of the first harvest, sold in Rotterdam in 1864, was of very high quality. Encouraged by this success Nienhuijs obtained more credit from his patrons, the trading company Pieter van den Arend & Co. of Rotterdam, and in 1865/66 three other planters settled in Deli.

The European tobacco, nutmeg and coconut plantations expanded rapidly. By 1871 the sultan of Deli had granted concessions for 17,900 bouw (12,702 ha) to a total of twenty entrepreneurs. The largest landowner was the Deli-Maatschappij, founded in 1869, whose second director (after Nienhuijs) was J. T. Cremer, who later served as Colonial Minister in the Netherlands from 1897 to 1901. The workers on the plantations were brought from China and later from Java, since the Malays and Karo refused from the start to work as coolies. By 1870 3000 Chinese coolies were working on the plantations.

From 1871 the sultan started granting land not only from his own region (Deli proper) but also from the bordering Malay and Batak regions which had their own rulers. The sultan regarded their land as his property under his personal control, but according to the *adat* the sultan had little power over these regions. The Karo regions in the *dusun* were obliged to support him in case of war for payment and in legal matters such as capital offences or conflicts between villages they turned to the sultan as a higher court. Traditionally the sultan derived his power mainly from the strategic position of his region at the mouth of the Deli river and from the recognition he received from the sultan of Aceh. However, according to the *adat* he had no control over the land belonging to the Malays or Batak without the agreement of the ruler. The flagrant violation of the *adat* caused the Karo affected by it to rise in revolt and burn tobacco-drying sheds. They joined under the leadership of the ruler of Sunggal and barricaded themselves in Timbang Langkat. The sultan asked the colonial government for help and on 10 May 1872 a company of soldiers and artillery were dispatched from Riau to Deli. The uprising, known as the "Batakoorlog" or *perang Sunggal*, caused the Dutch many difficulties and was suppressed only after two requests for reinforcements from Batavia with the latest military equipment (Veth 1877: 152–70; Sinar 1980: 10–25; Pelzer 1985: 93ff).

The Dutch learnt their lessons from this war. New rules were laid down for the granting of concessions with some protection at least for the rights of the people, and the Malay ruler, called the *datuk*, or the Batak *pengulu*, the "oldest in the village", received a third of the rent. Moreover, the administration was reorganized and in 1873 the residency of "Oostkust van Sumatra" with Bengkalis as the seat of the Resident was established. An "Assistent-Resident" was appointed for Deli. In 1887 Medan became the capital of the East Coast.

Nevertheless the situation remained precarious. The tobacco plantations extended further and further into Karo territory, and the government's measures to protect the native population were evaded by the plantation owners. The government officials were regularly presented with lavish gifts (Pelzer 1985: 114f).

From Deli the plantations expanded further into the territory of the east-coast sultanates of Langkat in the west, Serdang and Asahan in the east and into the region Batubara. In the highlands of these coastal states was the region settled by the Simalungun who watched the activities of the Dutch and especially of the Malay rulers with increasing annoyance, and from the 1880s there were open expressions of unrest here too. Of the four Simalungun states it was Raya which caused the Dutch the most problems. In 1887 troops from Raya attacked the small Malay state of Padang, whose ruler, Tungku Mohamad Nurdin, had been deposed by the sultan of Deli. The Raya under the leadership of their *raja*, Tuan Rondahaim, now gave the ruler their support. The sultan of Deli wanted to mobilize his army against him, but the Dutch prevented him because they feared a general uprising in Batak land. Tuan Rondahaim was ordered to the seat of government in Medan but he sent only a deputy who "behaved so impertinently" that he was taken prisoner (Tideman 1922: 44ff).

Since the Raya were also in dispute with their neighbouring state of Tanah Jawa, they gave up Padang for the time being, but in the same year they attacked Bandar Berjambu, the border village between Padang and Raya, and drove out the Malays living there.

As among the Simalungun so also among the Karo unrest towards the Malays grew. Not only because their sultans amassed vast fortunes from the granting of concessions, but also because the Malay rulers and traders were seeking to extend their influence to the Batak region. They had already taken over the vital salt trade and by the end of the 1890s the *datuk* of Hamperan Perak (a princedom in the Sultanate of Deli) had established a coffee plantation at Bandar Baru near the pass to the Karo plateau and claimed the sulphur from the Deleng Sibayak volcano. In 1899 there was violence when representatives of the Sultan of Langkat seized the monopoly of the resin trade with great disadvantages for the Karo Batak resin gatherers. Some Malay and and Chinese resin traders were robbed and murdered. The perpetrators sought refuge with the *pengulu* of the village of Batukarang one of the strongest opponents of the colonial government.

Throughout the 1880s and 1890s the East Coast had become very rich, as the planters made vast fortunes from their tobacco, and later rubber plantations. While they were not interested in extending their territory to the climatically unsuitable plateau, political contacts with the *raja* of the plateau were unavoidable simply for reasons of security. To this end C. J. Westenberg was appointed "Controller for Batak Affairs" in 1888, and two years later the Deli industrialists contributed 30,000 guilders for the building of a Christian mission, which was later also financed by the planters and was intended to help maintain political stability in the plantation region and prevent the Karo converting to Islam under the influence of Aceh (which had been at war with the colonial power since 1873) and become enemies of the government. However, the mission did not have the desired success. By 1905 only a hundred Karo had accepted Christianity. The Karo did not trust the motives of the missionaries and thought they were preparing the way for the planters. The first Christians were contemptuously called "white men's coolies" and were told they would have to fight in the war against the Aceh. The work of the mission was also made difficult by the influence of the Malayan *datuk* which had grown because of the support by the European planters and government officials and who openly declared that the Batak *pengulu* could not become Christians. It was thus the *pengulu* who were least well disposed towards the mission, and without their example hardly any Karo were prepared to convert to Christianity (Neumann 1902a).

The work of the mission was concentrated on medical work

9 The *sibayak* Pa Mbelgah of Kabanjahe. Karo plateau, c. 1910

and immunization against smallpox, which recurred periodically and claimed many victims especially in the *dusun*, as well as building schools, though at the beginning these were poorly attended.

The attitude of the independent Karo and Simalungun to the colonial administration was contradictory. Their chiefs came regularly to the Malayan "autonomous administration" of the sultans of Deli at Medan, or to the European government officials at Bangun Purba, where the "Controller for Batak Affairs",

C. J. Westenberg, had his headquarters. The Karo were not at all inclined to submit to the Dutch government, since they could see the fate of their brothers in the *dusun* who had been robbed of their land under European and Malay rule.

Whereas the Karo had a clear sense of independence, some of the *raja* of the Simalungun were more willing to place themselves under Dutch sovereignty and grant their land as concessions to European planters.

The difference in attitude between these two neighbouring Batak tribes may be explained by a difference in social organization. Karo land was divided into numerous independent political conglomerations called *urung*, usually consisting of a mother village and the daughter villages founded from it. In 1905 on the plateau there were eleven *urung* and twelve independent villages which did not belong to any *urung*. The head of an *urung* was a *raja urung* or *sibayak*, who was primus inter pares. He combined the roles of commander in chief, supreme judge and political leader, though in fact his power was small since the really important political units were the villages under the leadership of a *pengulu*. These were frequently subdivided into sections of villages (*kesain*), which were under their own, relatively autonomous *pengulu kesain*. Thus the political structures were very decentralized and "grass-roots" orientated.

In Simalungun on the other hand there were only four *urung*: Tanah Jawa, Siantar, Pane and Raya. These were subdivided into *karajaan* which mostly consisted of a few villages and were under a *tuan*. The *raja* of the four *urung* and the *tuan* enjoyed a much greater respect from their respective subjects, and they ruled their subjects and particularly their slaves (*jabolon*) in an almost feudal manner. While the Karo village land was owned by the villagers in common, the Simalungun *raja* and *tuan* regarded land as their personal property.

So it was not surprising if some of the Simalungun *raja* followed the Malay example and made themselves rich by granting concessions to tobacco companies.

In the 1880s the tobacco companies had spread throughout almost the whole of the east coast. As cultivable land became scarce the planters turned their attention increasingly to the fertile Simalungun piedmont zone. In 1884 they were granted concessions for the first time in the Simalungun country of Tanjung Kasau. This annoyed the *raja* of Siantar who regarded this territory as part of his state.

A year later it became known that the German American Baron von Horn had come to a secret agreement with the *raja* of Siantar giving him exclusive rights to concessions. The Baron even cherished the idea of asking the German government for support in establishing a German protectorate in Simalungun. News of this made the Dutch colonial government reconsider its

resolution of 1885 to plan no further territorial expansion for the time being. Three years later the *tuan* of Tanjung Kasau signed a declaration submitting to Dutch sovereignty, and shortly afterwards the *raja* of Siantar and Tanah Jawa followed his example. After 1891 a government decree prevented the annexation of any other regions for a few years, and it was not until 1904 that the states of Pane and Raya became part of the Dutch colonial territory.

The secret agreement of the *raja* of Siantar clearly shows that some at least of the Simalungun *raja* were interested in making their land available to European planters.

From 1889 onwards Controller Westenberg regularly toured the plateau inhabited by the Karo and Simalungun in order to foster political contacts and settle conflicts. The inhabitants of the plateau also had to rely on friendly relations with the European administration, since they still had their traditional trade with the coastal region. Their main export was horses, but also exported other livestock, resin and rattan in lesser quantities. From the coast they obtained, among other products, their vital salt. An easy means of putting political pressure on the plateau was to close the passes, and frequent use was made of this.

The aim of the Dutch policy was to create stable political conditions on the plateau with the minimum of administrative and financial expense, and have the Karo as allies if Aceh were to launch an attack across the plateau on Deli. So they encouraged the Karo to act together against bands from Aceh and Gayo and Alas land, who occasionally threatened the plateau, and also supported some endangered villages with firearms and ammunition.

Political relations were, however, almost entirely restricted to the eastern part of the plateau. The most notable of the *raja* the Karo plateau were the *sibayak* of Kabanjahe, the half-brothers Pa Pelita and Pa Mbelgah. They were violent enemies of each other, and each strove to increase his influence in order to outdo the other. The government's policy was to strengthen one party in the long term so that it gained a clear supremacy and could then represent all the *urung* as a trading partner with the government. The government supported Pa Pelita, who was very friendly towards it, but it soon realized that his influence was too small for him to gain a dominant standing within the eastern *urung*.

The Dutch administration had made hardly any contacts with the western *urung*. The influential *raja* here was the *pengulu* of Batukarang in the populous *urung* of Lima Senina. Si Kiras, otherwise known as Pa Garamata, had already aroused the hatred of the government by constantly refusing to have any dealings with it. The increasing influence of the *sibayak* of Kabanjahe aroused the mistrust of many; people suspected him of playing into the governments hands and of intending to relinquish independence. When in 1902 the mission received permission to build a post on the plateau, Pa Pelita made land in Kabanjahe available for a mission house. Many *urung* then banded together and attacked Kabanjahe, the population of which had already fled. The village was looted and the wood for building the mission house was taken away as booty. After this the government's policy of moving the eastern *urung* to support Pa Pelita had failed.

In 1904 in the course of Colonel von Daalen's notoriously bloody military expedition the lands of the Gayo and Alas were subjugated, and in large areas half the population perished. Some of the troops returned through Karo land to Medan. Pa Pelita and Pa Mbelgah, who had meanwhile become reconciled at the government's instigation, had accompanied them and been very helpful. At this the rage of the western *urung* against the two *sibayak* increased, and once again a large number of *urung* formed an alliance under the leadership of the *pengulu* of Batukarang and attacked Kabanjahe. Kabanjahe formed a counter-alliance and to begin with was successful in battle. However, the *urung* led by Kiras Bangun received reinforcements from the village of Lingga which joined the opposition after its population had driven out their *sibayak*.

The *sibayak* of Kabanjahe called on the government for help, which was given because the government saw that their policy had now definitely failed. There was the danger not only that the missionaries could not settle on the plateau, but also that the fruits of the policy of the previous years would be lost, since it was certain that the *raja* of Si Pitu Kuta and Si Lima Kuta, both *urung* in Simalungun, would be forced to withdraw their recent submission to the colonial government.

On 7 September 1904 a column of 200 Dutch colonial troops entered the plateau. After a week the energetic resistence in Batukarang was broken. The *urung* of the Karo plateau had to swear an oath to wage no more wars and pay damages of 14,733 Spanish dollars (Westenberg 1904; Schadee 1920).

In the districts of Simalungun which remained independent no such opposition had formed, but the Dutch were still irritated by the *raja* of Siantar who had accepted Dutch sovereignty in 1888. This *raja* Sangnawalu had signed the document of submission when he was still a minor and under the guardianship of his uncle and one of the magnates called Bah Bolak. Sangnawalu was thought to be stubborn. In 1901 he converted to Islam and attempted to make the rest of his family change their religion too. The conversion of a Simalungun *raja* to Islam represented a very real threat to the Dutch who feared nothing more than a religious war of resistance following the pattern of Aceh. In 1906 Sangnawalu was removed for misuse of his office and sent into exile together with Bah Bolak. His son, Riah Tuan Kadim, was taken to the missionary in Purba to remove him from Islamic influence, and in 1916, after changing his name to Waldemar

10 The house of Pa Mbelgah, with a skull house (*geriten*) and a dovecote in front of it, c. 1910

Tuan Naga, he was appointed head of the native administration.

In 1907 the four *raja* of Simalungun and four of the *raja* who had been legitimized by the Dutch administration, were forced to sign the "Korte Verklaring" (Short Treaty) by which they were officially incorporated into the colonial empire. In eastern Sumatra the Dutch practised a policy of indirect rule. Most of the traditional *raja* were allowed to stay in office, but their rights were reduced. In Karo land with its many small states the administration revived the ancient institution of the *raja berempat* ("the four *raja*"), which had developed there under Aceh influence as it had throughout Batakland, but which for the Karo had remained little more than a name. The *raja* and village chiefs were given administrative duties. Their legitimation came from the colonial government and not, as in the traditional society, from the people. Administrative centres were set up, and a state apparatus with a police force and prisons was formed (the administration of the law remained largely in the hands of the traditional courts with the village chief or *raja* presiding). In 1907 compulsory schooling was introduced.

Schooling in Simalungun was firmly in the hands of the Rheinische Mission, which had begun its work among the Simalungun in 1904. In Karo land, however, schools were run by Deli Mission of the Nederlandsch Zendelinggenootschap which in the same year extended its activities to the Karo plateau.

After the submission of the independent Batak lands the mission was able to achieve greater success than before, but the *raja* continued to oppose the mission because they feared a loss of their power, which was legitimized by religion. In its first years under colonial rule Karo land experienced an enormous economic boom due to extensive vegetable growing (see Chapter 2). In Simalungun the profits from the boom, which occurred there too, went mostly to the European planters and the regions in which the Toba Batak immigrants grew irrigated rice, while the plateau of Simalungun remained a marginal region in economic terms. In 1908 taxes began to be collected and every adult male was required to contribute up to 52 days labour a year for building roads through Karo land. In one of the rare written sources a Karo expressed his displeasure:

The sun is high in the sky,
we are working on this road,
if we want to go to the field hut
the foreman says it is not eleven o'clock yet;
then we suffer most,
O friends and fellow clan members.

How could it not be,
for hunger and thirst are combined,
as we stick the great spade
into the winding mountain pass.
(Lament, Tropical Museum, Amsterdam No. 137–644)

Taxes and forced labour were largely unknown in their traditional society, so it is not surprising that the drastic changes caused a deep psychological crisis for the Karo with their strong sense of independence.

Their discontent first made itself felt in 1908. The resistance was centred in the *urung* of the western Karo plateau. Led by *sibayak* Pa Tolong of Kuta Buluh several hundred men arrived on a number of occasions at the Assistent-Resident headquarters at Seribu Dolok to express their displeasure at forced labour and taxes. The movement spread quickly and the population refused to accept their tax bills or to start road-building. It was only through military intervention and after the banishing of Pa Tolong that the unrest was put down.

In the following years the mission stagnated, particularly in Karo land, where in 1920 there were still only 379 Christians. This was largely due to the *parhudamdam* movement, a pan-Batak, messianic movement which started in 1917 in north Toba from where it spread via Simalungun into Karo land. The followers of the *parhudamdam* believed in the resurrection of *Si Singamangaraja XII*, a religious and political leader of a section of the Toba Batak, who after a long pursuit finally fell into an ambush laid by the colonial army in 1907 and was shot. After his resurrection a new happy state was supposed to begin once the Dutch had been driven out, which would coincide with a natural disaster in which only the *parhudamdam* followers would be spared. The movement opposed Dutch rule, Christianity, taxes and forced labour. By 1920 the movement had collapsed because

of lack of organization, but it did have some after-effects. The *parhudamdam* movement was the first time that the wind of national consciousness blowing across Indonesia affected the Batak.

The *parhudamdam* movement was mainly supported by the disadvantaged in the new society. The magicians and healers (*guru* and *datu*) also played a large part in it, since they saw their privileged position in society threatened. Messianic influence was evident in the movement, but it was also political. Even in the years following its defeat the Karo still refused to send their children to the mission schools, which were therefore all closed in 1920. The population, who were aware of the usefulness of a modern education built their own schools, made the school benches, got the teaching materials and were quite prepared to pay much higher fees than those asked by the mission schools. The people had become more self-assured and began to take hold of their own future.

The years after the *parhudamdam* movement were years of political stability and the consolidation of the colonial administration. But the population began to organize themselves, form associations and political parties, and establish their own press. In this period the foundations were laid for the active participation of the Batak people in the development of a modern, independent Indonesian society. The mission made only slow progress. The Simalungun Batak did not convert to Christianity in large numbers until the formation of their own Simalungun Batak church in independent Indonesia (GKPS, Gereja Kristen Protestan Simalungun), and the Karo only after 1965, when under the anti-communist Suharto government "atheists" (i. e. those who were not members of one of the four recognized montheist religions) could easily come under the suspicion of sympathizing with the banned Communist Party.

While the Karo Batak developed a strong sense of self-confidence because of their economic strength based on market gardening, the numerically weaker Simalungun group failed to become a politically relevant factor in north Sumatra. The fertile piedmont region was firmly in the grip of the plantation economy and of the Javanese and Toba Batak immigrants. Already by 1930 37 per cent of the Simalungun population was living on the plantations (Pelzer 1985: 87) and it was only on the small and economically weak plateau that the Simalungun were still in the majority.

In 1942 the Japanese invasion brought to an end the Dutch colonial rule over the Simalungun and Karo Batak, which had lasted less than forty years. Hardly anyone shed a tear for the former colonial rulers, but nobody could have foreseen that the following years were to go down in history as the years of greatest suffering for the Batak.

Chapter 2   The Economic Foundations of the Society (Uli Kozok)

This chapter is mainly concerned with agricultural production, which still plays the dominant part in the Batak economy. A more comprehensive discussion of the very complex economy of northern Sumatra in its national and international context cannot be attempted here, and consequently important issues regarding the economy and political development have had to be omitted, such as unemployment and underemployment, the role of public service as an important employer, and other themes which do not specifically concern the Batak people.

Pre-colonial economic systems

Sources for the pre-colonial period all date from the initial phase of colonial expansion into Batakland. The colonial officials, missionaries and explorers to whom we owe the earliest accounts of the Batak were, of course, only able to describe what they saw and heard at the time. Their accounts may mention features that only appeared after contact with European culture. Any attempt to reconstruct the pre-colonial economic system is therefore a bold undertaking and liable to contain errors. Moreover, the culture and in this case the economic conditions of Batakland in the period before the direct political and military expansion of Dutch colonialism from the mid-19th century to the first decade of the present century had already come under indirect European influence, which should not be underestimated. It should be remembered that maize – an important staple food of the Batak – is of American origin and was spread through South-East Asia by Europeans from the 16th century onwards. The same is true of tobacco, the chewing and smoking of which was widespread – and still is. John Anderson, an Englishman who visited the small east coast state of Deli in 1823 on behalf of his government, reported that Karo from the plateau were engaged in the spice trade with the British colony of Malaya and had even laid out pepper plantations specially for export (Anderson 1971).

Batakland covers an area larger than Belgium and has a very varied pattern of settlement. Large areas of the country have never been settled and are covered in dense primeval forest, while in some districts the population is concentrated in a very small area. A number of factors have contributed to this very uneven distribution of the population.

Northern Sumatra is divided geographically into three zones which run through the land from north to south. The western and eastern coastal strips are inhabited by Malays, so only the mountain and piedmont zones are relevant for our purposes. The mountain zone consists primarily of the volcanic Bukit-Barisan range which runs through Sumatra from north to south with its foothills. Fourteen of its peaks are more than 2000 metres high. Within this mountainous zone is a high-mountain region which is unsuitable for human settlement because of the steep slopes, and rice, the principal food, cannot be grown above 1500 metres. This high- mountain region has a severe climate and is mainly covered with tropical rainforest which changes at 1800 metres to "mist forest".

Despite these limitations the mountainous zone is the most populous area because within the zone there are a number of plateaux and high valleys where the population has always concentrated.

The northern part (the Karo-*dusun*) of the piedmont zone towards the east coast is much fissured by mountain ridges and deep valleys running from the high mountains to the coast and therefore, although its soil is good, has few inhabitants.

Besides climatic and geographical factors soil conditions are also a decisive factor. Predominant are the grey and reddish yellow podzol soils typical of the tropics, which are very acidic and contain little organic material. Only through slash-and-burn cultivation can these soils provide satisfactory yields. More fertile are the latosol soils which occur in the Simalungun piedmont zone, on Samosir, in the highlands of Sibolga and south west of Lake Toba.

Andosol soils which are found on geologically young volcanoes, are extremely fertile. The eastern Karo plateau consists of this soil and is one of the most fertile and heavily populated regions of Batakland. In the pre-colonial period 65 per cent of the land here was under cultivation, 20 per cent was covered with primeval forest, and 15 per cent was uncultivated, mainly grass steppe. At the beginning of the 20th century there were already more than 30,000 people living here in an area of only 400 sq km. The corresponds to a population density of at least 75 inhabitants per sq km (see table; Volz 1909: 275ff).

Alluvial soils formed of eroded material from plateaux are particularly fertile if the eroded material comes from volcanic areas. Soils of this type are found only in isolated cases in Batakland. Of importance are the alluvial zones on the shores of Lake Toba, in particular on Samosir and the southern shores around Balige which form a huge *sawah* (paddy-field) area. At the turn of the century there was a population of over 90,000 living here in the heart of Batakland.

River valleys are only suitable for cultivation if the soil is not cut into too deeply. For this reason high valleys with fertile alluvial zones in the valley bottom, such as the Silindung valley, have always been favoured settlement areas. The Silindung valley had a population 45,000 in 1910.

Originally almost the whole of Batakland was covered with primeval forest. Centuries of human settlement have drastically altered the face of the landscape. At the beginning of the colonial period the different regions offered a very varied picture. The piedmont zone towards the east coast and almost the whole of Pakpak land was still covered with forest with individual settlement clearings consisting of several small villages. Near the villages were dry rice fields (Indonesian: *ladang*, Batak: *huma* or *juma*), and near the settlement areas the primary forest had already given way to looser secondary forest and small grass steppes.

The eastern Karo plateau consisted, as we have mentioned, almost entirely of cultivated land. The largest Batak villages of all, many of which had more than 1000 inhabitants, were located here. The western plateau was less heavily populated and was largely covered with forest. At various places the forest had been so frequently burned that they soil was carstified until finally only a hard grass (Indonesian: *alang-alang*) could grow their. These grass steppes, which cover large areas in some parts of Batakland, are always the result of human activity.

The Simalungun plateau is similar to the eastern Karo plateau but was more heavily forested. The mountains were all covered with forest, but the steep slopes which descend from the plateau to Lake Toba were completely treeless steppe.

Central Batakland (Toba) was still thickly forested, except for the plateaux (cultivated land and grass steppes), the paddy-field region on the southern part of Lake Toba, Samosir and the high valleys of Silindung and Batang Toru (both south of Lake Toba).

Mountainous southern Batakland (Angkola and Mandailing) was thickly forested and only the river valleys were inhabited. The flat treeless steppe of Padang Bolak, covering 1600 sq km, is also part of the southern Batak region and has almost no settlements. Presumably primeval forest once grew here too. The deforestation has led to a definite change in climate with months of drought followed by severe flooding. It is not known how such extreme weather conditions could have entered the natural ecosystem. From other regions we know that slash-and-burn cultivation in a densely populated area, or wars, which were frequently the consequence of disputes over the lessening land, led to the desolation of extensive stretches of land.

The staple food is rice, mainly grown on unirrigated fields. Only the Karo and, especially, the Toba use irrigated paddy-fields to a significant degree. The latter often use wooden irrigation pipes which are laid using the combined labour of several neighbouring villages. Paddy-fields are the most intensive form of cultivation. They can be worked year after year, but because of the cool mountain climate produce only one harvest a year. The productivity of irrigated cultivation with a yield (in multiples of the quantity of seed used) of 25 to 100 (in the fertile piedmont zone of Karo land this could even reach 200), is incomparably higher than unirrigated cultivation. Unirrigated rice in the highlands produced yields of no more than 30–40, only in the more fertile and warmer regions could yields of 60–100 be achieved (Joustra 1910: 286, 303; Tidemann 1922: 118ff).

On an unirrigated field as a rule no more than two to four harvests are possible before the soil is exhausted and needs to lie fallow for eight to ten years. During this fallow period the fields are usually used as pasture for livestock. Unirrigated and irrigated fields are worked in the same way. The field is broken up with sticks and/or with a hand-plough drawn by a woman, then smoothed with a rake and (in the case of the Karo) with a wooden club (*gudam-gudam*, ill. 14b). Other agricultural implements such as transverse spades and various sorts of hoes are also used. Occasionally the fields are fertilized with cattle dung and earth from the village (rich in organic material because of the pigs, dogs and chickens that run loose there), which means that the period of cultivation can be extended and the fallow period shortened. This more intensive form of the land use was not practised by the Simalungun and Pakpak.

In areas where sufficient primary and secondary forest was available, as in Pakpak land, in the Karo and Simalungun *dusun* and parts of Mandailing, unirrigated fields were thus often laid out as part of slash-and-burn cultivation.

The following is a description of slash-and-burn cultivation as practised by the Pakpak, who use the method as almost their only form of cultivation.

The unirrigated rice fields were laid out by the villages on a continuous area. The *permangmang*, a magician who specialized in agriculture, would look for a suitable piece of forest. The villagers then marked the area which was then divided by the *pertaki*, the village chief, between the various families. These then erected a small bamboo sacrificial altar on the land allocated to them. The *permangmang* determined the day for the felling of the trees, which were burned about a month later. Only a few big trees, fruit trees and those with bees" nests were left standing. Around the complex a fire-break was left which was first cleared of trees and undergrowth. Under the direction of the *permangmang* the boundaries of the land of the individual families were marked by putting down branches. A fence was then built around the complex by the community to protect the crops from wild boar. The wild plants were pulled up and piled together with what was left of the wood and burned. In the middle of their field each family planted some sugar cane, medicinal herbs, cucumbers and pandanus to weave mats from. Before the *permangmang* fixed the day for sowing he held a ceremony after which the village was closed for four days. This was the period of *rebu* ("taboo") when nobody was allowed to leave or enter the village. After the days of *rebu* a festive meal was held. Only then could sowing begin. First the field of the *permangmang* was sown by the community together. Afterwards came another two days of rebu. As a rule the ground needed no further working. The most important implement was the dibble with which the men made the holes into which the women scattered the seed. The *permangmang* had huts built where the families lived in the last weeks before the harvest to protect the ripe rice from birds. Any further work on the field was done by the women, while the men gathered forest products or planted benzoin, a fragrant, incense-like resin, which like the other products was traded on the coast. When the rice was ripe the *permangmang* would hold a feast for which a buffalo, a cow or merely a pig would be slaughtered. During these rebu days nobody was allowed to walk on the fields so that the spirits would have a chance to taste the fruits. At the beginning of the harvest the women brought to the *Boraspati Ni Tano* ("Spirit of the Earth") an offering in the form of rice or betel-pepper. For harvesting the women used a small knife with which they cut the rice stem by stem. Threshing was done by treading, and the rice grains were then stored in round barrels made of tree-bark or in rectangular wooden chests in the village granary. Three months after the harvest the harvest festival or *kerja tahun* took place, guests were invited and offerings presented to the spirits of the ancestors while the *gendang* orchestra played (Ypes 1932: 118ff).

This slash-and-burn cultivation, as practised by the Pakpak, was perhaps the most suited to their circumstances. The infertile soil was improved by the ashes, and the relatively low population density made it possible to have long enough fallow periods for the land to recuperate. Most of the Pakpak villages were temporary and were abandoned when there was no more land to be planted nearby. A new village would then be founded on a different site. The necessity of moving the villages with the fields resulted from the difficulties of reaching fields laid out in the forest.

Toba and Karo fields were usually situated on a treeless plateau and, even if they are several kilometres from the village, they can still be reached quickly in the grassland. As well as dry rice fields the Karo and particulary the Toba also make use of paddy-fields which are worked permanently. The settlements are consequently tied to them, and the villages in the steppes are fixed and usually consist of fine, large wooden houses, whereas the Pakpak, Simalungun and Mandailing do not usually build massive houses.

The most commonly cultivated crop after rice was maize. In Simalungun and Mandailing it was in fact the staple food of the poorer people. The tuber cassava was also of some importance, and various vegetables together with indigo (for dying textiles) and fruit trees were grown in gardens which were usually laid out in a ring around the village. An important fruit tree was the sugar palm the sap of which was used for making an alcoholic drink called *tuak* and for making sugar, while the fibres provided a durable material for covering roofs. In warmer places (below 900 metres) coconut palms were also grown. Cotton was grown in the Simalungun country of Tanah Jawa, but because European yarns and textiles very soon supplanted the native product, little is known about cotton growing. In Pakpak land *kemenyan* trees were also planted to provide benzoin resin, almost all of which was sold to Malay dealers on the west coast. The most frequently gathered forest products were rattan, various resins and honey.

11 View of Berastagi from Mount Bukit Gundaling. Karo plateau, 1989

The distribution of population related to geographical conditions and agricultural methods in the Batak lands in the pre-colonial period.

	Karo	Pakpak	Simalungun	Toba	Angkola Mandailing	Padang Lawas
1	Ladang (Sawah)	Ladang	Ladang	Sawah/ Ladang	Ladang	Ladang
2	permanent fields	migratory cultivation (slash-and-burn)	permanent fields and migratory cultivation	permanent fields	permanent fields and migratory cultivation	permanent fields and migratory cultivation
3 a	high plain	mountains	plain	high plain	mountains	plain
b	mountains	high plain	high plain	mountains lake shore		(steppe)
c			mountains	high valleys		
4 a	high plain +	rivervalleys –	plain +	lake shore +	river valleys +	river valleys –
b	river valleys +	high plain –	high plain –	high valleys +		
c				high plain –		
5	120,000 (24/km²)	25,000 (6/km²)	60,000 (10/km²)	300,000 (38/km²)	100,000 (18/km²)	40,000 (5/km²)

1. Main type of rice cultivation. Ladang = dry field cultivation; Sawah = irrigated field cultivation.

2. Economy of rice cultivation. Permanent = the fields are constantly replanted after being left fallow for a period. Changing (slash-and-burn) = the fields are abandoned after a few years and new fields are created by slash-and-burn technique.

3. Geographical nature of the region. The proportions of the total area are indicated in diminishing order (a–c).

4. Preferred settlement areas in the country. "+" = soil of superior quality; "–" = inferior quality. Density of population indicated in diminishing order (a–c).

5. Population in 1905 (based on estimates, in all approx. 645,000). In Angkola/Mandailing and in Padang Lawas the precolonial population was about 20 per cent less than the figures given. The population density is given in brackets.

Livestock was particularly important in the grass steppes. Buffalo, cattle, horses, goats, dogs, chickens and, above all, pigs were kept. The larger animals were mainly used for transport or export. Most loads were carried by people and only rarely would water buffalo be used to pull the plough – and this was almost exclusively confined to the Toba paddy-fields. Hunting wild boar and roe-deer was almost wholly a leisure activity.

The Batak villages were almost entirely economically independent. Anything needed could be purchased in the many markets which were held at regular times and places in the open air under the shade of a large tree. In Karo land alone there were more than twenty markets mainly dealing in imported goods. The most significant import was salt which was carried from the coast through the mountain passes to Batakland. Other imports included iron and gold, textiles, yarns, salted fish, and, in the early colonial period, matches and paraffin. Home-produced items such as betel, betel lime, tobacco, sugar, palm wine, coconuts, limes and other fruit were also sold. Before the currency reform in 1908 prohibited the use of old coins, various currencies were in use: Spanish and Mexican dollars, Chinese and Japanese coins had largely replaced barter (see ill. 254).

The most important trading partners of the Batak were the Malay coastal states. The main exports were livestock and forest products. The transport network consisted only of narrow footpaths linking the villages and markets. At the villages (*bandar*) on the border of the Malay coastal states export duties were levied.

There was some specialization of crafts between different villages and regions, which to some extent derived from the distribution of resources. Weaving was very widespread; only the Pakpak acquired their clothing mainly from the Karo, Malays or Toba. The weaving of mats and bags was practised in all villages by young women. More specialized was the blacksmith's craft; only a few villages had blacksmiths, who produced implements for daily use such as knives, hoes and other agricultural tools, as well as weapons. Goldsmiths and silversmiths were even rarer. The Toba and Karo in particular were famous for their delicate filigree work. The production of pottery was not highly valued and was confined to a few simple household items. Samosir and a few villages in Padang Lawas were small centres of ceramic production.

As we have mentioned, the differences between the various sections of the population within Batakland can be explained by a number of factors: the climate which limits the growing of rice to below an altitude of about 1500 metres, a very hilly landscape with deep river valleys hindered the exchange of goods and agriculture is impossible on steep slopes without very expensive construction of terraces and irrigation systems. Only fertile soils are able to provide sufficient food for a relatively dense population. Considering this it is surprising that the piedmont zone of Simalungun despite its advantages (fertile soils, an uninterrupted, slightly sloping landscape) was sparsely inhabited. There seem to have been historical reasons for this. The Batak spread in all directions from their "original homeland" on Lake Toba. The first areas to be settled were the plateaux and the high valleys. Only after the Simalungun had been living on the plateau for a long time did groups of them move into the piedmont zone. The Karo Batak tell the same story. According to their legends the piedmont zone was settled only in relatively recent times from the plateau. The reasons the leaving the homeland may have been social and political conflicts, pressure of population and shortage of land, and perhaps the ambition to become *pengulu* of a newly founded village, as the immigration of the Toba in the first decades of this century showed. Unlike the Simalungun and Karo Batak, the Toba Batak had no land in their immediate proximity which they thought suitable for reclamation, and they adopted a different strategy to confront the pressure of population: an intensification of agricultural production by using irrigated paddy-fields.

12 Chinese vegetable seller on a plantation in the lowlands. East Coast, c. 1930

The colonial period and its effect on the economy

The Dutch found Batakland of only small economic interest, and it was mainly political calculation which determined the annexation of the free Batak lands. The first country to submit to Dutch rule was Mandailing in 1835/36. The reasons were political and military: the *padri* war (see chapter 1). This did not, however, prevent the colonial power from forcing the population in 1841 to grow coffee and sell it the government at a fixed price. Mountainous Batakland was not suitable for plantations like those that had been established since the 1860s on the east coast. However, in the *dusun* of Karo and particularly of Simalungun the plantation economy spread. This took place at the expense of the population who gradually lost more and more rights to their land, while the Malay rulers, especially the Sultan of Deli, became rich from the rents. In Simalungun the *raja* and *tuan* of the plantation region received the rent, but later the colonial government changed to giving them a fixed salary instead. By 1938 a third of the area of Simalungun belonged to European plantation-owners. Thousands of coolies were brought over from the Malay peninsula (mainly Chinese) and Java, because the native population were unwilling to work as dependent coolies. By 1921 there were 44,000 coolies working on the plantations in Simalungun, and former coolies had settled in new villages near the plantations.

This enormous growth in population was accompanied by an increased demand for food in the plantation strip on the east coast. To boost rice production the colonial administration provided land for the Toba Batak, who were experienced in irrigated paddy-field cultivation and laid an irrigation system for them. Between 1907 and 1921 c. 25,000 Toba and Mandailing immigrated to the land of the Simalungun, who soon became a minority in their own country (in 1921 42 per cent).

In the first years after the annexation of the Batak lands the colonial administration had a transport system built by the forced labour of the population. This linked the newly established administrative centres with each other and with the principal ports of northern Sumatra, Medan and Sibolga, thus laying an important foundation for the further economic development of northern Sumatra.

In 1911 an experimental planting of European vegetables was undertaken on the Karo plateau. The Karo took up this opportunity to develop their economy with enthusiasm, and by 1917 they were producing 350 tonnes of potatoes and 20,000 cabbages a month as well as other vegetables and flowers which were exported to the plantation area on the east coast, to Penang (Malaysia) and Singapore. The agricultural products were transported on the 81 km road to Medan, which was completed in 1909. By 1918 there were 1000 ox-carts, which indicated that the Karo had invested about 30,000 guilders in means of transport. The population on the Simalungun plateau reacted less enthusiastically to the opportunity to grow vegetables, but their exceptionally high taxes forced them grow produce for the market (Clauss 1982: 55).

In the other regions of Batakland, too, a market economy developed, though less quickly, superseding the traditional economic systems and their branches. Cotton production, which had been important in pre-colonial times in Simalungun and Padang Lawas, for example, was destroyed by the European imports.

Because compulsory deliveries made coffee production in Mandailing unprofitable for the population, it was slowly but perceptibly declining by 1908. Only when compulsory cultivation was abolished did coffee growing begin to flourish, and it also spread in Pakpak land and Simalungun. In the 1930s production increased to 4000 tonnes with a value of 3—4 million guilders.

In Tapanuli particularly many small farmers followed the example of the European plantations and went over to growing rubber. Between 1921 and 1927 exports of rubber produced by small farmers increased from 204 to almost 5000 tonnes.

The colonial administration was concerned to encourage food production for the rapidly rising population by extending the irrigated field cultivation especially in Mandailing and Simalungun. The rearing of livestock, particularly in the steppes of Padang Lawas, was energetically promoted, and the swiftly developing farming economy was supported by a system of credit. People's banks, such as the "Tobaneesche Landbouwbank", gave agricultural loans especially to the settlers who immigrated to Simalungun. The improved infrastructure with telephone and telegraph communications, mainly created for the plantations, also benefited the population, and a native press, which although it was predominantly regional (i. e. tribal), brought news to Batakland from all over the world.

The mission, which was firmly established in the social life especially of the Toba Batak, was rather sceptical about this development. A missionary of the time complained:

"The greatest worry for the mission on Sumatra is of being flooded by the new culture. How different the conditions on Sumatra have become. The missionary used to drive along narrow bush paths and as a rule was accompanied on his way by screaming apes. He crossed rivers by rough tree trunks or on a rope spanning a river, while his boy followed him and made the horse swim across. Now at the same place the piercing whistle of a locomotive is heard. On the newly laid roads the grand 'motors' of the raja roar past. Chocolate coloured bicycles spin past hooting loudly. In Silindung the traveller's eye pauses in amazement on a well appointed tennis court. Telephone wires

13 Agricultural implements: weeding tool (*guris*), length: 22 cm; ricecutting knife and double knife

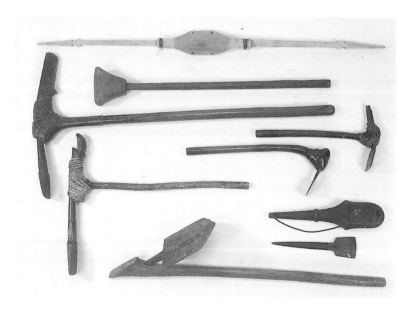

14 Agricultural implements: yoke (a), wooden club (*gudam-gudam*) for breaking up lumps of earth, axes with handles (c-f), wooden box for axe blades (g), hoe (h). Karo Batak

have been strung between the villages. The cinema of the Japanese attracts curiosityseekers in droves. The Chinese hotelier beckons with his wretched gramophone." (Bieger 1917: 92)

The mission, because of its otherworldliness and almost paranoid fear of "Islamic influence", is to some extent guilty for the relative backwardness of Batakland. Many older people can still be found there who cannot speak Indonesian, since fear of the spread of Islamic ideas made the mission for a long time prevent Malay (i. e. Indonesian) from being taught in the schools, although it was the lingua franca and language of administration.

Not all were involved to the same extent in the economic boom. Those most favoured were the *raja* appointed by the colonial administration, together with their families, as well as the new elite consisting mainly of government officials, mission staff and traders, and including the considerable number of Chinese who had followed in the wake of the Dutch – mainly as traders, but also skilled craftsmen and farmers – and were in competition with the still inexperienced Batak. Those who were not fortunate in finding a comfortable place in this new society were forced to earn their now indispensible cash by doing work for a daily wage as wellworking on their own field. The lucky ones were able to get hold of the four guilders needed to buy their release from unpaid compulsory labour for up to 52 days a year.

The basic economic structures which still determine economic life today were created during the colonial period. Then as now there existed three forms of production. First, subsistence economy is still of great, though diminishing, importance. This is the growing of rice and other agricultural and garden produce independently of the market, for one's own needs in a family concern, supplemented by the keeping of chickens, a few pigs and perhaps a water buffalo. As a rule some family members also have a second trade in order to earn the money needed to buy necessary industrial products, schooling for the children etc. There is wide range of possible jobs: small trader at the market, small craftsman, bus driver, wage-labourer in road building or agriculture etc.

The second form of production is the growing of produce intended exclusively for the market. Besides vegetables and fruit, coffee and cloves are the most common products. This cash-crop production is widespread and the predominant form of production on the Karo and Simalungun plateaux. Their vegetable producers are faced with extreme fluctuations in market prices with the result that vegetable-growing has in many cases become a game of chance. Singapore and Malaysia are the most important markets. The export trade is mostly in the hands of Chinese dealers, who also give credit for the production and have thus made many farmers dependant on them. The pricing policy of these dealers is an important factor in the fluctuation of prices. There are also suppliers from overseas who flood the markets in

15 Ploughing a field with a water buffalo. Toba region, 1989

16 Village scene with water buffalo. Gurusinga, Karo plateau, 1984

37

Malaysia and Singapore with their state-subsidised agricultural produce (even European Community produce is shipped there 10,000 km away) put the small farmers of northern Sumatra at a disadvantage, since they have to import seed, artificial fertilizers and pesticides from the industrialized countries. Intensive use of fertilizers has made the fallow periods unnecessary, and two or three harvests a year are possible. The monoculture of cabbage, potatoes and tomatoes demands the massive use of pesticides and artificial fertilizers. The ecological consequences of this intensive cash-crop production are progressive deforestation and erosion because of the demand for more and more areas for farming, as well as impoverishment and over-acidification of the soil. The possibilities of using tractors are limited because the fields are often too small or too steep, so the hand-plough is still used today, and garden tools are also generally little changed.

Lastly, the third mode of production is industrial capitalist plantation farming. The main products are rubber, palm oil, cocoa and tea. The once flourishing tobacco industry has declined greatly since the smoking of cigars, for which Deli tobacco provided the wrappers has become less popular. Most of the plantations were nationalized after independence, but after 1965, under the Suharto government, many were re-privatized and are now again owned by multinational concerns. The former Javanese contracted coolies with no rights are now free wage-labourers, but their lot has not changed much, and they are often still treated like slaves. Today the Batak still do not work as plantation labourers. They usually take the better posts on the plantations as senior salaried staff etc.

There are practically no industrial businesses in Batakland; they are almost all near the coast in and around Medan. Only a few small businesses in the food and semi-luxury goods sectors have been established in the regional centres. An exception is P. T. Indorayon, which makes raw material for paper and has recently been heavily criticized in the local media for deforesting vast areas, thus leaving them to become steppe, and discharging their unfiltered effluent into the Asahan river, which is now an ecological disaster. The biggest industrial project in Batakland is P. T. Inalum, a Japanese-Indonesian joint project for manufacturing aluminium. The electrical energy needed for this is provided by the dammed Asahan river, the only outlet from Lake Toba. This project, too, is not uncontroversial, because it is planned on a huge scale and at full capacity may reduce the level of Lake Toba by up to a metre. North Sumatra is economically one of the most important regions of Indonesia. This is almost entirely due to the plantation region of the east coast. However, agriculture on the fertile Karo and Simalungun plateaux is an important source of income which has brought their inhabitants a certain amount of prosperity, whereas central Batakland, the cradle of Batak culture, is one of the most underdeveloped parts of Indonesia.

17 Women and children on the front balcony (*turé-turé*) of a house. Karo plateau, c. 1910

Chapter 3 Traditional Foundations of Society

Rulership and equality: a contradiction?

So far as we can tell from the few historical sources available, the six Batak tribes never had a common political leadership encompassing them all. Early travellers speak either of an almost anarchic state of affairs, or else depict the *raja* (the village chiefs) as the absolute rulers of their subjects. The title *raja*, coming as it does from the Indian Sanskrit language, evokes associations with the *raja* of the subcontinent whose great power is shown by their gorgeous palaces and fabulous wealth show their enormous power. The Batak, however, have never had a central power controlling the whole Batak region, nor was each of the six Batak peoples ruled by a single political institution. The Batak *raja* often ruled a very small area and they were rarely despotic autocrats who enslaved and exploited their subjects.

The Karo Batak were never ruled by a single omnipotent ruler. Only in the urung, the largest political units, there was the *raja urung* or *sibayak*, who usually had authority over their "subjects" merely in time of war. The situation with the Pakpak Batak was similar.

Only the Toba Batak had a sort of priest-king, the *Si Singamangaraja*, whose "title" was hereditary (Joustra 1926). The twelfth *Si Singamangaraja* was an important figure in the period of the expansion of missionary and colonial territory. He was a committed opponent of the Dutch colonial power and for a long time resisted with arms the attempts of the Dutch to capture him. In 1907 he was shot dead in Pakpak country, and his body was publically displayed in Tarutung. His death marked the end of resistance to the Dutch, and thereafter the Rheinische Mission also made an increasing number of converts.

The influence of the *Si Singamangaraja* was largely restricted to the religious sphere, though the religious and the political are often impossible to separate. The term "priest-king" and "priest-prince" indicate the *Si Singamangaraja's* ambivalent function, but his secular power should not be overestimated, for he had very little significance in the daily life of the Toba Batak. True, he occasionally appointed village chiefs (van Dijk 1893; Helbig 1935: 92), and he was recognized as the head of the Toba by the Sultan of Aceh who provided him with an official seal, but he exercised his secular influence mainly in the struggle against the mission and the Dutch. On his death the office of *Si Singamangaraja* lost power and influence. His male heirs were mostly exiled from the Batak region, and his whole family were converted to Christianity. His limited secular power was also shown by the fact that by no means all the Toba Batak recognized his authority.

Besides the *Si Singamangaraja* the Toba had only their village chiefs, or *raja*. Their status was usually that of *primus inter pares* and their power was very restricted and merely based on the fact that the *raja* came from the family which had founded the village and owned the surrounding land. The raja was responsible for receiving, lodging and looking after strangers visiting his village. He represented the village in the outside world. His advice concerning the distribution of land was influential. He had a central role in the sorting out of legal disputes, laying down sentences and receiving fines, which could also be paid in kind. Without the permission of the *raja* nobody could move into the village, nor could a family leave the village to move to another region. And yet his power was restricted; he could not make decisions without the agreement of the elders and of his *boru*, which represented the village kinship group which took its wives from his family. In the Batak social system there are precisely regulated relationships of dependence between the "wife-givers" and "wife-takers", and the rights and duties of the two kinship groups towards each other are clearly defined, so that even a *raja* has obligations to his *boru* (his wife-takers) laid down in the unwritten law, or *adat*. A village chief cannot "rule" his *boru* – in so far as he can be said to rule at all.

A *raja* had real power only over the slaves (*hatoban*), who were not freed from slavery until the incorporation of the Batak lands into the Dutch colonial empire. In his role as leader of a festival, religious ceremony or military campaign the *raja* was called *suhut* (host and organizer of a celebration). For a *raja* to be recognized in all these functions what counted was not so much his formal legal rights as his charisma, his excellent knowledge of the *adat*, his generosity and justice as well as his persuasive powers of oratory. Seen from the outside, the division of village society into the family of the founder of the village, the "free citizens" (*anak mata*, who were mostly related to the village founders), and the immigrants and slaves seemed very hierarchical. In reality, however, this had only limited effects on the village communities. A *raja* who neglected his duties to his villagers soon found that his "subjects" left him to seek a new village with a fairer *raja*. If he was incapable, a *raja* could also be removed from office and replaced by another male descendant of the founder chosen by the elders of the ruling family (*marga*) and the *anak mata*, or free citizens.

18 View of the east coast of Samosir northwards. Lake Toba, 1989

19 View of the south-west coast of Lake Toba towards Bakkara, 1989

Above the level of the village *raja* the Toba also had *raja* who were responsible for a number of villages. These were usually new villages founded from a mother-village. The *raja* of this mother-village became the senior chief, or *raja ihutan*, taking the chair at meetings of the *raja*. Alongside the secular "rulers" the Toba also had the institution of *raja parbaringin* appointed by the *Si Singamangaraja*, whose function was primarily restricted to ritual.

The rulership structure of the Simalungun differed markedly from that of the Karo, Toba and Pakpak in respect of the power of the ruler (van Dijk 1893). The Simalungun region was divided into four smaller states each led - or even ruled – by an independent *raja*. In the lands under their control these *raja* appointed chiefs who bore the title of *tuan*. With the help of these *tuan* the *raja* governed their states in an almost feudal manner. Their power enabled them to exploit their subjects, to lease land to European planters for a lot of money – without regard to the population living there. The life of the simple country people in all the Simalungun states was made worse by taxes and forced labour. The large scale (by Batak standards) and lavish decoration of the great "palace" of the *tuan* Purba in Pematang Purba, now an open-air museum, show the power and wealth of its owner (ill. 31). Below the *tuan* in the hierarchy of village chiefs, were the *panghulu dusun* and *pertuanan* who were closely related to the *tuan* (van Dijk 1893: 183).

The rulers of these four Simalungun states based their legitimacy on the fact that they were appointed by the Sultan of Aceh. For a long period Aceh was the most powerful state in northern Sumatra and extended its influence far to the south. The sultans regarded Batakland as their "backyard". Occasional military actions ensured at least a formal claim to power, expressed most forcefully by the fact that the Sultan of Aceh appointed "rulers" acceptable to himself in the Karo and Simalungun regions - the *raja berempat* of the Karo and the *raja na ompat* of the Simalungun. Both terms mean "the four *raja*". The sultan invested the *raja* he had appointed with insignia, consisting principally of various gold objects such as rice bowl, spoons, pan, armband and lance. At the same time they received the title of raja from him (van Dijk 1893: 179ff).

While the four Simalungun *raja* were able to expand their power to the extent that they could be regarded as monarchs, the Karo *raja berempat* had long since lost their influence (see chapter 1). It was not until 1907, after the annexation of Karo country, that the Dutch revived the institution of the *raja berempat* and instigated an administrative reform by appointing four *raja* or *sibayak* as authorized government officials.

The structure of rulership in Mandailing and Angkola following the annexation of the regions around the middle of the last century followed the pattern of the colonial administrative system (Heyting 1897: 245ff). The region was divided into districts and sub-districts, with local chiefs appointed by the Dutch. However, colonial government was based on traditional Mandailing rulership structures, allowing the ruling aristocracy (*namoramora*) to keep their position. This meant that the *raja pamusuk* not only remained leaders at local level, they were also appointed by the Dutch to be heads of the larger administrative units. To a large extent districts and sub-districts followed the pattern of earlier structures above village level, and when it came to the question of succession in office the colonial government followed local customs and ensured the succession of the eldest or youngest son (an unwritten law among he Mandailing in order to keep the rulership for the nobility).

The diversity of the Batak peoples was therefore apparent in their political systems. In the northern part of Batakland existed rulership structures based from the direct influence of the Sultan of Aceh. These structures had been forgotten by the Karo, but among the Simalungun they were firmly rooted, while the Toba Batak *Si Singamangaraja* received his insignia from the Sultan of Aceh, but had not been able to extend his power beyond the world of ritual. In southern Batakland the Batak rulership structures remained, but were made to conform to colonial requirements.

At village level the highest bearers of office always played a subordinate role. Among the Simalungun and the Mandailing this was greater than among the Toba and Karo, but in everyday life it was the *raja* of the home village who was most important. However, as the example of the Toba shows, he was part of a network of social dependencies which meant that it was relatively rare for an autocracy develop. Various social strata existed within the village: besides the ruling family (*marga raja*) there were free citizens (*anak mata*) of other family groups (*marga*). Slaves (*hatoban*) and those in debt bondage were recognizable as separate social classes long after slavery had been abolished. Despite this apparent hierarchy of social stratification membership of a particular class was not necessarily a decisive factor in daily life. A Batak derived his social status from belonging to the ruling and land-owning family, but it was possible to gain prestige and influence by having particular skills or success in business. So a rich *anak mata* could assume a more respected and powerful position in a village than an empoverished *raja* who was unable to fulfil his obligations to the villagers and visiting strangers.

Most of the slaves lived in the *raja's* house and were obliged to work in his house and fields, though they could have positions of trust in the family and were generally well treated. Debt bondage was the fate of those who could not meet their financial obligations. Only the *raja* was entitled to take someone into debt bondage, if he could not pay his gambling debts or fines, for example. Prisoners of war and foreign debtors who were captured suffered a far worse punishment: they were placed in the block. Their legs were confined between two wooden beams, and they remained in this position until their relatives ransomed them or they died. Persons placed in the block were fed only sporadically and nothing at all was done for their personal hygiene.

Inhabitants of a village who were not slaves had the right to attend all meetings and decision-making. An important element in making decisions affecting the village as a whole, as in the distribution of land or legal disputes, was that everyone – including the *raja* – strove to find solutions which were accepted by all and could be supported by all. This search for a compromise could take a long time, but no decision could be made without the various claims being reconciled. If claims were not sufficiently respected or a "lazy" compromise was reached this often led to acts of revenge and was frequently a cause of warfare between villages.

Among the Batak, therefore, rulership and equality are not mutually exclusive. The institution by which the ruling *marga* appoints the *raja* of a village does not determine the actual rulership situation in a village. For even the power of a magician-priest (*datu* or *guru*), with his skill in white and black magic, should not be underestimated. Every free citizen had the opportunity of participating in political decision-making, or was free enough to turn his back on the work of a bad *raja*. The primary interest of a raja, who represented the village to the outside world, was to own as big a village as possible. His prestige grew with the number of inhabitants and the economic prosperity of his fellow citizens. A *raja* who was unjust or too selfish soon made himself unpopular and his people moved away from him and the village. Hence the villages of unpopular or incapable raja show a high fluctuation in population.

20 Rice granary (*sopo*) next to another *sopo* which has been converted to a house. The open surface of the *sopo* is used in the daytime as a work place and at night as a place for guests and unmarried men to sleep. Toba region, near Porsea, 1985

43

21 The village of Huta Bolon on the east coast of Samosir. Lake Toba, 1985

22 The village of Huta Siallagan near Ambarita, Samosir. The stone benches, tables and figures date from the 1930s. Photographed in 1985

23 Huta Bagasan. Uluan district, Toba region, 1985

24 The village of Dokan. Unlike the street villages of the Toba, the Karo houses are always built parallel to each other. Karo plateau, 1989

25 Monument for a *raja* or *sibayak*; height: 85 cm.
Karo Batak

26 Bone house (*geriten*); height: 47 cm.
Karo Batak

27 Model houses: (a) *jambur*, height: 60 cm;
(b) house of a *sibayak*, height: 90 cm;
(c) rice-pounding house (*lesung*); height: 55 cm.
Karo Batak

The village as the focus of life

All the Batak peoples regard their village as the navel of the world, and as far as the masses of the population are concerned the larger political units described in the previous section are of only secondary significance. In daily life what is important are one's personal – above all one's family – relationships in one's own village. One's position in village society is determined by one's membership of the land-owning and ruling family of the founder of the village, of the class of free citizens (*anak mata*) or – formerly – of the slaves. This in turn determines the rights and duties of each person in daily and ceremonial life. One's social position is also determined by the social relations between the individual inhabitants of the village. Reciprocal obligations based on what – to Europeans at least – appears a complicated family system, are regarded by the Batak as desirable institutions for maintaining and constantly reinforcing the network of social relationships in the village.

Relationships of kinship between various families among the Batak are also established by marriage. The choice of a partner is subject to the unwritten laws of the Batak kinship system, some of which are very strict. All Batak have to choose their partner from another family group; marriages within the same family are not allowed. These family groups, called *marga* by the Toba and *merga* by the Karo, are the most important criterion in the various Batak societies. Of decisive importance to a Batak is the family his wife comes from – in other words, his "wife-giver" family. Just as important is the family which the daughters of his own family marry into – the family that becomes his "wife-taker". This means that every married Batak - apart from his own family – has kinship and hence close social relationships with two other family groups: the *marga* which his family serves as wife-giver, and the *marga* which, as wife-takers, choose their wives from his family.

The type of kinship relationship also determines the rights and duties of the individual to the wife-giver group and the wife-taker group. A Batak has a subordinate relationship towards his father-in-law and his father-in-law's family (i.e. his wife-givers) and has particular duties to perform for them, providing certain sorts of assistance, for instance. His relationship with his own son-in-law (his wife-taker) is correspondingly that of a superior. Every Batak therefore has a role both as a superior and a subordinate to his fellows. It is one of his most important endeavours to maintain this network of relations and dependence between the individual family groups, and marriage connections are particularly useful for this.

In peasant societies another important criterion is the ownership of agricultural land, together with the power of to allocate ownership and rights of use, and this is of great significance in kinship relationships. Temporary rights of land use, for example, are transferred to a daughter by her family in the course of marriage negotiations, but they revert to the family of the wife in the case of divorce, so the field does not become the property of the husband. Property rights and rights of use are therefore additional factors in the close network of relationships between the inhabitants of the village. In daily and ceremonial life kinship relationships and the social positions that result from them decide what obligations the individual has towards his fellows.

The maintenance of these relationships between the various marga is thus a guarantee of the ideally frictionless functioning of a village society. The reciprocal relationships of dependence also influence the process of political decision-making. As we saw in the previous section, the political leader of a village, group of villages or a region is usually far from being an absolute ruler. There are of course local differences in the "power" of a *raja*, a *tuan*, a *pengulu* or a *sibayak*, but without general acceptance from his relatives and fellow villagers the political power of an unjust "ruler" diminishes very rapidly. In spite of the close network of relationships within a village the individual families are still free to turn their back on their home village and join another village – the Batak have generally been able to "vote with their feet".

28 Almost square house in a semi-modern style roofed with fired clay tiles. Silalahi, west shore of Lake Toba, 1989

The layout of a village

Although the conditions of life in the villages of the various Batak peoples seem very similar, there is much variety in the layout of the villages and the architecture of the houses between the six Batak cultures. Most of the Toba Batak and Karo Batak villages are permanent settlements made possible by the intensive cultivation of irrigated rice fields or fertile vegetable gardens, whereas the settlements of the Angkola, Mandailing and Pakpak are designed to be less lasting. These semi-permanent settlements are based on the unirrigated agriculture practised by these peoples, where the type of economy characterized by slash-and-burn demands a frequent change of land and long fallow periods. Regions in which irrigated rice growing is possible produce better yields and therefore support a larger population. In fact, so dense is the population that some of the villages are within hailing distance of each other. Each village usually has no more than ten dwellings built close together so as to keep the area of land cultivated a large as possible by using the minimum for housing. In the regions with unirrigated cultivation small villages with only a handful of houses predominate, but also common are single settlements in the immediate vicinity of the *ladang* fields. What all villages have in common is that they are always located as close as possible to the fields, and above all to a watercourse. The supplying of households with drinking water and washing are among the most important tasks given to young girls.

The political situation in a particular region has a great influence on the siting and layout of a village. In troubled regions with frequent or long-lasting wars it is wise to fortify the village and/or build it in a strategically favourable location. In remote and economically disadvantaged regions fortifications were unnecessary. The villages of the Pakpak in the Pegagan and Kepas districts are unfortified, but in the Simsim region they have high bamboo fences and a fortified entrance (Volz 1909: 301). Toba Batak villages, however, were formerly strongly fortified. Earth ramparts set with bamboo fences, fruit trees and suchlike formed an impenetrable wall around the houses. There were only two entrances and these could be closed in emergencies.

In some regions the stone ramparts of large ashlar blocks were built, as can still be seen at Huta Siallagan, part of the village of Ambarita on the Samosir peninsula in Lake Toba. But it would be quite wrong to draw general conclusions about the layout of Toba Batak villages from this particular example, as travel literature and travel prospectuses usually seem to, since this method of building is restricted to the Toba heartland around

29 Mortar and stone sarcophagus of the Simarmata *marga*. Lumban Pangaloan, Samosir, 1989

30 Fortification (3.5 metres thick) of a village near Bakkara. West shore of Lake Toba, c. 1930

Lake Toba. Karl Helbig, who travelled through southern Batakland in the 1930s, mentions passages made of layered stone walls linking neighbouring villages on Samosir and near Bakkara on the shore of Lake Toba and serving as defences between them (Helbig 1938: 280). In the densely populated regions with irrigated rice cultivation a village's security precautions against night-time attacks had to be greater than those of villages in isolated but stategically superior sites. The building of massive stone walls and high earth ramparts in the fertile and therefore populous Toba regions reflects these special security needs. No universal rules apply to village fortifications: there are records of rectangular and round examples, made of earth, stone or dense bamboo hedges, or even simple wicker bamboo fences (Volz 1909: 266).

Besides political circumstances, geography too influenced whether or not a village was fortified. Villages in strategically favourable sites – for example, on the crest of a hill or in dense primeval forest – could do without the labour-intensive construction of ramparts and walls. Most village fortifications were no longer needed after the Dutch annexation and "pacification" of Batakland and in course of time they were demolished. In the district of Uluan, south east of Lake Toba, on the western shore of Samosir and in the valleys north of Bakkara a few village ramparts can still be seen.

More important than the differences between fortifications are the differences between the arrangement of houses in the villages. Toba Batak houses ideally stand side by side with the front gable facing the village street. On the opposite side of the street stand (or stood) the rice granaries each belonging to a house. A traditional Toba village thus has the outward appearance of a linear (street) village. The open area between the houses (*jabu*) and the rice granaries (*sopo*) is called *alaman*. It is used as the working area, for communication and as a place for drying rice. Karo Batak villages are not linear (street) villages but more like conglomerate villages – though this term is not quite correct since it gives the impression of an unorganic haphazard structure, whereas the basic structure of traditional Karo villages is a unified one. All the houses are grouped around the centre where the rice pounding house (*lesung*) and assembly house (*balé*) usually stand. The family houses, rice granaries and ossuaries (see below) stand parallel with each other facing in the same direction determined by the flow of the nearby river (Huender 1929: 511). The layout of Pakpak villages is similar to that of Karo villages (Volz 1909: 29). Clear influences from the Minangkabau are apparent in the layout of villages and construction of houses by the Mandailing. The houses run parallel to the village street – not with their gables facing the street, as in Toba villages.

The influence of the Dutch colonial rule and the changes brought about in modern times have made it almost impossible to describe traditional village structures of the Batak peoples without constantly making reservations. The last decades have brought so many changes to the whole of Batakland that authentic, closed village structures are now almost nowhere to be found. Villages have grown beyond their earlier boundaries as the population has increased. Old houses have had to be demolished, or have become so delapidated that they are kept only as uninhabitable shacks, until they are torn down by the next storm. All over Batakland house-types that are easier to build have supplanted the traditional multi-family houses. Today there are only a few settlements in Batakland which still give a reasonably accurate impression of Batak village life. Of these the small hamlets in the irrigated rice growing area of Toba country have best preserved their traditional structure. This is not due to any special feeling for conservation, but rather because there is no room for the hamlets to expand, and even here modern house types are replacing the old traditional *rumah adat*.

31 Main building in the palace precinct of the ruler (*tuan*) of Pematang Purba. Simalungun Batak, 1985

48

Domestic architecture

Just as the layout of villages varies between the different Batak peoples, so also the architecture of their dwellings (*rumah*), rice granaries (*sopo*) and assembly houses (*balé*) varies. These three types of building types are customary among all the Batak peoples but with differences in their exterior appearance and interior division. Besides these buildings there are a few building types which are built and used by only one Batak tribe and are completely unknown to the other tribes. Much of the following description already belongs to the past; the traditional architecture of the Batak is vanishing. Cultural influences from neighbouring peoples, the rapid linking of long separated villages by the modern transport network in the colonial and modern periods have resulted in massive changes in the architecture. In the 1920s corrugated iron was increasingly used as roofing material at the instigation of the Dutch, and in a short time completely replaced the shingles made of fibrous material from the sugar palm (called *ijuk*), which had hitherto been used, and the more rarely used fired clay roof tiles. Other building types which had long been built by the coastal Malays were cheaper to construct and maintain than the traditional dwellings. They present less of a fire hazard and as single-family houses they are more in keeping with the modern trends towards individualism which have also affected the Batak.

Big houses in which several families lived together used to be the usual form of dwelling for all the Batak. These communal houses were not divided up into separate rooms: the living space was an area running through the building which was subdivided at night by hanging mats or cloths which ensured the individual families at least some privacy. The location of the living area of each family was not arbitrary but reflected the degree of kinship with the master of the house. The building of such large communal houses was an expensive undertaking accompanied by many religious ceremonies which were supposed to ensure not only success in the building of the house but also a harmonious atmosphere among its future inmates. With the adoption of Christianity these ceremonies were forbidden and the building of houses in the Malay kampong style encouraged. These have a simple square or rectangular ground plan set on a concrete base or low pillars. The living area is made of simple wooden-wall construction with cut out windows, a wide doorway and a veranda built on the front. They are lived in by a single family and are divided internally into living room, bedroom and kitchen. The rice granaries (*sopo*) which used to be common have also fallen victim to these changes. In Toba villages each house used to stand opposite its *sopo*, but in the last decades the *sopo* have either collapsed or have been converted into dwellings. The following description of the most important forms of building concentrates on the architecture of the Toba and Karo Batak.

Toba Batak architecture

The traditional dwelling house of the Toba (*rumah adat*; toba: *jabu*) is a rectangular building on pillars, which is reached by steps from below. The house is locked in the evening by means of a trap-door set into the floor which can be bolted from the inside. The substructure of the house consists of massive wooden pillars which rest on flat stones as protection against damp. The number of pillars varies from six to eight lengthways. On the front of the house stand two transverse rows of pillars to support the entrance through the trap-door. The pillars are linked together by inserted planks, which not only give stability to the vertical pillars but also form an enclosed substructure which is traditionally used for larger livestock. Between the two middle posts of the front are the stairs for access to the house. At the side the cross-planks can be removed to allow the water buffalo to enter the stall (Boer 1920, Domenig 1980).

The elevation of the house is clearly divided into three: stall, living area and roof. Typical of the Toba houses is the steeply rising roof with eaves which extend below the substructure. The enormous roof is in the shape of a saddleback with sharply projecting gables, so that the roof extends beyond the substructure not only at the sides but also at the front and back. The front gable projects much further than the back. The space under the roof is closed off with triangular gables. The one at the back is undecorated but the gable at the front is richly ornamented with carvings.

The floor of the living area is placed about half way up the pillars. Two massive wooden planks (*pandingdingan*) and two similar transverse beams (*parhongkom*) form the framework for the floor – they too are richly carved. The sides and rear of the house traditionally have only a small window apiece, which means that the interior is very dark. The living room is about two metres high, access to the space under the roof, which is used as a storeroom for provisions and valuable objects, is by a step ladder made from a tree trunk and occasionally given figural decoration (as can be seen in the very unusual steps in ill. 145). In the roof space of some houses the place for offerings to the ancestors (*debata idup*) is hung up. We shall return later to this frame, called *raga-raga*.

32 Model of a house (*rumah adat*); length: 95 cm, height; 71 cm. Toba Batak

33 Modern type of *rumah adat* with windows, doors and steps in front. Huta Bolon, Samosir, 1985

34 Models of rice granaries (*sopo*); length: 90 cm, height: 70 cm. Toba Batak

35 Old house with garish new paintwork. Lumban Tonggatongga, Uluan district, Toba region, 1989

36 Woman pounding vegetables in a communal rice-pounding house (*lesung*). Karo plateau, 1984

37 House in Lingga. Karo plateau, 1989

38 House in Gurusinga near Berastagi, 1984

39 Rice-pounding house at Seberaya, 1985

40 House, with a bone house beyond it. Ajijahe, Karo plateau, 1984

These large *jabu* have room for several families. Each family has its own hearth at the front of the living room, though kitchen extensions at the back of the house, the result of Dutch influence, have now taken the place of this division of the interior. In Toba villages as a rule the family of the house-owner, the family of the married eldest son, and the family of a married daughter live together in one house. Widowed sisters of the house-owner may also live there. Each family has its own living area in the house, the long hallway in the centre is used by them all.

Another smaller type of house appears to have originated only in the last decades. It is used by a single family and does not have the complicated construction of a trapdoor with interior steps. Instead the door is cut into the front wall, with broad steps – and sometimes even a handrail – leading up to it. The substructure therefore no longer needs the second row of house pillars at the front. As well as the wider entrance, there are also windows cut into the front wall and side walls, so that modern houses are better lighted and ventilated. The new form of the gables which is now filled with openwork wooden panels also improves ventilation in the house.

This house type should not be confused with the rice granaries (*sopo*), many of which have been converted into houses. These sopo had an open-air work area at the side half the height of the substructure, and were entered by means of tree trunks with steps cut into them. To convert *sopo* into houses side walls are inserted without otherwise altering the structure of the building, and the entrance has to by cut in the front wall.

In traditional *sopo*, now very rarely still in use in the Toba region, the weight of the house and roof is supported on six massive wooden piers. large round wooden disks at their upper end prevent rodents from entering the storeroom up in the roof. The platform beneath the roof has a carved framework like the *jabu*. It serves as a work area, a meeting place for young and old and a sleeping place for the unmarried young men and strangers who are passing through the village. In the sopo of a *raja* village assemblies were held. The roof construction of a *sopo* is almost a smaller version of that of a *jabu*. A trap-door is let into the floor of the storeroom, and notched tree-trunk ladders are provided for access. Today rice is stored in the *jabu* so the *sopo* are unnecessary or are used for storing building materials or firewood. The area beneath the building is railed off, like that of the residential houses, by the insertion of planks and is also used as a stall for larger livestock and pigs.

41 Fenced stone sarcophagus in Huta Raja. North-west Samosir, Lake Toba, 1989

42 Roof of a rice granary (*sopo*) with traditional roof shingles. Toba region, c. 1930

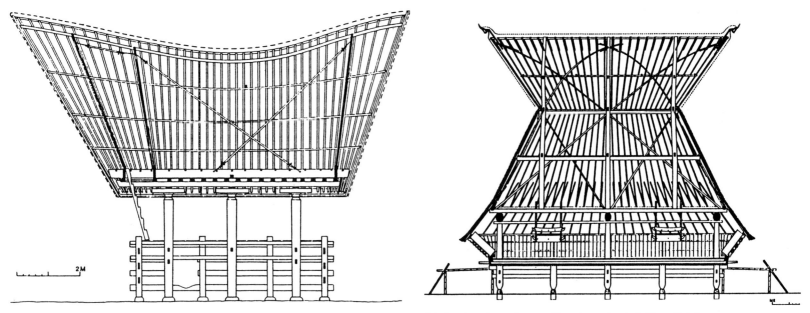

43 Section through a rice granary (*sopo*). Toba Batak

44 Section through a dwelling (*rumah adat*). Karo Batak

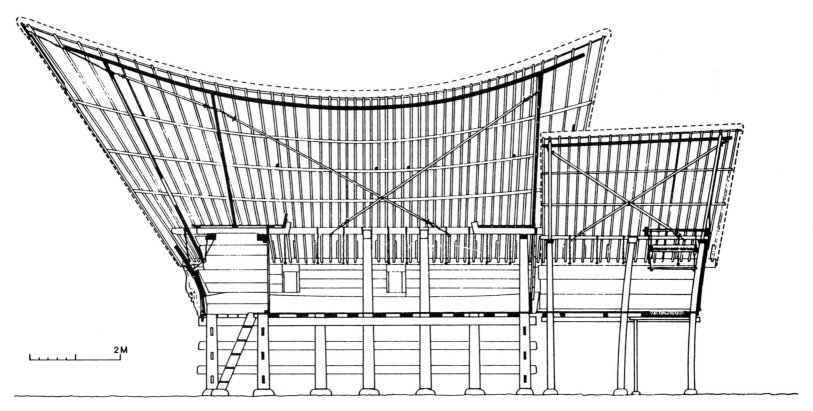

2M

45 Section through a dwelling with kitchen extension in the semimodern
style. Toba Batak (all three drawings are from Domenig 1980)

46 Hamlet hidden between trees. Toba region, 1989
47 View from the Sibayak volcano to the Sinabung volcano. Karo plateau, 1985
48 View from mount Pusuk Buhit northwards to the Karo plateau, 1985
49 Mounting a new television aerial in the village of Dokan. Karo plateau, 1989

Karo Batak architecture

The Karo Batak have the greatest architectural variety of all the Batak peoples. Dwellings, granaries, assembly houses, ossuaries and rice threshing houses are the usual building types and each is built in a variety of forms. The greatest range of variation is found with the dwelling houses (*rumah*). Two distinct systems of defining house types are used: by type of roof or by type of substructure. The roofs can be divided into two groups. The first is based on the gabled hipped roof in which the narrow ends of the roof slope down below the projecting gable (see ill. 38). The second sort of roof rests on an almost square substructure and the four sides of the roof all rise uniformly (see ill. 27). The appearance of both basic types may be varied by the addition of a contrasting upper part. A particularly splendid roof – a type rarely seen in the villages – is the *rumah anjung-anjung*, in which yet another miniature building is set on top of this upper part. This can be clearly seen in the model house (ill. 27b). Such a roof form is used by a *raja* or *sibayak* to show off his wealth. The old house of the well-known *sibayak* of Kabanjahe, Pa Mbelgah (see Chapter 1) even has a wooden equestrian figure on top of the topmost miniature building (ill. 10).

In the classification of buildings by their substructures the most important factor is how the main supports are anchored in the ground. The *rumah pasuk* rests on pillars rammed straight into the ground. In this building cross-braces are only inserted at the dwelling level (see model house ill. 27). The *rumah sangka manuk* rests on a log-cabin-like substructure supported on stone blocks. Holes are bored in the ends of the interlocking cross-beams for the corner posts of the house which taper downwards. These corner posts thus stabilize the cross-beams of the substructure. The substructure of the *rumah sendi* most resembles that of the Toba houses. The pillars stand on stone blocks as protection against rot and they are linked together by means of horizontally inserted planks (see model house ill. 26). The Karo too use the space beneath the houses for keeping livestock.

On the front and back of dwellings are bamboo platforms (*turé-turé*) which are each reached by a ladder. These platforms are used by the young people for evening rendezvous, in the daytime they are used as a work area and in addition for storing tools and the chicken cages. The living areas of the house is divided in two by a long beam in the middle. On each side of the hall, which in older houses was lower, there are two hearths. Up to eight families live in a traditional Karo house with two families to each hearth. Above each of the hearths hangs a square frame (*para*) in which firewood and kitchen utensils are kept. The

50 Overgrown roof made of *ijuk*. Dokan, Karo plateau, 1989

hearth is a square wooden box filled with earth and set into the floor. There are five hearthstones so arranged that the two families share the middle one. The basic symbolism of the number three recurs in many fields of Batak culture. Here the three hearthstones stand for the three pillars of the kinship system (called *dalihan na tolu* by the Toba): one's own family, that of the wife-takers and that of the wife-givers (see p. 60f). The communal hearthstone in the centre represents the link between the two families which share the fire.

The Karo house also does not have any division of space for privacy. A family's living space (Karo: *jabu*) is divided into a living area at the front and a sleeping area by the wall of the house, which has mats or cloths hung around in the evening. Like the Toba the Karo use the roof space for storing tools and firewood. Each of the side walls of the house has two double windows so that each family has a window. On the wall above the sleeping area are two shelves; the lower one is used for valuables and clothes, while the upper one serves as an "altar" for the most important family deities (Singarimbun 1975: 60).

Once again the division of the interior into eight family areas and the allocation of these areas to particular families is not arbitrary. Two of the living areas are of special importance: those situated to the left of each entrance are lived in by a member of the ruling family (*merga*) or by one of his *anakberu* (wife-givers). The relationship the residents of the remaining six areas have to the master of the house can vary considerably since there are no binding rules (ibid.: 63ff). Unlike the Toba house *jabu* which are used only by extended families, the traditional houses of the Karo can be lived in by members of quite separate families, though these usually have some relationship to the master of the house either as wife-givers or wife-takers.

The alignment of a house towards a point of the compass is based on complicated religious ideas. The long horizontal beams which frame the living area are giant tree trunks whose bases must always meet in the corner which belongs to the master of the house. The tops of the tree trunks meet at the opposite corner of the house where the *anakberu* of the master of the house has his living area (ill. 52). Houses are usually built so that this corner of the house is always to the east. Depending on whether the house is built in a north-south or west-east direction, this corner of the house will be located either north-east or south-east (Domenig 1980: 127).

The rice granaries are always built at right angles to Karo houses. Called *sapo pagé* (*pagé* meaning rice that has not yet been unhusked), these are usually rectangular buildings supported by four pillars on a log-cabin-like substructure. They are therefore similar to the *rumah sangka manuk* (see above). Like the

residential houses the rice granaries rest on stone blocks to protect them against damp. The roof is of a simple cantilever construction and the triangular gables, which are often decorated, have no weight-bearing function. The entrance to the granary is from above. A trap-door like that in the Toba *sopo* is not customary. The interior is usually divided into four equal compartments each of which is used by a family. Karo granaries do not have wooden disks as protection against rodents like those used by the Toba, because the substructure is built so massively that it is difficult for rodents to get in. Karo granaries have also become rare.

Granaries which unmarried men and visiting strangers use for sleeping are not called *sapo pagé*, even though rice is stored in their upper storey, but *jambur*. Their construction is, however, usually the same. In the daytime women occasionallly use the open work areas of a *jambur*. The assembly houses used for all sorts of village meetings and feasts are open on all sides with nothing but a gabled hipped roof. Nowadays these large bright halls are built on a concrete base; their substructure was formerly the same as that of the *jambur*.

A Karo peculiarity is the building of skull-houses or ossuaries (*geriten*) in which the bones of long dead ancestors were – and are still – kept (see Chapter 4). They are built on a square groundplan and their substructures are based on the various forms of house construction with a roof usually of the gabled hipped roof type (ill. 40). The model skull-house (cf ill. 62) shows a form of substructure which used to be common but cannot now be found, consisting of a single massive central support. The *geriten* were built for the influential, rich and eminent dead by their wealthy descendents (Singarimbun 1975: 24). Poorer families kept the skulls and larger bones of their ancestors in the roof space above their family sleeping place.

Like the Simalungun and the Pakpak, the Karo Batak had special houses for storing communally used rice blocks. In these rice-pounding houses (*lesung*) the women and girls of a village met in the mornings and evenings to prepare the required quantity of rice for the two main meals, unhusking it and making it into flour, or pounding the vegetables. In the southern Batak lands each family has its own pounding block consisting either of a large wooden trough or a large lump of rock. These pounding blocks stand in front of each house or are taken into the house after use.

The *lesung* in the northern Batak lands was a roofed structure built on piers and open at the sides. On the platform stood one or two tree trunks hewn into rectangular shape and with one or two rows of depressions on the upper side. The *lesung* had an important social function for the women. They could meet there regularly for a chat, and it was a relatively unobtrusive place for boys and girls to meet and get to know each other.

The use of the past tense in this description of the *lesung* is necessary because nowadays they are no longer built and the old existing examples are either not used or cannot be entered because they are in a dangerous state of dereliction (see ill. 318). Small square blocks of stone are now used by each family individually, as in the southern Batak lands, and the greater part of the rice harvest is taken to be milled at the rice mills which are found in all the larger villages.

Throughout the Batak region modern house types have replaced the traditional forms. Simple undecorated wooden houses with corrugated iron roofs, which in villages with an electricity supply are surmounted by the inevitable television aerials, are cheaper to build and maintain. The social control which was always exercised by the other residents in the *rumah adat*, no longer exists in the modern one-family houses. The family's increased demand for space which results from the acquisition of modern furniture such as suites, cupboards, chairs, tables and beds with mattresses, can only be satisfied in a traditional house by expanding the living area, so that a family no long occupies one eighth of a Karo house but instead perhaps a quarter or even half of it, and the number of families living in a house is reduced. Another important reason for the rejection of the old style of building is expressed in a comment that is heard again and again: the old buildings are simply old-fashioned, people want to live like the people in the towns. The ventilation in the *rumah adat* is particularly unsatisfactory and the acrid smoke from the fire can escape only slowly. Because of this Batak household utensils that have been used for a long time are always covered by a black smoky-smelling patina of soot.

51 Transporting rice to the granary (*sopo*). The large discs are supposed to prevent rodents gaining access to the granary. Toba region, c. 1930

52 Plan of a *rumah adat* showing the direction of the four great beams. The living area of the house owner and his family is marked B. Karo Batak (taken from Domenig 1980)

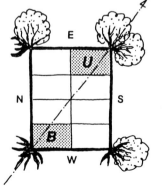
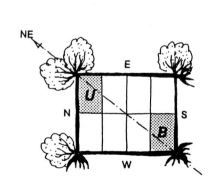

Dependence on the family

Forms of kinship

Who are you? Which family do you come from? Where are you from? Where are you going? Such questions always preface any conversation between two Batak meeting for the first time. They are necessary in order to establish what one's kinship to the stranger is and thus how one should behave towards him. A Batak considers it sensible and necessary to allocate to any stranger he meets a clearly defined place in society. We have already emphasized how important family relationships are in the community of the village and in particular of the house. Now we shall turn to the complexities of the Toba and Karo kinship systems.

In general terms the kinship systems of the various Batak peoples are similar. True, the terms used for the family relationships differ, but the basic structure of the patriarchal extended group is the same everywhere. In ethnological terms the Batak kinship system is one of patrilinear lineages with subordinate clans and sub-clans. These kinship groups are called *merga* by the Karo and *marga* by the Toba. This term gives no idea of the rank in the clan hierarchy. The *merga* or *marga* is a patrilinear kinship group. Ideally it is exogamous, i.e. the men must choose their wives from another unrelated *marga*. The rules were once strictly observed but are no longer obeyed in every respect.

The clan structure is derived from an old division into moieties – halves of a family whose common ancestor is – at least according to the beliefs of the Toba Batak – *Si Raja Batak*, who lived in the distant past on the holy mountain of Pusuk Buhit on the west shore of Lake Toba. His sons are the ancestors of the two halves of the family, *Lontung* and *Sumba*, which have split into innumerable large and small *marga*. The family trees (called *tarombo*) can be very complicated and are constantly updated by genealogists. Great store is set by their completeness. The genealogies of the Toba Batak are not only the best known but also the most extensive. They give a compelling idea of the common kinship of all the Batak and incorporate the other Batak tribes into their *tarombo* thus creating a very complex and intricate system. The Karo on the other hand know only few family genealogies or myths which indicate kinship with the Toba.

Information about ancestors assumes mythological dimensions after only a few generations. Off-shoots can often be traced only as far back as the great-grandfather, so one should not expect the historical accuracy of western birth certificates or parish registers.

53–57 Marriage at Paribun near Barusjahe, Karo plateau, 1985. (55) Presentation of gifts; (56) a book is kept of all the financial and material contributions made by the guests; (57) the laying on of traditional cloths is supposed to bring the couple luck

59

The Batak are more concerned with establishing who can be counted as an ancestor on the basis of male heirs and what social status this indicates. The *tarombo* are moreover an indispensible source for the kinship relationships of the individual groups. They make clear which sub-clans have split from which clan and in which generation this occurred. The individual ancestor in this system is not necessarily of great importance, more important is to be able to find out the position of one's *marga* in the family tree.

The place of the individual in the *marga* is much more impenetrable, mainly because of the size of some *marga*. Among the Karo Batak, for example, they can have several tens of thousands of members. The Karo have five large *merga*: Karo-Karo, Perangin-angin, Ginting, Sembiring and Tarigan, each of which is divided into 13 to 18 sub-clans. This means that the Karo Batak belong to one of only 83 sub-clans or extended families (Kozok 1989: 10). Taking the findings of the last census in Indonesia which included ethnic grouping (1930) and adding an average increase in population of two per cent one can estimate that there is a Karo population of more than 500,000. This means that statistically (!) each sub-clan has a average membership of more than 6000.

The relationships among the Toba Batak are far more impenetrable than the five large *merga* of the Karo, are too complex and intricate to be explained here in detail (see Vergouwen 1964: 5–16). We have already mentioned the enormous number of *marga* into which the two family halves of *Lontung* and *Sumba* have divided.

For all the Batak the most important social unit is the "family" which consists of all the descendants of a common forefather who lived three or four generations earlier. This unit is smaller than a sub-clan and is called *saompu* by the Toba. Depending on the extent of the descendents' knowledge a *saompu* can also contain all the descendants up to twelve generations. Among the Karo usually only the direct descendants of a grandfather belong to a family (which they call *sada nini*). Both these terms nominally limit direct kinship to the generation of the grandfathers (*ompu* and *nini*). The members of this kinship group form a unit and still live as close neighbours in rural areas. But there is no social compulsion, prescribed by the *adat* for instance, to do so. The smallest unit in Batak society is the nuclear family, consisting of the parents of a married man, his wife and his children. Karo Batak call the nuclear family *jabu*, the Toba Batak *ripe*.

Establishment of kinship relations: marriage

For the Batak the marriage of a man and woman is not a private matter, it joins two *marga* and defines the relationship between these kinship groups in accordance with the *adat*. There have been no changes in this to the present day. All the Batak agree that there are certain preferred relationships between partners which are intended to continue an already existing relationship between two families into the next generations. As has already been mentioned Batak society is patrilinear. Ancestry is almost exclusively defined on the father's side. Children receive their father's family name – just as they usually do in western societies – and are counted as members of the father's family.

When a young man wants to get married it is considered desirable that his wife comes from the same family as his mother came from. This connection preserves the relationship with the kinship group of the wife-givers (Toba: *hulahula*; Karo: *kalimbubu*). To the parents of the bride he becomes a wife-taker (Toba: *boru*; Karo: *anakberu*). An ideal match is thought to be the marriage beween a man and a daughter of his mother's brother, but marriage with a "parallel" cousin, i. e. the daughter of his father's brother, is strictly forbidden as incestuous. Also forbidden are marriages with women of families which have an *boru* relationship with the family of the bridegroom, i. e. who take their wives from his family.

In simple terms men of *marga* A take their wives from *marga* B. *Marga* B take their wives from *marga* C, who take their wives from *marga* A. In this cycle of exchange the *hulahula* or *boru* relationships remain constant. This is of course a very abbreviated and idealized presentation, but the principle is clear: three family groups are always of central importance to a Batak: the family of his father-in-law (*hulahula*), the family of his son-in-law (*boru*) and his own family (Toba: *dongan sabutuha* – "those who come from the same womb"; Karo: *senina*). Two other kinship groups, deriving from the marriages a generation earlier, are also important : the family of the brother of the bride's mother (Karo: *puang kalimbubu*) and the family of the wife-takers in the mother's clan of the father-in-law (Karo: *anakberu menteri*). These two kinship groups play an important role in ceremonial life, but nowadays they often have only a secondary role in everyday life. The equivalent groups are also important for the Toba. This means that in a network of relationships, which seems barely comprehensible to us, a Batak is connected with at least five different kinship groups.

In the past the young couple generally used to move after marriage to the village or house of the husband's parents, but this "patrilocal residence" is no longer strictly observed. However, the rule that if possible one should always make one's home where there are already close relatives living still applies today – even in the cities. After marriage the wives retain the *marga* names of their own family and it is impossible to tell from their names which man they are married to. It is true that on marriage the wife passes into the "possession" of her husband's *marga*, but she still retains her *marga* of origin, which is also important as the "mother clan" of her children, since the *hulahula* or *kalimbubu* relationship to the male relatives of the mother is also of significance for her children.

The customary law (*adat*) of the Batak permits polygamy, i.e. a man may have several wives at once (polygyny). This still occurs very occasionally among the Christianized Batak, but even in the past the polygynous family was the exception, because only rich men could afford to pay for a second marriage. While the first wife followed her husband to his village, the other wives stayed in their parents' houses. A husband's relationship with his second wife would therefore be as a visitor living with her for short periods at a time. Polygynous households were rare, for understandable reasons, but if the wife's sister was widowed and the husbands of the two women came from the same *marga* the widow could marry her sister's husband and would then live in the same household. This form of widow's marriage is called levirate. In this way the widow remains in the *marga* of her husband. She can also be married to another male relative of her husband if he has no brother, or if one of the two does not wish to enter into this relationship. If the wife dies her husband can marry her sister or another female relative of his wife (sororate).

This custom, which may seem hard for us to understand, is based on a sense of responsibility for the surviving dependents who have to be supported and should continue to live in the same kinship relationship to the *marga* of their dead spouse. This is particularly important if there are children or if difficulties concerning the ownership of property (land or house) mean that it is difficult or impossible to loosen the network of relationships linking the two kinship groups. The possibility that the husband's family could demand the return of the bride-price, which they had presented to the wife's family before the wedding, may play a part in this. Childless widows usually go back to their families and are taken into the household of a brother or some other close male relative. The Batak regard their fate as very unhappy: to have no children is considered the greatest possible misfortune. Childlessness within marriage is also considered a misfortune. Men need offspring – above all male offspring – to continue the *marga* and secure their social position in the land of the dead (see Chapter 4), and can separate from an infertile wife

after a few years without any problem, send her back to her family and ask for a specified part of the bride-price back. To the family of the bride this is regarded as a disgrace and it is the wife who is found to be at fault. The social status of such women is always underprivileged since women derive their social respect and prestige from motherhood and their efficiency in agricultural work. This attitude is changing only slowly.

Batak usually marry before they are twenty. Some of the marriages were - and still are – arranged by their families without the children having any say in the matter, and the proportion of marriages between cousins as described above has declined (Singarimbun 1975: 157f). Marriages not arranged by the parents are mostly based on the free choice of both partners. The only restrictions in the choice of a partner are that he or she cannot belong to the same *marga*, that laws are not violated, and that the choice does not reverse already existing kinship relationships between two *marga*. In rural areas the choice of partners from the same village predominates. The choice is influenced more by the degree of acquaintance, possibilities of contact, pre-existing social relationships among the parents etc. than by love – but love matches are by no means excluded. Among the Karo there is even an accepted way for a young couple to marry despite the refusal of their parents: they elope together and hide in the house of an *anakberu* who is obliged to provide protection and assistance until the two families agree to the marriage. In the other method of choosing a partner the respective parents of the prospective bridegroom and bride play a crucial part. The negotiations about the prospects of the courtship and the terms of the wedding are conducted entirely by the parents, though the son usually lets his parents know which girl he wants to marry, so he is in full agreement with the negotiations. The conduct of the courtship and the possible reactions of the bride's family are laid down by the adat and last several months. If all participants agree, the courtship then ends in a marriage ceremony.

An important element of the courtship is the negotiation of the bride-price. This word gives the impression that the bride is being bought, in fact the family of the bride is receiving compensation of their daughter whose working capacity will pass to her husband's family after the marriage and whose fertility will serve to perpetuate the husband's *marga*. The bride-price (Karo: *emas*; Toba: *tuhor*) is not a purchase price, even if it increases the greater the social status of the bride's parents and – interestingly enough – the greater the quality and length of the girl's education. If the negotiations are crowned with success a preliminary bride-price will be paid and the marriage is initiated with a small ceremony (*mukul*) in which bride and bridegroom eat from a single bowl. This marks the completion of the first part of the wedding; the couple is considered to be married and they can formally live together. However, the next part of the wedding celebrations laid down by the *adat* is the more important. It legalizes the new kinship relationship between all the participating groups or relatives on the male and female sides.

This ceremony, to which several hundred guests have to be invited, is independent of the official church or civic ceremonies. Without the *adat* ceremony the ties of kinship between the families involved are not considered to have been established. Depending on the family's financial situation the ceremony may take place years after the actual marriage, and indeed at many such ceremonies the children of the couple participate. The *adat* marriage of a Karo couple usually takes place in the bride's village. All the kinship groups of the husband and wife gather on the day of the ceremony at the assembly place or *balé* of the village. The seating arrangements at a wedding are precisely laid down. The direct families (*senina*) on the bride's and bridegroom's side sit opposite one another, each flanked by their *anakberu* and *kalimbubu*. With them sit the *anakberu*, the wife-takers, who are required to give particular assistance, to the left of the *senina*. Here a book is kept of the individual financial contributions to the wedding (see ill. 56). The bridal couple themselves sit on decorated cane chairs at a small table in front of the bridegroom's kinship group, with the bride seated on the bridegroom's left, i. e. on what is considered the subordinate side (Singarimbun 1975: 169).

A Karo wedding ceremony lasts several hours. The presentation of the bride-price is a very complicated procedure because the total sum is not paid all at once by one person but is presented in precisely determined portions among the various kinship groups present in strict sequence (ibid: 171–8). After this the various *kalimbubu* of the bride's parents (i. e. the male relatives of the bride's mother) present their gifts in return, mostly consisting of household goods. These gifts, which could be called a dowry, include mattresses and pillows as well as kitchen utensils (see ill. 55). A communal meal prepared and served by the bride's *anakberu* establishes and strengthens the new ties of kinship. As in other parts of Indonesia a communal feast is a central element in the building of social relationships. After the meal the bridal pair make a formal "first visit" to the individual kinship groups, and the party then breaks up. This ceremony laid down by the *adat* is also a way of officially announcing the marriage to all relatives and having it legitimized by their presence, the acceptance of the portions of the bride-price and participation in the communal meal.

Toba marriage ceremonies differ in many respects from those of the Karo, but their essentials are the same (see Vergouwen

1964, Niessen 1985b). Among the Toba too a bride-price is laid down as a preliminary to the marriage and it is presented at the official *adat* ceremony in the family circle. These gifts – called *piso* (knife) – from the *boru* (wife-taking) side of the bride's parents and their kinship groups, consist of money, rice or other objects of value. *Piso* are from the bridegroom's family and as such are the male element as opposed to the female-orientated return gifts (*ulos* = cloth) from the bride's parents. These also include money, but mainly consist of cloths and agricultural land. The size of the bride-price is determied by the return gifts and vice versa, though the return gifts often exceed the bride-price in value. The significance of the cloths will be discussed in chapter 6. The Toba, too, regard the primary purpose of the marriage as being to continue one's clan by the birth of as many male and female offspring as possible. The sons can preserve a flawless family genealogy by marrying, while the most important function of a daughter is to create strong social ties with another clan, whose members are obliged to give extensive help to members of the bride's family. The close relationships initiated by an *adat* marriage not only affect the young couple but also determine the relationships between all the family groups. For this reason divorce is not very common among the Batak.

Most marriages which end in divorce do so in the first or second year. Marriages which survive these early years and produce children usually prove to be very lasting. Early divorce is usually connected with the inexperience of the young couple, but divorces also occur when marriages remain childless. Before a divorce takes place everything possible is done to find out the cause of the childlessness. As we have seen, the fault is usually looked for first in the wife. A female healer (usually a *sibaso* – see Chapter 4) is called in. If her arts fail with the woman, she may also examine the man's sperm, if he agrees.

A divorce is always preceded by a family meeting in which the reasons for asking for a divorce are aired in public. Representatives of all the kinship groups involved are present. Only after these attempts at arbitration and reconciliation have proved fruitless is the case taken before the village chief (*kepala desa*). If his attempts to patch up the marriage are unsuccessful, then the district head (*camat*) is called upon as the next instance. The court of final appeal is at the next administrative level (*kabupaten*) and it grants the divorce (Singarimbun 1975: 185ff).

Even after a divorce the children are still counted as part of the father's family. They stay with his family, even if their mother returns to her family. Only children which are still being nursed can stay with their mother until they are weaned.

For the individual Batak it appears therefore that there is relatively strong social pressure to marry, have children and keep the marriage going. Man and wife establish a household of their own fairly quickly after marriage but they cannot avoid the close ties of kinship. Even now daily and ceremonial life is imbued with the *adat* and it is impossible to escape the network of relationships built up over generations with the *boru* and *hulahula* kinship groups. Every Batak is involved in this network of reciprocal dependences and obligations from the moment he is born, since the parents' kinship ties pass to their children at birth. A Batak, therefore, receives ties of kinship with other clans in two ways: from birth he has the *boru* and *hulahula* relationships of his parents, and on marriage he is also linked with those of his bride's parents. Because, in agricultural areas at least, the choice of partner is usually made from the same village or its immediate vicinity, not only is there social control on a large scale, but also in its more positive aspect: social security. In earlier decades this was certainly more important than it is now, but even in the larger towns, where a very high percentage of Batak live (in Medan, for instance), the kinship system and traditional values and norms have changed very little.

59 Fetching water in bamboo canes is an important task for young girls. Karo plateau, c. 1930

58 View into a Karo house. Over the fireplace hangs a wooden frame (*para-para*) in which firewood and utensils are kept. Kabanjahe, Karo plateau, c. 1910

Chapter 4   The Old Religion

Gods, spirits and "souls"

The religious ideas of the Batak reflect the various cultural influences they have experienced in the course of the last few centuries. Our knowledge of the pre-Christian forms of Batak religion is derived mainly from the writings of German and Dutch missionaries who became increasingly concerned with Batak beliefs towards the end of the last century. Their primary purpose of was to justify European missionary activity and scientific objectivity took second place. A paternalistic attitude towards the "heathen", "animists" and "godless" was the determining factor which coloured their limited methods of observation and interpretations. Nevertheless their accounts are still an important source for understanding old Batak forms of religion.

The various Batak cultures differ in their pre-Christian religious ideas as they do in many other aspects of culture. There is incomplete information about the old religious ideas of the Mandailing and Angkola in southern Batakland, and we know very little about the religion of the Pakpak and Simalungun Batak. For the Toba and Karo on the other hand the evidence in the writings of missionaries and colonial administrators is relatively abundant, and consequently the religious ideas of these groups will be at the forefront of the present chapter.

In Chapter 1 we mentioned the various influences which had affected the Batak through their contact with Hindu, Hindu-Buddhist or Hindu-Javanese traders and settlers in southern Batakland, or the east and west coast near Barus and Tapanuli. These contacts took place many centuries ago and it is impossible to reconstruct just how close they were at the time and how far the religious ideas of these "foreigners" were adopted and reworked by the Batak. Many elements of Batak religion go back to these contacts, or at least were strongly influenced by them, as can be seen from the names of gods, oracular methods, technical terms used in the "language of religion" (poda) etc. Many Indian Sanskrit words have entered the Batak languages, though not by a direct route but by way of a south Sumatran language (Voorhoeve 1958: 247; Parkin 1978). Waldemar Stöhr, a scholar with a deep knowledge of ancient Indonesian religions, reaches the following verdict on the possible Hindu origin of many old Toba religious concepts: "One can only conjecture to what extent the intrinsic characteristics of the deities were adopted, since nobody knows about the pre-Hindu (ancient Batak) world of ideas. A considerable probability attaches, however, to the 'conjecture' that Indian and Hindu-Javanese influence had a modifying effect on pre-existing concepts of gods and creation. Although this question is of importance for the cultural history of the Batak, it is only of secondary significance in the ethnology of religion, since, wherever the individual elements may have come from originally, they fused together in the Toba religious system and so became Toba Batak concepts, and should be regarded as such" (Stöhr 1965: 56).

A further difficulty in examining the old religious ideas of the Batak is the Christianization of the Toba and some of the Karo. In the case of the Toba the acceptance of Christianity already lies several generations in the past, which means that Toba living today usually have only a incomplete picture of the religion of their forefathers. In the case of the Karo the situation is far better (from our point of view) since the percentage of those belonging to the Karo religion (called perbégu or pemena) is still very high. A 1980 statistic showed that about 12 per cent were Moslems, 31 per cent members of Christian churches and sects, and the remaining 57 per cent adhered to the traditional religion (Beyer 1982: 101). Of these, 47 per cent were listed as "secular animists" – which simply means that these Karo were not prepared to provide precise information in answer to the relevant questions. It could also indicate a religious vacuum, a sign of the insecurity which results from the lack of state recognition of the perbégu religion (Smith Kipp 1974: 6). Nevertheless the ancient traditional religion has been preserved by a large section of the Karo population.

The religious ideas of the Karo differ from those of the Toba in several central points. For the Karo the most important thing is the worship of the souls of ancestors and natural spirits. Ideas about a world of the gods, a world-creating senior god etc., have remained only sporadically in the memory. Batara Guru is the most senior god, his son Tuan Banua Koling is the creator of the earth (Westenberg 1892). The names of the gods vary in the different sources and Christian and Islamic elements also occur, which suggests the influence of Aceh and the east coast. The gods are fairly unimportant in religious life, they receive no sacrifices and have no significance for the average Karo. Knowledge about the gods and the creation of the earth seems to be possessed only by the magician-priests (guru).

Here I shall concentrate on the cosmogonic and cosmological ideas of the Toba Batak. The differing ideas held by the Karo will be discussed only in passing (Westenberg 1892; Neumann 1902b, 1904).

There are many different versions in circulation. These were formerly passed down entirely by oral tradition but have now been written down in the local languages. There are also large collections of Batak tales collected by European scholars since the mid-19th century and recorded in European languages – mostly Dutch (for bibliography see Stöhr 1965: 47). As well as explaining the cosmogony, the main themes in these rich collections of myths is the further development of the world, and the origins of mankind and of the Batak people.

At the beginning of time there was only the sky with a great sea beneath it. In the sky lived the gods and the sea was the home of a mighty underworld dragon. The earth did not yet exist and human beings, too, were as yet unknown. All the surviving myths record that at the beginning of creation stands the god *Mula Jadi Na Bolon*. His origin remains uncertain. A rough translation of the name is the "beginning of becoming". The creation of everything that exists can be traced back to him. *Mula Jadi* the great lives in the upper world which is usually thought of as divided into seven levels or storeys. His three sons, *Batara Guru, Mangalabulan* and *Soripada* were born from eggs laid by a hen fertilized by *Mula Jadi*. Two swallows act as messengers and helpers to *Mula Jadi* in his act of creation. Their functions vary in the different versions. *Mula Jadi* begets three daughters whom he gives as wives for his three sons. This marks the appearance of a motif which we shall come across again in connection with the magician priest's magic wand: incest between brother and sister. Mankind is the result of the union of the three couples.

Besides the three sons of *Mula Jadi* there is another god, *Asiasi*, whose place and function in the world of the gods remains largely unclear. Waldemar Stöhr writes of him: "There is some evidence that Debata Asiasi can be seen as the balance and unity of the trinity of gods [i. e. the three sons of *Mula Jadi*]. In this sense he is nothing more than a manifestation of the highest god, Mula Djadi" (Stöhr 1967: 10). What all the five gods so far mentioned have in common is that they play a minor role in ritual. They do not receive any sacrificial offerings from the faithful and no places of sacrifice are built for them. They are merely called on in prayers for help and assistance.

The ruler of the underworld, i. e. the primeval sea, is the serpentdragon *Naga Padoha*. He too existed before the beginning and seems to be the opponent of *Mula Jadi*. As ruler of the underworld *Naga Padoha* also has an important function in the creation of the earth. In its role as the astrological god *Pane Na*

Bolon we shall encounter this serpent dragon again in the oracular tradition of the magician priests.

The origin of the earth and of mankind is connected mainly with the daughter of *Batara Guru, Si Boru Deak Parujar*, who is the actual creator of the earth. She flees from her future husband, the ugly son of *Mangalabulan*, and lets herself down on a spun thread from the sky to the middle world which at that time was still just a watery waste.

"She refuses to go back but feels very unhappy in the watery waste. Out of compassion Mula Djadi sends his granddaughter a handful of earth so that she can find somewhere to live. Sideak Parudjar was ordered to spread out this earth and thus the earth became broad and long. But the goddess was not able to enjoy her rest for long. The earth had been spread out on the head of Naga Padoha, the dragon of the underworld who lived in the water. He groaned under the weight and attempted to get rid of it by rolling around. The earth was softened by water and threatened to be utterly destroyed. With the help of Mula Djadi and by her own cunning Sideak Parudjar was able to overcome the dragon. She thrust a sword into the body of Naga Padoha up to the hilt and laid him in an iron block. Whenever Naga Padoha twists in the fetters an earthquake occurs" (Stöhr 1967: 11).

After the lizard-shaped son of *Mangalabulan*, the husband the gods intended for her, had taken another name and another form, *Si Boru Deak Parujar* married him. This marriage too offends the marriage rules of the Batak, for he is her paternal uncle, i. e. her "parallel" cousin, a union strictly prohibited by all Batak as incestuous. *Si Boru Deak Parujar* becomes the mother of twins of different sexes. When the two have grown up their divine parents return to the upper world leaving the couple behind on the earth. Mankind is the result of their union – again incestuous. The couple settle on Pusuk Buhit, a volcano on the western shore of Lake Toba, and found the village of Si Anjur Mulamula. The mythological ancestor of the Batak, *Si Raja Batak* is one of their grandchildren. After the creation of the earth and mankind the gods withdraw to the upper world. The underworld dragon *Naga Padoha* is under control, and mankind spreads over the earth.

However, living near the humans are other gods whose relationship to the gods of the upper world and the underworld dragon *Naga Padoha* is not quite clear. The serpent-shaped goddess *Boru Saniang Naga* is a water goddess who is at home in all rivers, in the sea and in Lake Toba. She is regarded as the sister of *Batara Guru* or the daughter of *Soripada* (Warneck 1977: 220), but since she lives in the water she is closer to *Naga Padoha*. She is called on for help and protection by people fishing, working in the fields, launching a new boat, or making a journey by boat across Lake Toba. Being a water goddess she also dwells in springs which are therefore ritually purified by the presentation of offerings. The *Pane Na Bolon*, the serpent-shaped god who is so important in oracles, also lives in the underworld.

An earth god to whom sacrifices are brought and who stands at the head of the list of deities invoked in prayers, is *Boraspati Ni Tano*, a fertility god. He is imagined to have the form of a lizard and sacrifices are made to him at the beginning of work in the fields. At every intrusion into the earth sacrifices are made to pacify him and to beg his blessing. As *Boraspati Ni Huta* he protects the village and as *Boraspati Ni Rumah* the house. This means that in venerating the lizard (which has already appeared in mythology as the son of *Mangalabulan*) three different nature deities are being venerated. Representations of this *Boraspati* are found on the façades of old houses, on the doors of rice granaries and on various objects belonging to magician-priests (ill. 144).

The *tendi* cult

In the religious world of the Toba and Karo Batak the gods, cosmogony and the creation of mankind are far less significant than the complex concepts connected with the term *tendi* (Karo) or *tondi* (Toba). It is very difficult to find an adequate English translation for *tendi*. Attempts have been made to use various circumlocutions to avoid using the Christian term "soul" or the animistic term "soul material", since these terms have proved unsuitable for describing the Batak understanding of souls. Stöhr (1965: 177ff) after considering possible translations of *tendi* and *bégu* comes to the following conclusion: "Probably the most useful translations of the terms are 'life-soul' and 'death-soul', because they are the least explicit and leave room for all aspects of the two concepts of soul."

A Dutch theologian (Leertouwer 1977) has recently reexamined the concepts of soul of the Toba and Karo Batak, basing his work on an intensive study of concepts of soul in Oceania (Fischer 1965). In his dissertation he states that what Stöhr calls the "life-soul" would be called in Fischer's terminology the "dream ego" or "spiritual double" (Leertouwer 1977: 220ff). Fischer himself defines the two terms as follows: "'Dream ego' and 'spiritual double' are the same thing seen from different sides, from within and without, in its function for the person himself and as an optical phenomenon for others." (Fischer 1965: 273)

Since Fischer regarded the two terms as merely two aspects of the same idea, it seems justified to use Stöhr's terminology –

"life-soul" for *tendi* and "death-soul" for *bégu* – in the present chapter.

Over the last hundred years numerous works on the history of religion have dealt with the Batak idea of the soul. The ideas expressed here are mostly based on theories that were valid or current in this period (Leertouwer 1977). All the works agree that to the Batak the "life-soul" and the "death-soul" are in the forefront of religious thought and that the world of the gods is largely insignificant in religious practice. Since the *tendi* (I shall use only the Karo term) are at the centre of religious thinking and also of daily life, the Batak have been said to have a "*tendi* cult" (Stöhr 1965: 177).

A person receives his "life-soul" (*tendi*) from *Mula Jadi Na Bolon* before he is born. The destiny of the individual *tendi* is decided by the *tendi* itself before birth. Various myths are woven around manner in which the *tendi* choose their destiny from *Mula Jadi*. What is significant is that the *tendi* themselves are responsible for their destiny. Warneck, a missionary and for a long time superintendant (ephorus) of the Batak Church, recorded two particularly expressive myths in his major work on Batak religion. Both are concerned with the choice of destiny:

"God presents him with all kinds of things to choose from. If the tondi asks for ripe pepper, then the person whom he animates will be a poor fellow; if he asks for flowers, then he will live only a short time; if he asks for a hen, the person will be restless; rags indicate poverty; an old mat, lack of fame; a gold piece, wealth; plate, spear, medicine pot indicate that he will become a great chief or understand magic arts."

"With Mula Djadi in the upper world is a mighty tree called Djambubarus. God has written on all its leaves. On one leaf is written 'many children', on others 'wealth' or 'respect' and so on. 'Contemptible life', 'poverty', 'wretchedness' are also written on the leaves. All the possible different fates of the person are entered on the leaves. Every tondi that wishes to descend to the middle world must first ask god for one of the leaves. Whatever is written on the leaf chosen by him will be his destiny in the middle world." (Warneck 1909: 49f).

The Karo Batak too know about the choice of destinies made by the *tendi* before birth (Neumann 1904: 104). Among the Karo and the Toba there are sometimes widely diverging versions of where the *tendi* dwells and how many *tendi* there are. According to the Toba a person has seven *tendi* (Leertouwer 1977: 44ff). These can, however, be reduced to two, since five of them are merely aspects of the second. In another interpretation these represent character traits of the *tendi*-owner (Warneck 1909: 62). The second *tendi* is found in the placenta and amniotic fluid of the new-born baby, and accordingly the afterbirth is given special attention after the birth of a child. It is usually buried under the house, is called *saudara* (brother) and is regarded as the person's guardian spirit. Similar ideas about the afterbirth are also found among the Karo, who also bury the placenta and amniotic fluid under the house and regard them as two guardian spirits (*kaka* and *agi*) who always remain close to the person. The idea that there are seven *tendi* is also found among the Karo, but is restricted to the magician-priests (*guru*); the rest of the Karo believe that a person has only one *tendi* (Westenberg 1892: 229).

All Batak regard the loss of *tendi* as a signifying a great danger for "body and soul". *Tendi* can be separated from their owners through inattentivness, or as a result of black magic by a magician-priest with evil intentions. In other words, the *tendi* is not tied to the body; it can also live for a time outside the body. The final loss of the *tendi* inevitably results in death. There are a variety of ideas about where exactly in the body the *tendi* dwells. It is present to a particularly high degree in certain parts of the body, especially the blood, the liver, the head and the heart. Sweat too is described as rich in *tendi*. It is believed that illnesses are connected with the absence of *tendi*, and the bringing back of the *tendi* is a main method of healing. The Karo, for instance, have gifts, called *upah tendi* (*upah* = wage, payment, gift), which they give to their *tendi* so that their *tendi* stay with them. These gifts may consist of a knife, a gong, a particular piece of clothing, a water buffalo or a small holy place (op. cit.: 230). The gifts are carefully cared for in order to keep the *tendi* satisfied. It must be emphasized that only the magician-priests are in a position to interpret and influence people's *tendi* correctly. If their endeavours are unsuccessful, then clearly the *tendi* has chosen another destiny for itself.

When somebody dies it is thought that the *tendi* vanish and the "deathsoul" (Karo: *bégu*, Toba: *begu*; I shall use only the Karo term) is set free. There is a fair amount of confusion about this point too. For a long time discussions of Batak religion were dominated by the question whether *tendi* became *bégu* on death, or whether *bégu* was just an aspect of *tendi* which carries on living in the land of the dead, while the rest of *tendi* dissolves into nothingness. It is certain, however, that after the death of any human being only the *bégu* continues to exist. People believe that they continue to live near their previous dwelling and have the possibility of contacting the bereaved and descendants. This can be made apparent in both positive and negative ways. Bad dreams, particular misfortune and such like may be signs that the *bégu* of an ancestor is not satisfied with the behaviour of its descendants. Any individual can attempt to pacify an enraged *bégu* by means of food and drink offerings and prayers. If this does not work, a magician-priest or a medium must be called in

to establish which *bégu* is responsible and what it desires from its descendants (see Chapter 4).

In the land of the dead the now Christianized Toba Batak recognized a hierarchy. A person's *bégu* had the same social status as person had when alive. In other words, the *bégu* of rich, powerful and influential people also had a prominant place in the land of the dead, if their descendants contributed to this by sacrifices. A *bégu* could advance to the status of a *sumangot* if a rich descendant (the male ones were particularly important in this) raised it to that status by means of a great ceremony and substantial sacrifices. At such festivals a vast number of pigs, cattle or even buffalo were slaughtered, and the *gondang* orchestra provided an accompaniment to this great event which could last up to seven days (Warneck 1909: 85). Stöhr (1965: 192) surmises that this *horja* feast was the occasion of the formation of a new kinship group, descended from the ancestor thus honoured (*saompu*; see Chapter 3). The bones of the ancestor were exhumed for the ceremony and reburied at the end of it.

The next level up from the *sumangot* was the *sombaon*, who were numerically much fewer than the *sumangot*, since they were the spirits of important ancestors who had lived ten to twelve generations earlier. They often lived in uncanny places and people took them offerings if they went near their abodes. To raise a *sumangot* to a *sombaon* another great festival was necessary. To this *santi rea*, often lasting several months, the inhabitants of the whole district came together. Animal sacrifice and the reburying of the ancestor's bones also played a central part in the ceremony (Warneck 1909: 85ff).

As well as the *bégu* of their dead the Karo Batak also have other categories of spirits which people can contact. According to Westenberg (1892: 221) the bicara guru are the death-souls of stillborn babies or of babies who have died before teething. It is possible to turn *bicara guru* into guardian spirits if particular misfortune has befallen the family of the child shortly after its death. With the help of a female medium (called *guru sibaso* by the Karo) the *bicara guru* can be made the family's guardian spirit for which a shrine is provided and to which sacrifices are regularly made from then on. Banana bushes and particular ornamental plants (e.g. a lily, Karo: *kalinjuhang*, or an Acanthaceae, Karo: *sangké sumpilet*) are planted at this spot and it is surrounded with a bamboo fence (ibid: 222). Such a holy place is called *ingan bicara guru*. Once a year the *bicara guru* is accorded a special feast, preceded by ritual hair washing (*erpangir kulau*).

The death-souls of members of the family who have had a sudden death (*maté sada-uari*) also act as guardian spirits for the family to the Karo. They include the victims of accidents, suicides, murder victim, people struck by lightning – those who have suffered a "bad death". To them a similar shrine is built where they are venerated and where sacrifices are made to them. A third but rarer category consists of the death-souls of dead virgins (*tungkup*). To be unmarried is always very unusual among all the Batak, and hence unmarried virgins have something mysterious about them. Their graves, called *bata-bata* or *ingan tungkup*, are kept in good repair for a long time by their relatives. They too are positive guardian spirits of a family. According to Neumann (1902b: 34) these three types of death-souls can also be venerated as *bégu jabu*, spirits which live in the house in the living area of the individual family, i. e. in the closest possible proximity to the family, with a place for offerings on the shelf above the family sleeping place, where they receive their food and drink offerings and their prayers.

Another category of death-souls which influence the Karo Batak consists of the personal guardian spirits (*jinujung*). Almost every person has his or her *jinujung* which makes its home either near the body or in the head or throat of its "host". People receive a *jinujung* in childhood and, unless they are unfortunate enough to lose it, they keep it for life. A *jinujung* can leave a person, in which case that person falls ill. A *guru sibaso* will call the *jinujung* back and while she is in a trance the *jinujung* will enter into her and speak through her mouth. According to Neumann (1902b: 36) a man has a female *jinujung* and a woman a male *jinujung*. Elsewhere he states that girls and boys mainly receive their *jinujung* at puberty (Neumann 1951: 87). I know of nothing to explain the antagonism between the sexes which underlies this.

Contact with the dead

The death of a Batak affects not only his close family but also the *marga* and the other inhabitants of the village. Death at a great age, and particularly with numerous progeny, is no less painful to the Batak, but as a rule an old person has achieved those goals in life which in Batak eyes are necessary for a happy fulfilled life after death. Ideally he has provided for his many male descendants, who will continue his *marga* and above all ensure that he is buried in accordance with the *adat* and ancestor-worship after his death. He has also through the marriages of his daughters further strengthened the ties of kinship with the bride-takers (*boru*) or has entered into new *boru-hulahula* relationships.

A sudden death at a young age, death in childbed or a similar "bad death" is much harder for the bereaved to understand, even though the idea that the *tendi* has chosen its own inevitable destiny is in a way a consoling one. Though the death-souls of those who have died suddenly or early are regarded as dangerous, the Karo believe that for their own family they take on the role of guardian spirits, *bicara guru* and *maté sada-uari* which have a predominantly positive effect (Westenberg 1892: 222ff). This does not apply, however, to women who have died in childbed: their *bégu* are called by the Toba *Boru Na Mora* and they are among the most feared of spirits of the dead (Winkler 1925: 66ff, 159).

At death the life-soul (*tendi*) leaves the human body through the fontanelle and the death-soul (*bégu*) is set free. The cult of the dead starts immediately after the death and may continue over many months and even years. Its main purpose is to bid farewell to the deceased and to make it clear to the *bégu* that it is now free and that its world is now quite different. Attention is also paid to the legal problems connected with death: all relatives with a claim to parts of the estate of the deceased come together to settle the questions of inheritance. If the deceased was rich, or even the *raja* of the village, negotiations over the division of the estate and the succession to the office can be drawn out over a long period.

The procedure of the burial – the treatment of the corpse, the type of coffin and the location of the grave, the extent and duration of the ceremonies – depend on a variety of factors. The Batak do not have a uniform method of burial, or a uniform programme for the funeral ceremony. Even within the individual Batak groups the cult of the dead can vary depending on family membership or social status. Burial in a suspended woven mat, a second burial after a few years in a stone sarcophagus or a stone urn in ossuaries, or the keeping of the remains in the family house, or the sending of the ashes on a soul-boat to the land of the dead – these are ways in which the Batak have dealt with their dead in the past, and in some instances still do so today.

The cult of the dead among the Karo Batak

Of the five great *merga* of the Karo Batak (Tarigan, Ginting, Sembiring, Perangin-angin and Karo-Karo) the Sembiring deserve special attention (cf Chapter 1). It seems fairly certain that the members of this *merga* are descendants of Tamil immigrants from south India, from whom they have preserved certain features in their cult of the dead. The *merga* names – Pandia, Colia, Depari, Milala, Berahmana and Pelawi – are not derived from the Batak languages but are of south Indian origin. Besides those mentioned the following sub-clans also belong to this group: Muham, Gurukinayan, Bunuhaji, Busuk, Keling, Pandebayang, Sinukapur and Tekang (Singarimbun 1975: 74). Within the Sembiring *merga* these sub-clans have a special position. They are called *Sembiring si ngombak* – those Sembiring who let the river carry away the ashes of their dead (ibid: 79). They are also forbidden to eat dog flesh, a food usually consumed by the Batak. This group within Karo Batak will feature prominently in our study of the cult of the dead, since their cult differs in many respects from that of the other Karo (see the detailed presentation in Sibeth 1988). A second group of sub-clans, Keloko, Kembaren, Sinulaki and Sinupayung, are also forbidden dog flesh.

All Karo who still follow the traditional religion (*perbégu*) hold the same beliefs about how the death-soul should be treated. All the attention paid to the welfare of the *tendi* in the person's lifetime is transferred to the *bégu* after his death. In this there is a mixture of veneration, anxiety and hope for support and protection more on a rational than an emotional basis. It is an absolute necessity for a Karo to give the *bégu* the requisite attention, since in his view the *bégu* are not in a far-away, separate land of the souls or of the dead, but live in a village of the dead which is thought to be situated not far from the cemetery. In the society of the dead they occupy the same roles they had when alive – in other words, death is merely a transition to an immaterial form of existence. Their status in the land of the dead is derived mainly from the sacrifices offered by their descendants (who ideally should be numerous), since they share these offerings with the other *bégu*. Only the male descendants ensure a *bégu* its social status and respect among the other death-souls. The *bégu* are not immortal, since death also rules in the land of the dead: a *bégu* dies seven times before it is changed into a straw and finally becomes earth (Neumann 1933b: 542).

Immediately after death various ritual actions are performed to make the *bégu* understand that from now on its world will be separate from that of its kin. Symbolically this is done among other things by turning round the mat on which the corpse is laid out so that the body lies with its head at the foot. Thumbs and toes respectively are tied together and the body is wrapped in a white cotton cloth (see also Neumann 1933b: 536ff). During the ceremony *perumah bégu* a *guru sibaso* declares to the *bégu* of the deceased, that it is definitely dead and must take leave of its relatives (Joustra 1926: 182). After that care is taken that the burial follows as quickly as possible.

Up to this point there are no essential differences in the ancient religious ideas of the Karo Batak. The differences become apparent and significant in the manner in which the body is buried. In the following description it must always be remembered that much has already been forgotten and has not been practised for a long time, as was already noted by Neumann (1933b: 535).

60 Cremation tower (*ligé-ligé*). For this ceremony the bones of the ancestors are disinterred and burned with the tower. Karo plateau, c. 1910

Formerly the body was veiled in a white cloth and bound into a bamboo split four ways, but today wooden coffins are used. The coffin is carried a few times round the house and usually by women to the cemetery with musical accompaniment from the *gendang* orchestra and the continual firing of guns (Joustra 1926: 182). At crossroads the coffin is put down and eleven people go round it four times to confuse the *bégu* (Smith Kipp 1974: 9). It is hoped that the *bégu* will then be unable to find its way back to the village. According to Neumann (1933b: 542) the cemetery for the ordinary mortals was always located downstream, while that for relatives of the aristocracy was upstream. When the funeral procession arrives there the grave is dug and the corpse laid flat on its back in it. Care is taken that the head lies towards the village so that – in the unexpected event that the body should get up – he will not be looking in the direction of his native village. The burial usually takes place in greatest haste and, leaving behind offerings of food and drink, the people depart from the spot very quickly.

The bodies of magician-priests and those who have died from lightning were buried sitting up with their hands tied together, unlike the usual method of burial. The palms of the hand were joined and a quid of betel placed between them. At the end of the 19th century the poorer Karo Batak and those who had died of epidemics were still being wrapped in a mat and hung from a bamboo frame (ill. 68). In other cases no grave was dug for the coffin, a mound of earth was piled around it, though this form of burial (*kubur*) was restricted to members of respected families (Joustra 1926: 183). The burial place of a great man could also be enclosed with large stones and protected with a roof made of *ijuk* (fibrous material from the sugar palm) (Westenberg 1897: 44).

Personal objects belonging to the dead person were not laid in the grave but on top of it. The only objects which could be termed grave goods were the quid of betel or a silver coin which, depending on the region, was placed in the mouth of the deceased (Müller 1893: 10; Neumann 1933b: 536). The favourite coins were Spanish dollars of the late 18th and early 19th centuries, also known as "Spanish mats" or "cannon dollars". Because of their high silver content these silver dollars were highly valued both as raw material for silver jewellery and as currency (see ill. 254). Mexican, Japanese and silver coins from the British Straits Settlements were also in circulation. Boiled rice in a little basketwork bag or a variety of cooking vessels was used as a food offering. These vessels were either laid on the grave or hung over it on a stick. Palm wine or water was placed on the grave in bamboo vessels. To these were added personal possessions of the deceased such as opium pipes, cooking vessels, tools etc. Since the *bégu* still remained for four days in the immediate vicinity, it was believed that it could be kept near the grave with the help of personal objects. There are also accounts of the practice of breaking off a corner from each of the objects placed on the grave or using objects that were already damaged. Karo Batak do not use any chipped plates, bowls, pots etc for fear of ill consequences, since only *bégu and hantu* (nature spirits) eat from such vessels (Neumann 1933b: 540f). This indicates another symbolic separation of the various spheres of life, which is characteristic of the cult of the dead.

As a rule the Karo did not mark the graves in a special way. The graves of insignificant people were given a simple marker for recognition, such as unusually shaped or coloured stones or bushy plants with a striking appearance. The graves were enclosed with a bamboo fence within which was planted *kalinjuhang*, a holy plant used in many ceremonies, and lemon grass (see p. 98, note 16). Graves of the members of respectable families were often given special decoration. A house or roof structure was erected over the burial place, and sacrificial offerings were placed on its beams or on the grave.

The graves were not especially looked after. At the beginning relatives still occasionally visited the grave, but thereafter it was left to its fate. For a large part of the Karo Batak village inhabitants the simple burial marked the end of any contact with the deceased, who then passed into oblivion, unless his *bégu* became discontented and brought misfortune to its descendants or appeared to individual family members in dreams. In such cases the help of the guru or the sibaso was called on to pacify the *bégu* again.

Boat-shaped coffins

When an ordinary villager died people tried to get the body out of the house, out of the village and under the earth as quickly as possible, and sometimes it was not even put in a coffin. But around the body of an influential, well-to-do inhabitant a lavish cult of the dead would develop. A coffin made of the wood of the *kemiri* tree (*Aleurites moluccana*) was carved for him in the shape of a boat with its bow decorated with the carved head of a hornbill. The dead body was rubbed all over with camphor, and its orifices stopped with camphor (Kruijt 1891: 352). The lid was then sealed with resin and the coffin was set up outside the house beneath the overhanging eaves. The fluid from the corpse was channelled through a hole in the floor of the coffin and down a bamboo pipe to the earth (ill. 61). This coffin, which the Karo call *pelangkah*, remained in this position until the last stage of the burial ceremony could take place. The time for this varied considerably – from one year to ten years or even longer. In the end the financial situation of the bereaved family was the factor that decided when the concluding ceremony was performed.

The existence of boat-shaped coffins among the Karo is puzzling since the Karo believe that the land of the dead, where the souls of the deceased dwell, is situated near the village, their burial places or prominent points in the landscape: mountains, waterfalls or springs etc., but not in some regions, which can only be reached by boat across standing or running water. Traditions and ideas which are conclusively connected with the boat-shaped type of coffin are not – or no longer – found among the Karo. It is interesting, however, that the use of boat-shaped coffins (*pelangkah*) was not obligatory for all sections of the population but was restricted to the more powerful and influential families. To the Karo influence, power and wealth were indications of an especially potent life-soul (*tendi*), and the death-soul (*bégu*) of a *raja* or *sibayak* were also considered to be very powerful. By treating it with particular honour one was sure of it as an effective guardian spirit which could keep away misfortune of any kind from the village. The keeping of the body in the village – outside the house in the gallery or under the eaves, but still in the immediate vicinity of the family – lends weight to this interpretation, especially in view of the fact that all other corpses were buried in the shortest possible time outside the village. One can certainly surmise that the boat shape of the coffin is a survival from forgotten notions of a voyage made by the soul in a boat of the dead to the land of the dead, such as are encountered among many other Indonesian peoples. As yet, however, we have no evidence for this thesis.

The decoration of the boat-shaped coffin with a zoomorphic stem also raises a few questions. In many instances the carving is of a hornbill (the model coffin shown in ill. 64 illustrates this type very clearly). Another motif used in the decoration is the head of the *singa*, a zoologically unclassifiable animal that is ridden, which seems to be represented in another model (ill. 63). Other depictions show a clearly recognizable horse's head. To the Karo the horse and hornbill are apparently closely connected. The hornbill is a symbol of bravery, endurance and swiftness (Steinmann 1939/40: 162).

The boat-shaped coffins (*pelangkah*) always remained in their place until their final burial. Not until sufficient financial resources were available was the second part of the funeral ceremony performed. The coffin was opened and the remains taken out. The skull and sometimes the larger bones are cleaned and deposited in a skull house (*geriten*). The rest of the body was cremated or reburied. The Karo call this ceremony *nurun-nurun*.

But even in this point the Karo did not have a uniform system. There are accounts that after exhumation the skull too was cremated. If the remaining bones were cremated the ash was either scattered or made into healing medicine or buried again in a wooden vessel (Sibeth 1988: 126f).

Wooden sculptures of two persons are attached to the lids of the boatshaped coffins: a male figure sitting or standing in front at the bow and a female at the stern. On almost all coffins the man is armed with a muzzleloading gun and is looking the direction the boat is supposed to be travelling – though a photograph by Tassilo Adam taken before 1920 (ill. 61) shows the armed man sitting facing backwards. The figures are nearly always clothed and their sex can usually be determined from their clothing. The man with gun in the bow has the same function as the men shooting at the burial ceremony: the firing of the guns is supposed on the one hand to keep away the harmful *bégu* and on the other prevent the *tendi* of the participants in the funeral from following the *bégu* of the deceased. The female figure at the stern is almost certainly a priestess (*guru sibaso*). Her hands which are usually raised in supplication point in this direction. Comparable figures (ill. 64) were also mounted on soul-boats of the Sembiring *merga* – one of the few parallels between the cult of the dead of the Sembiring and that of the other four Karo *merga*.

61 Boat-shaped coffin (*pelangkah*) with hornbill head by the side of a house with rich painted decorations. Karo plateau, c. 1910

Soul-boats in the funeral ceremony of the Sembiring

As has been mentioned above, the funeral customs of the Sembiring differ markedly from those described so far. The following description is in the past tense because the use of soul-boats has not been current among the Sembiring since the beginning of the present century. The *Sembiring si-ngombak* – those Sembiring who sent the ashes of their dead down river in a boat – cremated their dead soon after death. The ashes were gathered and kept in earthen pots, which according to informants in Seberaya (questioned in 1985) were undecorated and c. 30 cm in diameter. Not all the Sembiring cremated their dead however; the Sembiring Kembaren sub-clan did not countenance cremation on principle (Neumann 1933b: 546). The *Sembiring si-ngombak* also excepted magician-priests (*guru*) from cremation; they were buried in a seated posture (Joustra 1926: 182).

The funeral ceremonies of the *Sembiring si-ngombak*, called *pekualuh*, apparently took place in accordance with a strict chronological pattern, though writers cannot agree as to the precise number of intervening years. The times given range from once a year, every two or four years, every seven or eight years, every eight or ten years, up to a cycle of twelve years. The earliest known source speaks of an 13 month cycle (Sibeth 1988: 127). The *pekualuh* which the missionary Joustra was able to observe in September 1902 was the last of its kind to be held in the Karo highlands. After the annexation of the Karo highlands the Dutch colonial administration banned the ceremony, which lasted a whole month, on economic grounds.

One reason generally given for the fact that only members of the *Sembiring si-ngombak* held *pekualuh* is that it was imposed on them as a punishment for breaking the clan rules of exogamy. A second reason is more mythological: according to a story a Sembiring once presented the sultan of Aceh with a supposedly white elephant, although he had in fact whitened the animal with white earth or rice flour. When the deception was revealed he fled and settled in the Karo highlands. In another version the Sembiring attempted to sell a similarly whitewashed buffalo to the sultan as a rarity. The sultan directed him to Raja Rum, a Turkish sultan, who bought the whitened buffalo. Then, as in the other story, the deception was found out. In both versions the punishment was that the Sembiring could no longer bury their dead on Batak ground but had to transfer the ashes during the funeral ceremony to the Lau Biang river which flows into the Straits of Malacca.

Unlike the other Karo *merga* certain sub-clans of the Sembiring (and also a sub-clan of the Perangin-angin) are allowed to marry endogamously in the *merga*. Thus members of the sub-clan Milala are allowed to marry members of the other Sembiring sub-clans. According to information collected in 1985, this is connected with the attitude of the other four great *merga* who had forbidden their members to enter into marriages with Sembirings as a reaction to the war waged by the sultan of Aceh against the Karo highlands because of the deception described above. Another reason for *merga*-endogamy among the Sembiring is closely tied to the obligation of holding the *pekualuh*: the cost of such a ceremony was so high that all the family members including married sons-in-law and brothers-in-law were called in to finance it (Singarimbun 1975: 75). A man had therefore to think carefully before marrying a woman of the Sembiring *merga*, and the shortage of men from the other four *merga* willing to marry into the Sembiring would in the end have led to permission being granted for *merga*-endogamous marriages.

The funeral ceremony was preceded by numerous preparations which could begin once the *guru* had chosen a propitious day by means of his calendar. Six days before the ceremony the trees from which the soul-boat was to be made were felled. The work, with all the construction, was done in the forest or by the river. Boats were about two metres long and manned by four or eight small figures, each representing one of the dead. An eyewitness of the last *pekualuh* described the 14 boats which he saw at the ceremony in 1901, as follows.

"With small deviations the basic shapes are the same. They are massive, 1.2 to 2 metres long and, like the dolls, carved of kemiri wood. The projecting stem and stern terminate below in a fairly narrow scrolllike decoration. The boat is painted with the usual Batak motifs in red and black: the figures are coloured yellow with turmeric and hung with jewellery, wearing head scarves etc., so that it is possible to distinguish which represent men, women or children. The jewellery is later removed. The boat also has three tall, slender masts which are decorated below with models of Batak houses that are not bad, and at the top with loose decorations, including fish-trap-like baskets (hence called *tuwar-tuwar*) edged with white hen feathers" (Joustra 1902a: 550).

Clothing, jewellery and weapons of the deceased persons were hung in the boat. The subsequent procession ended on an open field near the river. The boats were put down on small mounds of earth before being each attached to a large bamboo raft. Not until it was mounted on bamboo raft was it complete and fully operative (see ill. 64). There are various versions describing where on the soul-boat the ashes or vessels were positioned. The ashes were either scattered next to the figure on the deck of the boat, placed in a pot under the corresponding figure on the bamboo raft or beside the figures on board the soul-boat. The model soul-boat (ill. 64) does not provide a solution to this question. In

my opinion the most plausible solution seems to be that the pots
were placed on the bamboo raft below the actual soul-boat. This
seems logical simply because of the lack of space on the deck of
the boat and also explains the construction of the boat on a raft.

At the end of the day of the ceremony, after intense mourning
around the dead, to the continual accompaniment of *gendang*
music and the firing of guns, the soul boats were brought back to
the village. On the sixth day of the ceremony, called *mata kerja*,
the soul-boats were carried back to the open field and set down
on the prepared mounds of earth (*pengelebaten*). *Gendang* music
accompanied the soul-boats on their way, but interestingly the
firing of guns was forbidden on this day. A food offering of a
living white hen was placed on the stern of the soul-boat. In the
afternoon the boats were carried down to the river. The number
of participants was greatly reduced at this point, since offences
against good morals were frequent. The order of precedence
of the soul-boats in their transportation and launching seems to
have been strictly laid down. Each sub-*merga* had its own
soul-boats, which were transferred to the river in the following
order: Colia, Pandia, Milala, Depari and Pelawi. The order of the
boats of the other sub-*merga* is not known. Before the departure
of the soul-boats the masts together with the clothes and
jewellery and the offerings were removed. Then the boats were
moved eleven times upstream and downstream. They had
scarcely left the bank before the spectators began to use all their
efforts to capsize them with stick and stones. No explanation for
this has come down to us. It can only be that by destroying the
boats, and with them the urns, people wanted to hasten the
transfer of the ashes to the river. This was possibly done to
prevent anybody further down river from gaining possession of
the ashes illegitimately.

If the grass by the side of the river had changed its direction
by 90 degrees in four months, this was interpreted as a positive
sign that the death-souls (*bégu*) had reached their destination
(information in 1985). Where that destination was still remains
unclear, but in the past the *Sembiring si-ngombak* apparently still
had the idea of a land of souls that could be reached by water.
The other Karo Batak did not have this belief, although they used
a boat-shaped coffin (*pelangkah*), because they believed the *bégu*
stayed near the place of burial.

62 Bone house (*geriten*). The string decoration on the outside shows a lizard
(see p. 115); height: 50 cm. Karo Batak

63 Model coffin with winged animal; length: 78 cm. Karo Batak

65 Model of a boat-shaped coffin with hornbill head at the prow. The middle rod channels the fluids from the corpse to the ground; length: 30.5 cm. Karo Batak

64 Model of a soul boat with a superstructure to ward off evil spirits; height: 132 cm. Sembiring Karo Batak

66 Original figures from a soul boat; height: 50–60 cm. Sembiring Karo Batak

67 Original figure from a soul boat; height: 66 cm. Sembiring Karo Batak

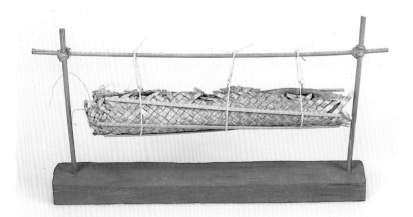

68 Model of a poor person's burial. This type was still in use up the turn of the century; length: 38 cm. Karo Batak

The Toba Batak cult of the dead

Even for the largely Christianized Toba Batak ancestor worship still has a central place in religious thought. The Toba do not, however, have such a variety of burial practices as the Karo Batak. Of particular importance to the Toba are the architectural structures in which during a great reburial ceremony the disinterred bones of the ancestors are finally laid to rest. We shall look at these in more detail later. The Toba Batak have been Christian for many generations, the majority of them organized in an independent tribal church (HKBP = Huria Kristen Batak Protestan). Since the arrival of Rheinische Missionsgesellschaft from Germany the Gospels have become a firm part of the religious system of the Toba, yet they see no contradiction between Christianity and the reburial ceremonies which hark back to ancient beliefs. The collective conversion of whole kinship groups, as practised by the German missionaries, tended to place little emphasis on personal religious conviction and was closer to the old formula *cius regio, eius religio*. As part of this collective evangelization the missionaries in the early stages allowed many elements from the traditional beliefs to continue – above all the *adat* by which the values and norms of Batak society were handed down. It was believed that the concepts from the old religion in the *adat* would in the course of time be replaced by Christian concepts. This form of Christian missionary activity has meant that many typical Toba Batak elements from the old religion have been preserved to the present day.

As in almost all cultures, the Toba cult of the dead has proved particularly resistant to change. For the Toba this certainly has to do with the fact that a death is not an individual misfortune for a small nuclear family but – as with the Karo – is of central significance for the members of all the various kinship groups. Burial, ancestor worship and reburial of bones are ceremonies through which they can give combined expression of their loss, and at the same time these social ceremonies serve to strengthen the reciprocal obligations and dependences of the three kinship groups (*dongan sabutuha, hulahula* and *boru*). Earth burial is customary among the Toba. In the past the coffin used was made from a tree trunk (ill. 69), which the more foresighted Toba would arrange to have made while they were still alive. Today such coffins are used only in rare instances (ill. 70), and simple panel coffins have supplanted the massive ones. The ready-made coffin is stored by the house under the eaves, or on the open area of the rice granary (*sopo*), until the day it is needed. In the past it was customary for the Toba to keep the coffin with the body of an influential man – a *raja* for example – on the gallery of the house (*bonggar-bonggar*) or on the open area of the *sopo* until the process of decomposition was complete, but this practice was prohibited by the missionaries, and since then all deceased have been placed in their coffins soon after death and buried in the cemetery outside the village. Burial in mats was mainly used for those Toba who could not afford a coffin carved from a massive tree trunk (Winkler 1925: 55).

News of the death of a relative, neighbour etc. quickly travels around the neighbourhood. All the people affected by the death pour into the village where the deceased lived to take part in the lamentation of the dead (*andung*). In well-to-do families this can last up to a week during which all the participants are looked after at the expense of the bereaved (Winkler 1925: 130). Before he could be buried, the deceased person had to be measured. This was not just to obtain the precise measurements for the coffin and the grave but because if the length of the body is not measured then the *bégu* (I shall keep the Karo spelling) could grow enormous amd become a malignant *bégu nurnur* (Warneck 1909: 78). At the burial an animal is slaughtered on each day and the "essence" of the flesh is given to the *bégu* in the land of the dead. Without this sacrifice the *bégu* does not obtain entry to the circle of the respectable dead. The meat is shared among the relatives and villagers present and the bones of the slaughtered animals placed on the grave when it is filled in. The poles on which the coffin was carried are stuck into the foot of the grave and on them is hung the cooking pot in which the funeral meal was cooked (ibid.: 71f). The wealthy dead had their personal jewellery put into the grave with them, and their burial places could be marked with roughly carved sculptures in stone or wood (Warneck 1904: 76). Songs of lament (*andung*) accompanied all stages of a burial. For a few days food and drink offerings were brought to the grave for the death-soul, which was thought to remain there until the process of decomposition ceased. Thereafter people no longer bothered about the burial place.

69 Making a coffin from a tree trunk. Toba region, c. 1930

70 Coffin next to a house in Huta Gaol. Uluan district, Toba region, 1989
71 Masked dancers, c. 1930
72 Masked dancers. Karo plateau, 1930

Masks in the cult of the dead

In the past mask dances were often performed during the funeral ceremonies. Such dances are also found in other Batak regions: among the Simalungun as well as the Karo. In all three regions masks appeared at the burial of influential persons. Usually there were two masks, one representing a man and the other a woman, which were accompanied by a hornbill or horse's head mask (*huda-huda*). We have very incomplete information concerning the cultural and religious origins of these mask dances. The masked dancers make their appearance during the lamentation and perform their dances in front of the deceased's house to *gondang* accompaniment. In their hands they carry wooden hands which are relatively roughly shaped but can have moveable fingers (ill. 72). The mask-wearers then escort the coffin to the cemetery where they finally take off their masks and lay them on the grave. In the case of the Simalungun the masks were then kept in a little house erected over the grave. Presumably they were to keep away evil spirits and accompany the death-soul of the deceased on its way to the land of the dead. Simalungun masks are flat half-masks tied in front of the face, decorated with hair made from animal fur or *ijuk* (the fibre from the sugar palm) and often painted with a pattern of lines or dots in gaudy colours, while the large masks of the Toba and Karo are made from a tree trunk and are pulled over the head of the dancer. Historical photographs often show a colourful confusion of masks and costumes originating from a variety of Batak groups, which suggests that by that time (in most cases the 1930s) these dances were already assuming "folk" characteristics.

73 Masks. (a) flat mask. Simalungun/Toba border region   (b) flat mask, Simalungun Batak; (c) with hands, and (d) Karo Batak; (e) height: 55 cm. Toba Batak

The jointed doll (si gale-gale)

If a Toba man died without a male descendant this was regarded as a very great misfortune since the *bégu* of a man who died childless could only occupy a very subordinate position in the land of the dead. Moreover the performance of the lamentation and burial in accordance with the *adat* was put in question. In the all-important area of ancestor worship it even meant that the deceased would never be able to rise to the higher ranks of *sumangot* or even *sombaon*. Similarly it was considered a great misfortune if all the sons had died before their father. In order to perform the burial in accordance with the *adat* it used to be permissable for the Toba to substitute a jointed doll (*si gale-gale*), dressed to represent a predeceased or imaginary son. We do not know when this *si gale-gale* was invented by the Toba. The first mention of this jointed doll in the sources dates from around the end of the 19th century, but it is believed that the practice originated in the mid-19th century in the vicinity of Balige (Tichelman 1950: 8). The use of the *si gale-gale* was very rarely observed by Europeans, not even by official and missionaries who lived for a long time in the region. Today the dances with *si gale-gale* dolls are performed as a tourist attraction on the Samosir peninsula (ill. 74). The *si gale-gale* is moved by an operator pulling strings which are passed through the body. By means of these strings the figure can turn or nod its head, stick out its tongue, shut its eyes, turn and bow the upper half of its body and even execute dance movements with its arms and hands. One *si gale-gale* (Museon, The Hague) with a moistened ball of moss inside its head was even able to shed tears.

Reburial of bones after some years

The lamentation, mask dances and burial did not, however, mark the end of the cult of the dead. A second ceremony followed, at least for those dead who were held in honour by their descendants and whose family had the necessary financial means to undertake the reburial of the ancestor's bones. This usually took place after one or more generations. This form of ancestor veneration is still practised by the Toba today. In a ceremony lasting several days the bones of a particularly honoured ancestor and those of his descendants are exhumed, cleaned, mourned and finally laid to rest again in bone houses. Formerly large stone sarcophagi and round stone urns also served as grave houses (ills. 76ff), but these stone containers were not used throughout the Toba region, only on the Samosir peninsula and the area immediately around Lake Toba. We do not know how old this custom is. Attempts of scholars in the 1930s to relate this regional use of stones to a presumed thoroughly Batak

74 In Tomok, 1985

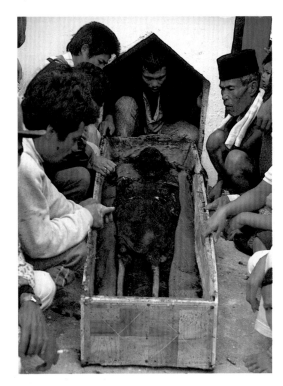

75 Exhumation of a woman who died four years previously. Toba region 1989

megalith culture tend not to seem very convincing when the evidence on which they are based is examined more closely. The large blocks of stone used for these stone sarcophagi, called *parholian*, were broken from the cliffs and hollowed out, and a lid was made which could consist of one or more parts. A female figure is usually seated on the lid holding a bowl in her hands. The lower part of the sarcophagus is carved at the front with the massive head of a *singa*, a mythological beast, with its tail hanging down at the back, and it was therefore thought of as a *singa* in whose body the bones of the ancestor found their last resting place. The sarcophagus could even stand on large paws (ill. 5 in Stöhr et al. 1981: 50). Below the open mouth of the *singa* and under its protection stands a male figure possibly representing the male primeval ancestor of the *marga*. In this case the woman on the lid is probably the female half of the primeval parents.

Stone urns, found in the immediate vicinity of the *parholian* and possibly made at the same time, can sometimes be as tall as a man and are occasionally decorated with a squatting figure in stone on the round lid (ills. 77, 80). Many old stone urns and stone sarcophagi are still in use today, that is to say the bones of ancestors are still stored in them. It is said of others that the families have taken out the bones of their ancestors and reburied them in another place. This is partly due to Christian beliefs and partly a wise precaution to keep the bones out of the hands of strangers – probably anthropologists and tourists (information: C. Schreiber 1990).

More common than these stone sarcophagi were the little wooden houses built in the style of the *rumah adat* which could contain the bones of one or several ancestors. Reminders of these *joro*, as they are called, are to be seen in the small cement constructions which decorate modern grave houses (ill. 78). These are architectural structures in concrete and cement (called *tugu*) which are simpler to make yet more elaborate. They are appearing throughout Tobaland in greater numbers and increasing in height. Based on the form of the old stone sarcophagi they originated at the latest in the 1920s as simple ossuaries built of brick with an outer rendering of cement. These structures, which were then still known as *tambak* were painted and decorated with *singa* heads on the front (see Chapter 6). A early version is described by Warneck (1915: 357):

"These bone festivals are among the most popular in the Batak calendar because everybody is given his due. Finally the bones are buried and a high mound is raised over the grave which is often decorated with a cement structure."

Since the 1950s the building of such structures has increasingly become a matter of prestige for individual families. In order to take away their connection with the old religion and emphasize their character as memorials they are now called by the Javanese word for boundary stone: *tugu* (information: D. Gröpper 1990). An impressive *tugu* is a way of expressing the power, wealth and importance of the *marga*.

The construction of such *tugu* and the reburial of the ancestors can almost ruin a *marga*. The enormous expense by Batak standards (Simon 1982: 202f) is usually met by financial contributions from those members of the family now living outside Batakland who have obtained well-paid government posts or achieved a certain prosperity by some other means. The attachment of all Toba Batak to their home is so great that they wish their last resting place to be in their native soil, and the financing of the most splendid *tugu* possible with the associated ancestor ceremony help pave the way for the donors themselves to be also transferred to Batakland after their death to take their rightful place in the *tugu*. For financial reasons today usually several bodies are reburied at the same time.

76 Famous stone sarcophagus of the Sidabutar *marga*. Tomok, Samosir, 1985

77 Stone urn and its owner, who estimates that it is 300 years old. Pansur Simbolon, Samosir, Lake Toba, 1989

78 Cement *tugu* in the form of the old grave houses. Simanindo, Samosir, Lake Toba, 1989

79 Stone urn with its lid open. Pansur Simbolon, Samosir, c. 1920

80 Stone figure from the lid of an urn with remains of paintwork; height: 94 cm. Toba Batak

81 Grave of the last *Si Singamangaraja* but one. Toba region, c. 1920

82–90 Transfer of bones at Huta Julu, Toba region, 1981: (82) exhumation
and (83) sorting of the bones; (84) cleaning and rubbing with betel
juice; (86) baskets and small wooden coffins; (87) slaughtering of
a water buffalo at the sacrifice post (*borotan*); (88) the holder of the
ceremony (*suhut*); (89) dance of the wifetakers; (90) dance of the
wife-givers

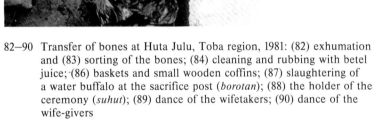

The programme of an ancestor festival

At the reburial ceremony which the music ethnologist A. Simon, a film team from the Institut für den Wissenschaftlichen Film at Göttingen and D. Gröpper were able to observe in Uluan country on the south-eastern shore of Lake Toba in 1981 71 bodies were exhumed and reburied in a newly built *tugu* in the course of a four day long festival (Simon 1982). At this great ceremony in the small village of Hutajulu the bones of an early ancestor of the Hutajulu *marga* and those of his direct male descendants with their wives were reburied. His great-great-great-grandson was the giver of the festival (*suhut*) and as such had to look after all the preparations and make sure that everything was carried out in accordance with the *adat*.

All the kinship groups receive written invitations to the ceremony and duplicated booklets inform the numerous guests of the planned programme of events. Since in this instance the ancestor had had two wives from different *marga*, two different wife-giver (*hulahula*) groups of the ancestor took part in the ceremony as well as the *hulahula* of his descendants. Also obliged to attend were the various *boru*, the representatives of those families which had taken their wives from the *marga* holding the celebration. They have to do all the work during the ceremony: preparing the site of the ceremony, assisting in the opening up of the graves, providing the participants in the ceremony with food and drink etc.

On the morning of the first day of the festival the graves in the cemetery are opened and the bones of the ancestors that are still there are removed (ill. 82). The unearthing of the skulls is presented as especially moving (Simon 1982: 189f). The bones are collected in baskets lined with white cloth and then ritually cleaned by the women using the juice of various citrus fruits. The rubbing of the skulls with betel juice seems in my opinion to go back to the former practice of offering the *bégu* a quid of betel. The exhumation and cleaning of the bones is accompanied by the singing of laments which Simon was able to record on tape. The bones are kept in the baskets in the tugu until the following morning. The remains of other ancestors buried in the cemetery of the town of Pematang Siantar were exhumed there and transported to Hutajulu. On the next morning the remains were wrapped in traditional cloths (*ulos*) and transferred from the baskets to small wooden coffins. After long speeches from the *suhut* and the representatives of the *hulahula* the coffins are nailed down and after communal prayer placed in the chambers of the *tugu*. A feast consisting of meat and rice follows and then traditional dances are performed.

"The programme of the dances is usually agreed on and fixed the evening before the ceremony begins. This is necessary because not only are one's own boru or hulahula present but also those of one's father, grandfather, great-grandfather, and if these were married several times the picture becomes even more complicated. It is easy to imagine how difficult it is to draw up a protocol for a ceremony like the one described here, since it is of great importance that none of the groups feels itself slighted or neglected." "As a rule the dances are spread over three days, beginning on the afternoon directly after the reburial of the remains with the suhut and his patrilinear line, dongan sabutuha. The second day is given over to the boru and the third to the hulahula, and during these the family of the suhut must always be present." (Simon 1982: 194f)

On the second day of the *adat* dance the representatives of the various *boru* present their financial contributions to cost of the feast within as part of their dance. The *boru* are obliged to make these donations and a book is carefully kept of how much each group has contributed. On the third day the representatives of the *hulahula* present unhusked and husked rice to the *suhut*. Dancing women take them into *suhut's* house in tall woven rice-bags carried on their heads (ill. 90). A book is kept of these too. At the concluding meal of the festival the slaughtered buffalo and pigs are divided up in accordance with the traditional rules and the individual participants receive the portions of meat allotted to each of them by the *adat*. The presentation of traditional *ulos* cloths to the group of the holder of the festival by its *hulahula*, the blessing of the *boru* by the giver of the festival, and of the *suhut* by his *hulahula* brings the festival to an end. A *gondang* orchestra seated on the gallery of the *suhut* house accompanies all the dances. The individual pieces of music and the dances to be performed are also determined by an established programme (see Schreiner 1970, Simon 1982 and 1987; chapter 6).

91 Bone houses (*tugu*) on Samosir. Lake Toba, 1989

Pa Surdam, a Karo Batak guru

(Juara Ginting; translated from the Indonesian by Uli Kozok)

In Karo society there are people who are accepted as having the ability to perform practices of the ancient religion. These include the art of fortune-telling, the carrying out of rituals and ceremonies, contact with the supernatural world, the treatment and healing of diseases, as well as other skills. The field of work covered by *guru* as such people are called[1] is hence very diverse, and *guru* are also differentiated according to their particular qualifications and specializations. There is the *guru pertawar* (healer and preparer of medicines)[2], the *guru pedadapken* (masseur), the *guru kalak mehado* (healer of mental illnesses), the *guru si beluh niktik wari* (the *guru* who knows the lunar calendar and can determine which days are propitious or unpropitious), the *guru persendungken* (who can tell fortunes by questioning the spirits), the *guru si ngogé gerek-gereken* (who can tell fortunes by reading signs), the *guru dua lapis pernin matana* (who can see the spirits), the *guru perseka-seka* (who produces noises in this larynx which reproduce the language of the spirits), the *guru si baso* (medium between the living and the dead, also called *guru perhoi* or *guru kemulun*), the *guru pertabas* (specialist in magic spells *mantras*), the *guru permangmang* (master of the art of singing mantras), the *guru peraji-aji* (who prepares poisons), the *guru penama-nama* (master of black magic), the *guru baba-baban* (who prepares amulets) and the *guru perbégu ganjang* as a *guru* is called if he follows a *bégu* which brings disaster.

This list gives a brief survey of the multiplicity of work which the Karo *guru* are given to do. In this chapter we shall restrict ourselves to one *guru* who lives in a village in the Karo highlands.

The Life of Pa Surdam

The *guru* described here is called Pa Surdam. He is about 75 years old and lives in the village of Barung Bertuk which has about 600 inhabitants and is 25 km from Kabanjahe, the main town in the Karo highlands[3]. Here he lives with his wife, who is about twenty years younger, and his seventeen-year-old and still unmarried daughter in a wooden house with a corrugated iron roof, which measures approximately four by five metres. The house stands in a field two kilometres distant from Barung Bertuk together with thirty others, which were originally built as field huts but have since come to constitute a sort of new village.

The woman who lives with Pa Surdam in this house is his second wife, whom he married in 1955, 36 years ago. The four eldest children are already married and live in another village. Only the youngest daughter is still living with them.

Pa Surdam's first wife died fifteen years ago. She was, in fact, his own stepmother, the second wife of his father, whom he married after his father's death.[4] Pa Surdam has a daughter by her who is married and lives in another village.

Every day Pa Surdam works with his wife in the field. When their daughter comes home in the afternoon from the senior school at Kabanjahe she helps her parents with their agricultural work. Their field, in which their house stands, is planted partly with coffee, partly with dry rice and maize. Sometimes Pa Surdam goes to the coffee house which is only 200 metres from his house, to drink a glass of tea or coffee. Around 5 pm, after having a bath at the village bathing place (a spring), he heads for the main village of Barung Bertuk. There he can usually be found in the coffee house conversing or playing a game of satur (the Karo Batak form of chess). On nine of the ten occasions I visited him in the coffee house he was playing chess and incessantly singing classical Karo Batak songs as he did so. Here in the coffee house he will often be asked by other villagers about the old legends and myths, about the performance of ceremonies and rituals, or the treatment of certain illnesses. Most of the people in Barung Bertuk consider him to be an expert on the traditional customs.

Although many are of the opinion that Pa Surdam knows much about the traditional world, rituals and illnesses, scarcely a single inhabitant of Barung Bertuk would ask for help from him in his role as a *guru*. The practices connected with the old religion are not held in high esteem by the Protestant Karo, and in any case they have some doubts about his capabilities as a guru, despite the fact that he seems to know much about the *guru* lore and can give convincing explanations for many phenomena.

The doubts they harbour about Pa Surdam are based on their own experience of his treatment of his own wife 15 years ago. At that time Pa Surdam spent a long time in Medan, where he heard from his daughter that his wife was showing symptoms of a psychological disorder. Sometimes, his daughter said, she talks to herself and laughs, cries for no reason or runs into the street and opens her clothes. The people who see her behaving like this believe that it is a reaction to possession by a spirit.

The people described to me how Pa Surdam treated his wife at that time:

"When Pa Surdam came home he looked at his wife for a moment. The he sent one of his children to buy a particular brand of cigarettes. He took one, lit it and placed the packet near his wife. Then he calmly smoked it, taking deep drags, as if he was enjoying it, blew the smoke in his wife's face and said: 'How good this cigarette tastes!' His wife felt the urge to smoke a cigarette and asked Pa Surdam for one. But he did not give her one, and instead took the packet away from her, when she

92 Chess players in a coffee house. Karo plateau, 1985
93 Chess is widespread among all the Batak. Model of Karo Batak playing
    chess; height: 17 cm; width: 28 cm

wanted to take one. Pa Surdam continued smoking and showed
even more clearly how much pleasure the cigarette was giving
him. Suddenly his wife flew into a rage and shouted: 'Shameless
son-in-law, pays no heed to his parents-in-law, I'm going!' Then
the wife suddenly collapsed in heap. Some people came and
stood her up again. Shortly afterwards she opened her eyes,
looked at Pa Surdam and asked, 'Have you just come?' She was
clearly surprised to see so many people in the house and asked
what had happened. Pa Surdam explained later that she had been
possessed by the spirit of her own father. Just imagine how easy
he made it for himself treating his own wife."

On Sundays, when most Karo do not work in the fields and
many of the Christians, particularly those that are married, go to
church, Pa Surdam spends the day in the coffee house in the
middle of Barung Bertuk. On such days he often takes a bamboo
flute (*surdam*) with him. One of his favourite songs is *ngandung-
ngandung* anak permakan, the lament of a shepherd boy bewailing
his unhappy fate.

Pa Surdam is not a Christian. To people not from his village
he admits that he is a follower of the *agama si dekah*, the old
religion, which is also called *perbégu* or *pemena*[5]. Officially Pa
Surdam is a Moslem, since the *kepala desa* (village chief) filled in
"Islam" on his identity card, when Pa Surdam would not decide
between the five recognized religions (Protestantism, Catholicism,
Islam, Buddhism or Hinduism). The *kepala desa* was however of
the opinion that Pa Surdam must choose a religion and so in the
end he wrote "Islam" on the card. The *kepala desa* is a Protestant.
When asked why he wrote "Islam" as the religion he declared
that whereas the Protestants and Catholics rejected the practices
of the old religion, Islam did not have an explicit ban. As far as
Hinduism and Buddhism were concerned the village chief was of
the opinion that they were not suitable religions for a Karo.[6]

Pa Surdam as a guru

As a *guru* Pa Surdam is active mainly outside Barung Bertuk,
particularly at Medan and Kabanjahe, where he is known as "the
guru from Barung Bertuk". Anyone needing his services will
generally send an *anakberu*, as is the usual practice among the
Karo, to make contact with Pa Surdam.[7] Pa Surdam then usually
comes to the house of the person who wants treatment or
the performance of a ritual. Occasionally, however, a patient will
come to Pa Surdam's house alone or accompanied by a family
member. In that case the treatment takes place there and if
necessary will be continued at the patient's house.

Pa Surdam treats his clients mainly by ritual means with the
support of magical powers, but I have also seen him on a few

94 Pa Surdam at a ceremony. Karo plateau, 1988

occasions use physiological methods of healing. He massaged one patient's sprained foot, after rubbing it with massaging oil (*minak*). He massaged a woman's belly to bring about an abortion. He gave one patient who was suffering from gonorrhaea (*pasar*) a medicine to drink (*inemen*), to another who had taken poison while eating he gave medicine in the form of a black powder (*pupuk*), and to another he gave a preparation to increase sexual potency (*tawar menci but*). On my last visit I saw how Pa Surdam in his own house applied a fluid with a cotton wool pad to a wound on a young man's foot and then bound it with a strip from a wrap-around skirt (*sarung*) which was no longer needed.

Most of the medicines which Pa Surdam prescribes for his patients are prepared by his wife. She gathers various parts of plants (leaves, fruit, seeds, barks, resin, roots and flowers) and prepares them in a variety of ways: as an oil using coconut oil as a base (*minak*), as a paste with spices as a base (*tawar*), as powdery pellets which are mixed in water and applied to the skin, using rice flour as a base (*kunung*), or in the form of a crystalline powder using broken rice and spices as a base (*sembur*).

To these medicines – particularly the *tawar* and *minak* types – Pa Surdam adds other ingredients with particular powers. Pa Surdam inherited some other medicines, above all *pupuk*, from his father. Because he only ever uses very small quantities of *pupuk* he still has a small supply.

The medicines of the *inemen* type are usually prepared by the patients themselves. Pa Surdam gives them a prescription and they can buy the ingredients at the market in Kabanjahe or Berastagi, where there are stalls selling spices and ingredients for traditional Karo medicine.

I was present at various ceremonies performed by Pa Surdam: *erpangir*, a purification ritual; *raleng tendi*, a ritual for calling back the *tendi* (soul) which has left the patient's body; *mère sembah-sembahen*, a sacrifice at a holy place; *ngulak*, a ritual to ward off magical powers; and *nggera bégu*, a ritual for driving away spirits (*bégu*). Some of these rituals are connected with treatment of an illness, while others keep illnesses away. Once I was present when Pa Surdam gave a man something as love philtre, and on another occasion I saw him give a medicine to strengthen self-confidence (*penetap ukur*) to man who wanted to go to look for work in the interior of the island of Kalimantan (Borneo).

Pa Surdam says that apart from the rituals that I witnessed he has also performed others. In the *ersilihi* ritual a human figure is carved from the trunk of a banana tree. The spirit threatening the life of the patient is fooled into believing that the figure is in fact the patient and in this way the patient's life is saved. *Ngeraksamai rumah* is a ritual for the ceremonial purification of a newly built house and *ngarkari* is a ritual to drive away malignant spirits threatening a particular group, e.g. a village.

The sources of guru lore

Pa Surdam has a number of skills which put him in the position of being able to work as a *guru*. He knows many mantras (*tabas*) as well as how to recite them in a sing-song manner (*ermangmang*) before beginning a treatment. Pa Surdam is a passionate flute-player, and knows how to incorporate his skilful playing of the bamboo flute (*surdam*) into the ritual; *tendi* in particular, and also guardian spirits (*keramat*), love the sound of the *surdam*. If a *tendi* has abandoned the body of a patient, the use of the *surdam* in the *raleng tendi* ritual can contribute to the *tendi* returning to the body of the sick person.[8]

As well as this Pa Surdam is skilled in the art of the dance. The *guru* dances which he performs in particular rituals, for example in the *ngarkari*, at which the *gendang* orchestra also plays, make a significant contribution to the participants' belief in its success. Pa Surdam is also skilled in the art of singing. Not just singing prayers with mantras, he also knows how to recite in a sing-song tone the old legends and myths which are important in the performance of a ritual so that the participants understand its background and can therefore experience the ritual more

95 A magician-priest (*guru*) at a ceremony where he skewers an egg and a
frog with his magic wand. Kabanjahe, Karo plateau, c. 1910

intensely. His knowledge of the history handed down in the myths, of nature, plants, and the objects which he uses in the rituals enables him to perform the rituals in a more complete way, even if certain conditions hinder the performance of a ritual.[9]

He frequently compares himself with other *gurus*. They often ask the patient to buy the necessary means for a healing ritual themselves. This means that the ritual is doomed from the beginning to fail. The patient either cannot provide the financial means, he can come to no agreement with his family[10], or the social situation of the patient do not permit the performance of the ritual (e. g. if the patient is a Christian). In such cases many *guru* refuse to perform a ritual. In Pa Surdam's view however, every ritual can be made to suit the individual needs and conditions of the patient. If a particular ingredient, a particular object, or a particular medicine is not available, then another can be substituted for it, providing that the *guru* has a comprehensive knowledge of the properties of the substance needed for the ritual. Even if it is not possible to find the best substance there is still no need to do without the ritual.

The tailoring of a ritual to meet individual requirements – the creation of an individual ritual – is one of Pa Surdam's strengths, but one which the people of Barung Bertuk regard as a weakness: "He does the rituals just the way he wants to."

In Pa Surdam's view a ritual or a healing is not an action which any other *guru* could have done. It is not enough for it to be done the way it was done in the past or the way one has seen another *guru* doing it. Then, according to Pa Surdam, not all the possibilities that are immanent in a ritual or a treatment are fully exploited. As an example he mentions the treatment of a sick man whose *tendi* had left his body (*la jé tendina*). A simple theory shared by many guru holds that "If the tendi has left the patient's body, then the *tendi* must be called back." The usual ritual for this is *raleng tendi*, which means, says Pa Surdam, simply performing a ritual in its usual sequence, in the way that people are already familiar with it. This is, however, nothing more than "writing out a prescription": someone whose *tendi* has left his body receives the *raleng tendi* ritual as his prescribed medicine. Pa Surdam believes that as a rule the *guru sibaso* (mediums), who are mostly women, perform a ritual in this manner. But in traditional healing of the Karo these *guru sibaso* served a *guru* as assistants. They are skilled in the art of singing, can see spirits, make contact with them, and let the spirits enter their own bodies. These abilities are not usually possessed by a *guru*, who functions as a healer, and since the *guru sibaso* frequently participate in rituals, many of them feel that they themselves are able to perform a ritual without any other *guru* being present.

For Pa Surdam it makes a big difference whether a ritual is performed to ensure someone a good future or as means of treating a patient. In a ritual done to bring someone success, the *guru* is nothing more than the director of the ritual which has already been planned by the person who wanted it performed. An example of this is the *ngerasamai rumah* ritual. After a house has been built the ritual is performed to ward away anything bad from the house and its inhabitants. The master of the house and his relatives have planned the ritual well in advance and ask a *guru* to perform the ritual because he understands more about ritual and everything to do with ritual.

In the treatment of illness, however, the ritual is performed on the basis of the *guru's* diagnosis. In his diagnosis the *guru* not only establishes what sort of illness it is and what has caused it, but also the appropriate type of treatment. An example is the loss of *tendi* which has already been mentioned. It is not enough to know that the illness is caused by the loss of the *tendi*, the *guru* also has to find out why this may have occurred. It may be an influence from the outside, such as black magic, a malignant spirit or the spirit of an ancestor. Perhaps there are also circumstances to be sought within the patient himself which have caused the loss of the *tendi*. The *guru* must now find out how this can have happened: whether the patient has broken a taboo, is under psychological pressure, or is hated by somebody. Attention must also be paid to the time when this began (so that it can be found out whether there will be complications in the healing process), and also the exact place where this occurred (so that characteristics of that place can be taken into account in the assessment). The *guru* also has to consider the psychological situation and the social environment of the patient: is he strong enough, which family does he come from (a *raja* family, *guru* family, craftsman family etc.), are there problems in the family or with relatives (and if there is a conflict, how strongly does the family support the healing process). And of course the financial aspect must also be considered (is the patient able to pay for the ritual), and there are many other factors which affect the process of healing, which the *guru* has to examine.

Before Pa Surdam decides which method of healing to use, he first discusses it with the patient or his family. He suggests various methods: first, the one that seems to him the most effective, but then others which he considers less so, but which may nonetheless be the best for the patient.

For Pa Surdam the decision to perform a ritual to call back the *tendi* of a patient, is not only the choice between various methods of calling the soul back to the body. The *tendi* can be called by the *guru* playing on a bamboo flute (*surdam*). It may feel drawn by the sound and return to the body. But if the

96-97 Ceremonies at the hot spring Lau Debuk-debuk. Karo plateau,
1984/89

98, 105 Offerings to the spirits of the spring, 1984
99, 100 Holy shrine and mortar. Karo plateau, 1985

90

101–103 The ceremony of *perumah jinujung* (see p. 216). Berastagi, Karo plateau, 1984

104 Rain-making ceremony (*ndilo wari udan*). Kutabuluh, Karo plateau, 1984

diagnosis reveals that the case is rather more difficult and the *tendi* are being held by certain spiritual forces (*tertaban tendi*) because a taboo has been broken at a holy place, then the *tendi* must first be freed from the power of these spirits. Only then can the usual ritual be carried out in order to call the soul back to the body.[11]

The manner in which the *tendi* are freed from the power of the spirits depends, according to Pa Surdam, both on the type of spirit holding the *tendi* and on the patient himself. First of all Pa Surdam will try to identify what sort of spirit it is – whether an evil spirit, a guardian spirit or the spirit of an ancestor – and then he will decide whether the spirit has to be attacked, whether an amicable agreement should be reached with it, or even whether the spirit should be made the patient's guardian spirit. If it turns out to be the spirit of an ancestor, Pa Surdam will ask the patient or his family how he should proceed. If the patient is of the opinion that the spirit should be turned into a guardian spirit (*jinujung*)[12], then the *petampéken jinujung* ritual will be performed. The patient can then become a *guru perjinujung* and with the help of his *jinujung* can carry out various *guru* practices, in particular as a *guru sibaso* (medium). Should the patient or his family decide that the spirit should be combatted, then Pa Surdam will proceed in that direction. For instance, he will beat with various holy plants on the patient's joints, and the struts of the patient's house (*basbas*), or break an egg representing the spirit (*ngulak*). Or he will attack the spirit by performing a war dance to the accompaniment of music as a sign of aggression (*perang-perang*).

An amicable agreement with the spirit can be achieved if the spirit is asked what it requires in return for the souls it has captured. A ritual is performed and the offerings demanded by the spirit are laid out (*meré kahul*).[13]

If the patient or his family are Christians, the spirit is not turned into a guardian spirit, because this could result in excommunication. If the patient is unable to raise the money for the offerings that the spirit demands, a goat for example, then an amicable agreement with the spirit will not be sought and instead it will be attacked and forced to give up the soul of the patient. There will be no consideration of feelings in this, if, for example, it is the spirit of the his own dead father that has taken the patient's *tendi* captive.

Two circumstances are helpful to Pa Surdam in his work as a *guru*. First, he possesses a guardian spirit (*jinujung*) which is at his side to give him advice and speaks to him with an inner voice or gives him sudden inspiration. And secondly he has an exact knowledge of the old myths and legends (*turi-turin*) which he can rely on in the exercise of his work.

An example in this connection is the *ersilihi* ritual in which a human figure is carved from the trunk of a banana tree[14], a figure representing a patient, who it is believed must die because a spirit is demanding his death. The purpose of the ritual is to hoodwink the spirit that is demanding the patient's death, by fooling it into believing that the figure is the patient.[15] The figure is therefore thrown into a river or a ravine in the course of the ritual simulate the death of the patient. If Pa Surdam considers that a spirit is striving for the life of a patient, he will make the figure out of *uncim* (trunk of the forest banana) and throw it into a ravine. This is based on the legend of Raja Bekelewet, according to which a spirit which dwelt in a ravine sought Raja Bekelewet's life. Raja Bekelewet hit on the ruse of making a figure out of *uncim* which the spirit took for Raja Bekelewet himself.

If, however, Pa Surdam believes that the life-threatening illness is caused by conflicts within the family, he will make the figure from the trunk of the *galuh si tabar* banana – a variety of banana that commonly grows in the village.[16] Here he is referring to the legend of "Land of the East and Land of the West" (*Negeri Kepultaken ras Negeri Kesunduten*) in which a child whose father wants to murder it is saved by a guru who carves a figure of the child from the trunk of the *galuh si tabar* banana and throws it to the father who thinks it is his child.[17]

In the first case, during the ritual Pa Surdam will sing mantras (*ermangmang*) which tell the story of Raja Bekelewet, and in the second mantras which tell the story of the "Land of the East and the Land of the West".

How Pa Surdam became a guru

The foundations for Pa Surdam becoming a *guru* were laid in his childhood. Until his fifteenth year he lived with his father who was a very well known *guru* in Karoland. His father specialized in healing people with psychological ailments. His patients lived in a hut which he had built in the middle of a field and also helped him with work in the field. Here Pa Surdam was often able to observe how his father handled his patients and how he performed rituals. His father taught him the Karo script (*surat Batak*)[18], so that he could read his father's bark books (*pustaka*). In the evenings his father would often tell him stories in which the roots of *guru* lore are embedded.

At the age of fifteen Pa Surdam left his home village of Barung Bertuk and settled in a village about 30 km away. There he spent his time with others playing dice, which was prohibited by the Dutch colonial government as gambling. To avoid detection by the police they played in a hut in the forest or in a cave.[19] In this way Pa Surdam met gamblers from the other parts of Karoland who were usually skilled in some *guru* arts, though only some of them were really *guru*. They spoke much about fortune-telling, history and stories, magic, sickness and other subjects, which at that time represented a sort of "science" (*pemeteh*). But they would never have thought of consciously relating this science with faith or religion, as we generally do.[20]

Between 1947 and 1949 Pa Surdam fought in the guerilla war with the people's army (*laskar rakyat*) against the Dutch occupying power. In this period he got to know almost all the regions of Karoland and had the opportunity to learn from various *guru* in different places. He says that his curiosity and his openness to the advice of other *guru* played a large part in his acquisition of a comprehensive knowledge of the arts of the *guru*. The people loved to share their knowledge with him, and in this way as he travelled around he deepened his knowledge and his abilities, which he later used as a *guru*.

Pa Surdam did not become a *guru*, however, until he had passed through a period of psychological disorder (*mehado*) and had acquired a guardian spirit by means of the *pertampéken jinujung* ritual. This happened in 1955. At that time Pa Surdam was living at Medan where he was indulging his passion for dice-playing. After he had been in Medan for a time a deep frustration became apparent and his thoughts were no longer clear. He got out his bamboo flute again, which he had not touched for a long time, played it, as he spent his time in a coffee house in Padang Bulan, a suburb of Medan.[21] He neglected his hair which grew down to his shoulders: so deeply was his mind disturbed, that he had not thought of having it cut.

One day he felt that a being, which he could not define exactly, was now commanding him to return to Barung Bertuk. So he made his way on foot up to the plateau. He had been under way for two days when he came to the turning to the village of Daulu (approximately 60 km from Medan) where a path led up to the volcano Deleng Sibayak (*deleng* [Indonesian: *gunung*] means mountain). On arriving there, and without knowing how it happened, he took the path in the direction of Deleng Sibayak. On Deleng Pertekteken hill, at the foot of Sibayak, he came across a place in which there was not a single plant growing. From this place – which is a holy spot (*sibiangsa* to the Karo – rose poisonous sulphurous gases from the volcano. The Karo believe that all creatures which cross the place die immediately.[22]

The same being that had told Pa Surdam to return to Barung Bertuk now commanded him to stay and meditate at this spot. He spent two weeks there in meditation without eating or drinking. At the end of the this period he felt his mind beginning to clear and he experienced great joy at his unusual experience. Using a knife he cut his hair and laid it under a stone not far from the spot where he had meditated. During his meditation two

guru had appeared to him, *guru* who play a major part in the legends of the Karo: Guru Penawar and Guru Pakpak. In the legend Guru Penawar is a guru who knows little about a *guru's* work but has in his possession a medicinal powder (*pupuk*) which he has obtained from god (*dibata*) and which can cure smallpox (*remé*) as well as restoring to life those who have died of smallpox. While Guru Penawar is far away healing people, his two daughters die of smallpox. When he returns home and wants to return his daughters to life, their bones have vanished. The spirit of the Deleng Sibayak volcano, Beru Kertah Ernala has taken away their bones out of pity for the daughters, so that Guru Penawar can no longer bring them to life again. In his disappointment Guru Penawar throws the medicinal powder, which he received from god, onto Deleng Pertekteken. This is the origin of the holy place (*sibiangsa*) on Deleng Pertekteken. Beru Kertah Ernala gave to the spirits of the two girls the holy sulphur spring of Lau Debuk-Debuk at the foot of Sibayak, and the Karo today bring offerings for them on the day before a full moon.

Guru Pakpak, as his name suggests, comes from Pakpakland. He is the *guru* who, according to some legends, discovered the measurement of time and made a magic wand called *tongkat malékat*. Many *guru* practices are based on the legend of Guru Pakpak, among them the art of using the *tongkat malékat* and the mantras for the magic wand which tell the story of why Guru Pakpak made it.

106 Sacrificial ceremony on Samosir. The *datu* stands in a magic sign in front of the magic wand and an altar structure. Lake Toba, c. 1920

While Pa Surdam was meditating on Deleng Pertekteken, Guru Penawar and Guru Pakpak offered themselves as his guardian spirits. On returning to his village, he told his wife and his relatives what had happened to him on Deleng Pertekteken. They came to the conclusion that the *petampéken jinujung* ritual had to be performed so that Pa Surdam could receive Guru Penawar and Guru Pakpak as guardian spirits.

Since then Pa Surdam has been recognized as a *guru*, although the ritual was conducted by Pa Surdam himself. The Karo call this "becoming a *guru* for oneself". Pa Surdam was able to conduct the ritual himself because he had already acquired much *guru* knowledge. For this reason all the *guru* in Barung Bertuk as well as the *guru* among his own relatives who were asked to carry out the *petampéken jinujung* ritual were of the opinion that no *guru* other than Pa Surdam's father could conduct the ritual and make Pa Surdam a *guru*, but by this time Pa Surdam's father was already dead. The ritual was therefore conducted by Pa Surdam himself under the direction of his father's spirit.

Pa Surdam and the current attitude of the Karo to the guru

Thus Pa Surdam explained to me the abilities he had as a *guru* and the practices performed by himself and other *guru*. Not only is Pa Surdam an excellent source of information for insights into *guru* lore but also for the culture of the Karo in general, particularly regarding the concepts on which the practices of the *guru* are based.

J. H. Neumann (1910) in his article on the Batak *guru* lists the characteristics of the Karo *guru*:

"He is a man of science, combining in himself all historical, medical, theological and economic knowledge. He is his people's walking encyclopedia." (p. 2)

"To perform a ritual well a guru must follow definite rules. ... First of all he must know the legend of the origin of the ritual, a legend often connected with the origin of the world. Besides this he must know which plants are needed for the performance of a ritual and also the actions and magic words which belong to a particular ritual. The first thing that a guru must know about a ritual is the story of its origin. This points us to another aspect of the guru's skills. He is the keeper of the old legends, traditions and myths which make up the literary heritage of the Batak. These legends are very worthy of attention, with their mixture of historical memories and descriptions of natural events, ornamented by the imagination of the writer and sometimes so muddled and distorted by a clumsy story-teller that they are incomprehensible." (p. 10)

Neumann's description does not fit all *guru*. Even in Neumann's time not all *guru* had the combination of characteristics he ascribes to them. Of all the *guru* I have met only one combining all the qualities described by Neumann, and that is Pa Surdam.

Neumann's description represents the ideal picture of a *guru* in the possession of all the qualities which as a rule are found only in a *guru mbelin* (*mbelin* = "great"). A *guru* is called a *guru mbelin* if he is skilled in all branches of *guru* lore and knows the legend of the origin of the world and of mankind (*turi-turin tuang tembé manusia ras pertibi*). This does not mean, however, that it is sufficient for a *guru* to be able to recite the legend of the origin of the world; *turi-turin* in this context means rather knowledge about the nature of the world and the forces that govern it ("force" in this context means no more than the nature, the essence, which the *guru* can activate by means of his knowledge). A *guru mbelin* must therefore be able to master and use the legend of the origin of the cosmos by having at his disposal a deep knowledge of nature of this world. This includes knowledge about the "forces" that link mankind with the supernatural world, and about the nature of kinship relationships, about *guru*, health and sickness,

107 Lamp with inset ceramic container for burning oils and resins; height: 35 cm. Karo Batak

108 Dancing *guru sibaso* at a *perumah bégu* ceremony in the house of Pa
Mbelgah. Kabanjahe, Karo plateau, c. 1910

the house, the mountain, to mention only a few of the many powers which find their fullest expression in the existence of the world and mankind.

For this reason a *guru mbelin* is also called a *guru si meteh turi-turin manusia ras pertibi* – the *guru* who knows cosmogony and cosmology. This knowledge makes a *guru* a *guru mehantu*, a "mighty" *guru*.

Because of the abilities and knowledge that he possesses as a *guru*, Pa Surdam should really be called a *guru mbelin*. However, nobody has thought to giving him this title. There seems to be a difference between the concept of *guru mbelin* in the traditional culture of the Karo, which I have described, and the everyday concept of a *guru mbelin*. In general the Karo tend to give a *guru* the title of *guru mbelin* if he is able to cure patients of chronic illnesses, and particularly if all the efforts of doctors have failed. Examples of such illnesses are cancer, tumours, kidney stones, leprosy, diseases of the liver, mental illness and tetanus. A *guru* will be regarded as a *guru mbelin* especially if he can cure patients when the doctors have given up all hope or if the doctors can offer no diagnosis. The Karo call illnesses of this sort "invisible" (*pinakit si la teridah*) – illnesses of a supernatural kind.

A *guru* is also regarded as a *guru mbelin* if he can use a powerful supernatural force to drive away malignant spirits or control nature by calling up or stopping rain, creating a storm, calling wild beasts etc.

It is clear therefore that in daily life the Karo do not follow the traditional concept of the *guru mbelin*, but instead put more trust in his success in practice. A *guru* is called a *guru mbelin* if he has "extraordinary" capabilities or can use stronger magic force than other *guru*. In their assessment of a *guru mbelin* the Karo tend to emphasize his abilities as a healer and his magical powers, while less attention is paid to his abilities in the field of ritual. This modern view clearly differs from the criteria which were used to assess a *guru mbelin* about thirty years ago, when the fields of healing, supernatural power and ritual all had equal status.

It is therefore understandable that Pa Surdam is not regarded as a *guru mbelin*. His abilities as a *guru* and his knowledge of *guru* lore, based in particular on exact knowledge of the cosmic order, are only effective in the performance of a ritual, rooted in the old tradition and largely unaffected by new concepts and ideas which have been brought into Karo culture through Christianity, Islam or general modernization.

As an illustration I should like to draw on my own experiences during fieldwork in a village in Karoland. I needed some information from the various *guru* of this village and so felt it necessary to interview a few of them. The village chief directed me to a female *guru* who in his view was the most capable in the village. When I spoke to some other people in the village, it seemed that they shared his opinion.

Later when I met this *guru* it turned out that she had only a very limited knowledge of the various practices of a *guru*; she admitted that her abilities were restricted to the healing of a few diseases such as kidney stones, or some illnesses of women and children, which she would treat with medicines prepared by herself. It was she who gave me the names of some *guru* who she thought would be in a better position to supply the information I needed.

The village chief could not believe that this *guru* in fact knew only a little about *guru* lore. He preferred to assume that she had perhaps kept some of her knowledge from me, because it is true that many *guru* are very unwilling to reveal their knowledge to people they have known for only a short time. Only after I had interviewed another female *guru* in the same village for three consecutive evenings and had told the chief that she knew quite a lot about *guru* lore, was he willing to believe that the first *guru* indeed only had the ability to cure certain illnesses without knowing the background of the practices she used.

In the view of the village chief, the ability to heal was directly related to the degree of knowledge of *guru* lore in general, and was also connected with the *guru's* ability to express his knowledge. Public opinion and the poularity of a *guru* is clearly an important factor in the assessment of a *guru's* capabilities by the village community. In the case of the first *guru* it should be added that many of her patients were people with kidney ailments from the town, who frequently came to use her and her medicines in order to save themselves the costs of an expensive operation. The very fact that a *guru's* patients come from the town even though in the view of the villagers people in the town have a higher standard of living and better education, can greatly contribute to such a *guru* soon being regarded as a *guru mbelin*.

The situation was different in the case of the second *guru*, who I thought had a far deeper knowledge. Most of the inhabitants of the village (the majority is Christian) regard her as something of a charlatan. At a *raleng tendi* ritual for calling back a lost soul they say "she just behaves as if she could see the *tendi*". Also they do not believe that a patient can be cured by a ritual calling back the lost soul. Only a few, predominantly older people, value her as a *guru* who knows a lot about her profession, particularly as regards the performance of a ritual. This *guru* has the ability to be possessed by her guardian spirit, which most people dismiss as play-acting which cannot be trusted.

In this way the traditional rituals and ceremonies are increasingly losing their significance, and this loss of significance

109 Sacrificial ceremony at Lumban Tonga. Altar structure with three
tunggal panaluan. Southern Samosir, Lake Toba, c. 1920

means that the *guru* who knows about the performance of a ritual and in particular about its background based on the principle of the cosmic order (*turi-turin*), have no future.

One of the central fields of *guru* lore, its cosmological-philosophical background, once so important, is disappearing.

It should be noted in conclusion that the attitude of the Karo to the *guru* and their practices has changed decisively in just one generation, the generation of Pa Surdam. Jokingly I once called Pa Surdam "the last representative of a past era". Pa Surdam laughed heartily.

[1] *Guru* is synonymous with the Toba Batak word *datu*. The practices of the *datu* and *guru* are the same. There is, however, a difference between the two which is connected with the term *sahala*. It is accepted that a Toba Batak *datu* uses magic power (*sahala*), whereas a Karo *guru* can be an ordinary man (or woman), who merely has a great knowledge of the traditional lore, or certain abilities such as healing the sick, without having *sahala* in the Toba sense.

[2] Among these there are *guru* who make only a few sorts of medicine, or only a single medicine. For example, the *guru pertawar penggel* makes medicine for treating broken bones, the *guru pertawar beltek* makes medicine for indigestion, and the *guru pertawar remé* heals smallpox.

[3] In this description the name of the *guru* and the name of the village have been changed to protect the data.

[4] According to the Karo *adat* it is possible for a son on his father's death to marry one of his father's wives, but not, of course, his own mother (*lako man*). Similarly it is possible for a man to marry the wife of his son if he dies (*gancih abu*). The social reason behind this custom is that women are thus provided for after the death of their husbands. Nowadays the custom has become very rare.

[5] The Karo Batak Christians call the old religion *perbégu*, meaning "worshippers of the spirits of ancestors". The supporters of the old religion prefer to use the word *pemena*, meaning "the first (religion)". After many supporters of the old religion had made their religion an officially recognized religion in the 1970s, calling it *Hindu-Karo* and organizing it in the *Parisada Hindu Dharma Karo*, they reverted to the term *perbégu*, but gave it a new interpretation. In the pseudoscientific work of Brahma Putro (1981) there is even the absurd thesis that the word *perbégu* is derived from a Hindu missionary from India by the name of Bhagavart Brgu, which the Karo pronounced first as "Perbrgu" and later as "Perbegu". Brahma Putro's "theory", which denies there is any connection between *bégu* (spirit, ancestor's spirit) and *perbégu*, is very widespread among the supporters of the old religion. I agree with Rita S. Kipp (1974: 5) that in the past the Karo had no abstract concept of a faith and consequently had no name of their own for their religion. The need to develop their own abstract concept of a faith, which regarded religious ideas as something separate from other aspects of life, seems only to have arisen after the Karo were confronted with a Christian community among their own people.

[6] The *pengulu desa* seems not to have realized that since the 1970s many supporters of the old religion have come together in the above mentioned Hindu community *Parisada Hindu Dharma Karo* with its own office at Kabanjahe.

[7] The Karo are divided into three kinship groups: the *senina* (members of same clan), the *anakberu* (wife-takers) and *kalimbubu* (wife-givers). In the performance of a ritual, as in other ceremonies, it is the *anakberu* that do the necessary work, preparing the site, fetching the *guru* and the musicians etc., while the *kalimbubu* let themselves be waited on.

[8] The sound of the *surdam* is soft and touches the emotions, especially when it is used to play a song such as the "Lament of the Shepherd Boy".

[9] The singing recitation of traditional legends is a forte of Pa Surdam. There is hardly anybody left in Karoland who is still capable of this art. I know two professional singers, but they do not sing traditional legends, they recite their own experiences as singers during the war of independence (1947–1949).

[10] As a rule a treatment, particularly a ritual, is only performed if the close family, consisting of the kinship groups of wife-givers (*kalimbubu*), wife-takers (*anakberu*) and the fellow clan members (*senina*) give their consent.

[11] Cf Steedly 1988.

[12] The guardian spirits are also called *teman erdalan* (fellow travellers) or *singarak-ngarak* (escorts).

[13] Cf also Ginting 1986 and Steedly 1988.

[14] The head is carved from the root and the body from the trunk.

[15] Some *guru* consider this ritual to be trickery used against the force that wishes to take the patient's life. Others are of the opinion that the ritual is a means of coming to an amicable agreement with this life-threatening force, since in a symbolical way the force does get the life of the patient in the form of the figure.

[16] These varieties of banana are often planted together with various holy plants – *besi-besi* (Curcuma longa), *sampé sempilet* (Justicia gendarusa LINN), *kalinjuhang* (Cordyline fructicosa, Backer), *selantam* (Graptophyllum Pictum GRIFF), *rimo mukur* (Citrus hystrix D. C.). The places where these are planted are called *nini galuh* (meaning something like "grandfather banana"), and are a symbol of the solidarity of a sub-clan or a group with common ancestors.

[17] Cf Ginting and Premselaar 1990.

[18] To this day Pa Surdam cannot read roman script, since he has never been to school or taken part in any of the government's literacy campaigns.

[19] Dicing (*judi dadu*) is the classic form of gambling among the Karo. In many legends dicing is a symbol for magnificence and manliness. A decoration on the exterior of the traditional Karo houses represents a bowl which is used to cover up the rolling dice (*tutup dadu*).

[20] In present-day usage *pemeteh guru*, which literally means "knowledge (lore) of the guru", is understood as "non-rational magical power".

[21] The population of Padang Bulan consists predominantly of Karo, who settled in the former tobacco plantation of Padang Bulan after the Second World War.

[22] Twice aeroplanes have come down on Deleng Pertekteken hill. The Karo believe this is because they flew directly over this spot.

110 Group of dancing women at a ceremony. Parsanggul Na Ganjang,
    western shore of Lake Toba, c. 1920

Chapter 5   Batak Script and Literature

(Uli Kozok)

Towards the end of the 18th century, when the first researchers began to gather ethnographic information about the land of the Batak, where no white man had yet set foot, they were very surprised to discover that this "primitive" cannibal people had a script and literature of their own.

William Marsden had published the Batak alphabet in his *History of Sumatra* as early as 1783, but scholars asked by collectors of curiosities about the origin of their exotic books written on bark and with wooden covers, would speculate about possible comparisons with hieroglyphics, Greek and Arabic astronomical symbols, or the Phoenician alphabet. It was not until the middle of the 19th century when H.N. van der Tuuk had studied the Batak language and literature in detail and published a grammar of Toba Batak, as well as a four-volume textbook of various Batak languages, that the literature of the Batak became generally known (Tuuk 1861 and 1862).

In 1925 the missionary doctor Johannes Winkler wrote a book about Batak magicians and healers (*datu*), which still remains the standard work on datu lore (*hadatuon*) and gives a great deal of information about the contents of the *pustaha*, as the Batak call their books written by *datu*. Petrus Voorhoeve, whose expert knowledge of all Batak languages has enabled him to compare manuscripts from all over Batakland, can rightly be called doyen of modern *pustaha* research. He has written a large number of books and essays about Batak literature, in particular about the *pustaha* and other Batak manuscripts. While Voorhoeve has been mainly concerned with editing and cataloguing manuscripts from Dutch, British, Irish and Danish collections, Liberty Manik has described and catalogued all the Batak manuscripts in German collections (see the many publications by Voorhoeve; Manik 1973).

J. Edison Sarigih (no date) also deserves a mention here for translating two complete *pustaha* into Indonesian.

Soon after the existence of the Batak script became known, researchers were quite sure that – like all Indonesian scripts – it had developed from an Indian script, but it has not yet been possible to identify which of the numerous Indian scripts this was. Today it is thought certain that the Batak script did not originate directly from an Indian model, but that it is far more likely that there developed by way of the ancient Javanese Kawi script an as yet undiscovered early Batak script, which was the basis not only of the Batak script but also of the scripts of Rejang and Lampung (South Sumatra).[1]

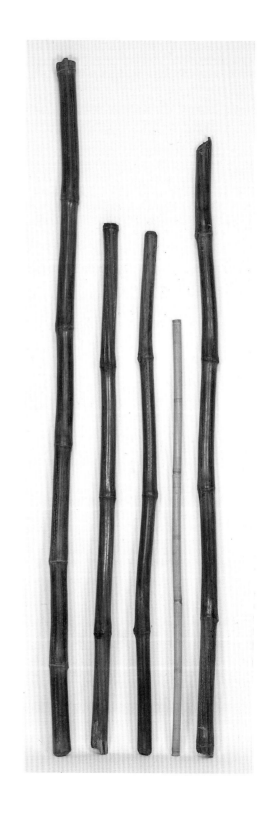

111 Inscribed bamboo rods; length: max. 195 cm

112 Bamboo bearing inscriptions: (d) lament (p. 107f); height: 23 cm; (g) lament (p. 110f); length: 18.3 cm; (h) threatening letter (p. 114); length: 30 cm. Karo Batak

Each of the five Batak languages – Angkola, Mandailing, Toba, Pakpak, Simalungun and Karo Batak – has its own alphabet. They are divided into three sub-groups: southern Batak (Angkola, Mandailing and Toba), central Batak (Simalungun) and northern Batak (Pakpak-Dairi and Karo). It is possible to communicate within each of these groups, since the languages differ only slightly from each other. However, the Toba and the Karo Batak, for example, cannot understand one another and therefore have recourse to a lingua franca. Nowadays the national language of Indonesia, *Bahasa Indonesia*, is used for this purpose, but before the establishment of this national language communication between the different linguistic groups was not easy, although very many Batak learned one or two other languages of neighbouring tribes besides their own mother tongue. The researcher Freiherr von Brenner reported in 1894 that many Karo Batak could also speak Malay. On the other hand even today one still meets old women, especially in remote villages, who can speak only their mother tongue.

Although the languages differ, the scripts vary only very slightly from each other. They consist of 19 to 22 radical signs, of which the consonants are always pronounced with an "a", and 6 to 8 diacritical signs which can change the "a" of the consonant radical signs to another vowel, lengthen the radical sign with another sound, or drop the "a" as a final sound. The script is written from left to right and from top to bottom. No punctuation is used, and even the words are not separated. Only the beginning of a new section is occasionally marked by an ornament (*bindu*).

I have reproduced the Batak alphabet in the following table in the form in which it is usually written. Unfortunately I have so far only created a printer-driver for the Karo and Toba script. So I cannot yet use my word processor to print those characters of the other Batak scripts which differ from those of the Karo and Toba, and have therefore filled them in by hand.

1. Radicals

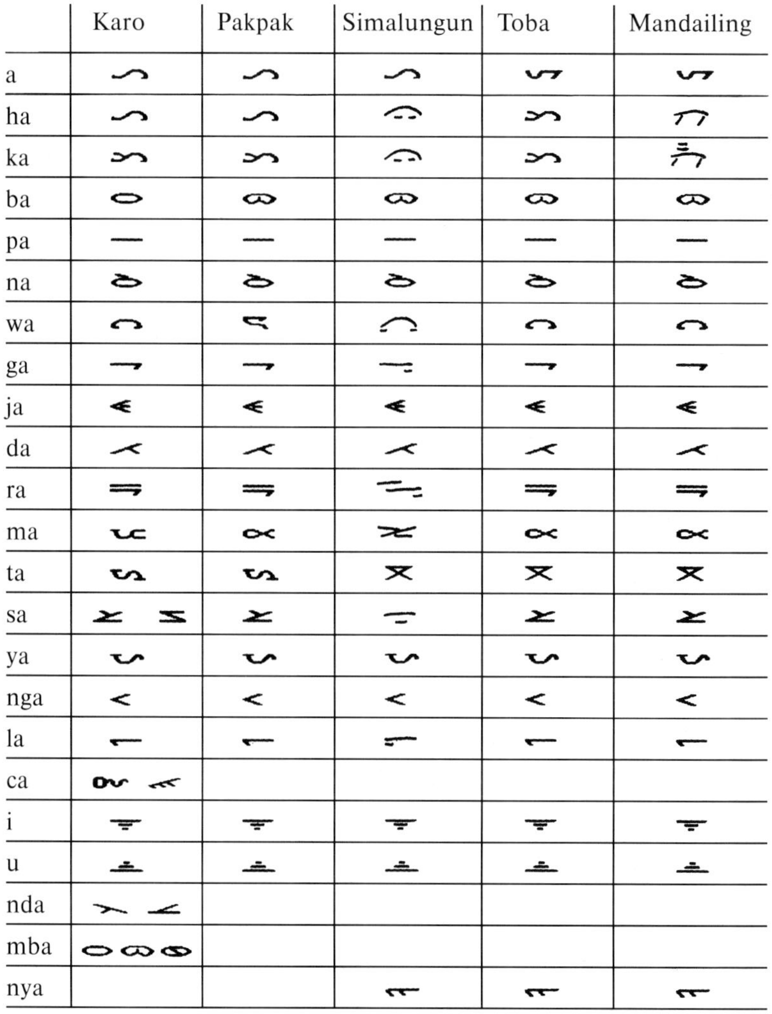

	Karo	Pakpak	Simalungun	Toba	Mandailing
a					
ha					
ka					
ba					
pa					
na					
wa					
ga					
ja					
da					
ra					
ma					
ta					
sa					
ya					
nga					
la					
ca					
i					
u					
nda					
mba					
nya					

2. Diacritical signs

Some diacritical signs are placed above, others after the radical signs. Because of the vocal diacritical as well as the privative sign the a-sound of the radical will change and even be omitted.

Toba and Mandailing:

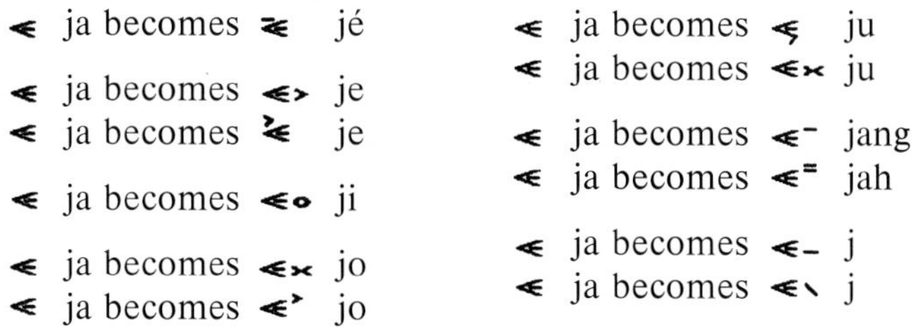

ja becomes jé   ja becomes ju

ja becomes je   ja becomes ju

ja becomes je

ja becomes ji   ja becomes jang

                       ja becomes jah

ja becomes jo

ja becomes jo   ja becomes j

                       ja becomes j

From this it is clear that in the script too there is a difference between the northern, central and southern Batak[2], and that the script is well suited to the range of sounds in each language. Only in northern Batak is there an unvoiced "e" (as "about" [əbaut]), and in northern Batak and Simalungun there is the consonant [x], written "h" and pronounced like the "ch" in "loch" [lox]. Simalungun script also has the peculiarity that the Karo Batak sign for "o" is used for the double vowel "ou", a sound which occurs frequently in Simalungun. The following are some examples of Karo Batak: *bapa* "father" is written [Batak script] ; *iluh* "tear" [Batak script] ; and "Batak" [Batak script].

A characteristic of Batak script is that if two consonants follow one another in a word and the vowel preceding the first consonant is not an "a" (that is, it is written with a diacritical sign), the diacritical sign for the vowel is placed after the second radical and before the privative sign. Thus, for example, the Karo words *merga* "clan" is written [Batak script] , but *perik* "bird" is [Batak script] . Nevertheless the script is relatively simple, as anybody can find out for himself: *Aku patonguntonunken surat sepulah siwah*_____

_____.
The solution (to this piece of Karo Batak script) can be found in footnote[3].

The principal writing materials used by the Batak are bast and bamboo. (The term "bark books" by which the Batak *pustaha* are commonly known is not strictly correct.) The bast of the *alim* tree (Aquilaria malaccensis) is removed in long strips, smoothed and prepared with a rice flour paste. These strips are then cut to the desired width and folded concertina fashion. The two ends of the bast strip are stuck to wooden panels which in many cases are decorated and serve as the binding. Plaited rattan cords are used to hold the book together. The ink is prepared from various resins, mingled with other ingredients and boiled over the fire to a viscous black mass. Occasionally a recipe for the manufacture of this ink is found in a *pustaha* (Sarigih n. d.: 33f). The ink is applied with a pen cut from bamboo, buffalo horn or the leaf sheath of the sugar palm.

Bamboo and bones are also used as writing materials, besides bast. The script is engraved with point of a knife and the fine lines are then blackened with soot.

The literature set down in this way by the Batak can be divided into the religious and the non-religious, although this difference is an artificial one reflecting our western point of view; to the Batak the religious element in their lives was omnipresent. I shall first discuss the literature which I call religious, i. e. which refers to *datu* lore.

The *pustaha* contain almost exclusively magic formulas (*tabas*), oracles, recipes for medicines and instructions (*poda*) for performing rituals and the production of various magic cures. Unfortunately these recipes and instructions are rarely written out in detail, since the *pustaha* written by the *datu* are notebooks for his own use and the texts are often hard to understand since they assume a certain knowledge of the subject matter beforehand. It is characteristic of the religious literature that, no matter where the writer come from, they are written in a sort of uniform language which P. Voorhoeve has termed "poda language", the "language of instruction". It is an archaic Toba Batak dialect which has retained many words no longer used in the spoken language.

The *pustaha* contain the basics of the *hadatuon*. Winkler divides this knowledge into the following categories:

1. the art of preserving life
2. the art of destroying life
3. the art of fortune-telling

These three "arts" make up the essentials of what is dealt with in the *pustaha*. The art of preserving life includes first of all medicine. In the *pustaha* in the Linden-Museum's collection we find for example recipes for medicines to combat infertility, dysentry, breast pains, the poison aji, as well as recipes for massage materials. Winkler also mentions medicines for the symptoms of shortness of breath, coughing blood, bloated body, diarrhoea, fever, rheumatism, bone fractures etc.

Since scientific knowledge was largely lacking, the causes for an outbreak of sickness were sought in the spiritual world. Illness was defined as disturbance of the harmony and equilibrium between microcosm and macrocosm. Consequently the most probable causes of illness were the spirits of the ancestors (*bégu*) who had not received offerings for a long time and therefore felt themselves neglected. Illnesses could, however, also be caused by the aggressive magic of hostile persons or by the disruptive intervention of other spiritual beings. As a protection used preventatively or after the onset of the illness, *pagar* were used. These consist of a variety of ingredients, mostly vegetable, prepared in a lengthy process. Some *pagar* were taken as a medicine, while others were hung up near the sickbed or in front of the house. *Pagar* could be used to protect an individual or the community in a house or a whole village (e. g. during epidemics, after harvest or in times of war) against hostile *begu*.

The *pustaha* also contain instructions on how to make *porsimboraon* amulets, usually of lead (*simbora*), which work in a similar way to the *pagar*.

113/114 Magic books (*pustaha*) containing texts written in ritual language. The magician-priest uses a *pustaha* as a reference work or notebook.

Another form of amulet is the *sarang timah*. A *pustaha* in the Linden Museum, Stuttgart (inv. no. 4141) includes instructions about a prophylactic medicine called *pagar sarang timah* with is supposed to prevent a person being hit by enemy bullets. A *sarang timah* usually takes the form of a triangular shoulder blade from a cow or a buffalo with ornaments and anthropomorphic figures on one side and a short text on the other. The Linden-Museum collection contains four such amulets (ill. 116). Three of these have only a few words on them; "I wish the lead to fly upwards or downwards" (inv. no. 4177); "Go to the right, upwards, downwards" (inv. no. 4176) and "Blocked be the lead, the bullets of my enemies" (inv. no. 121.512). Inv. no. A 30.819 is unusual, a leather cartridge bag with bullet-holder and twelve cartridges of bamboo (ill. 115). On it is inscribed the following text: "This is a lament (*bilang-bilang*) on leather which serves me as a cartridge bag, as a bag for the gunpowder against my enemies and as a *sarang timah* so that I [stay] well". The combination of *bilang-bilang* and *sarang timah* here is unique.

Finally mention should be made of *porsili*. These are roughly carved figures of human figures which are thrown into a ravine or a river so that the spirit responsible for the illness thinks that it is the patient who has died (ill. 169, 170). Texts concerning the making of *porsili* are included in many *pustaha*.

Besides the defensive magic preparations mentioned so far, *datu* also have the power to make offensive magic. The most important partner of the *datu* in this "art of destroying life", as Winkler calls it, was the *pangulubalang*, a spirit which the datu makes submissive to him by magic powers. Winkler reports that in order to gain a pangulubalang a child had to be kidnapped from a neighbouring village. At first this child was well treated and had to praise the *datu* and always be obedient to his will. Then a drinking horn was put to his lips and moulten lead poured into his mouth. From the body of the child killed in this way a substance is cooked in a magical way containing the child's soul which even after death was still bound by its vow to the *datu*. The *pangulubalang* is mainly used for taking into an enemy village in order to cause great damage there. Recipes for *pangulubalang* with a list of the necessary ingredients are found in many *pustaha* but these do not mention a human sacrifice and consequently it seems justifiable to doubt the authenticity of Winkler's account. Another piece of offensive magic whose manufacture is described in the *pustaha* is *pamunu tanduk*, a magic powder which is kept in a horn (*tanduk*).

It is interesting that the art of shooting is often the object of discussion in the *pustaha*. It is possible that the Batak first obtained firearms before the 16th century and have developed their magic of shooting since then. There are texts in which the various parts of the gun are described with instructions about how to hold a gun and about the method of shooting depending on whether the enemy is in the far distance or nearby. The art of making bullets is also described (see ill. 115). These instructions are always accompanied by ritual actions, oracles and magic fomulas referring to shooting, so they do not constitute an exact training in marksmanship in the modern sense. The instructions are often illustrated.

The art of fortune-telling occupies a large space in the *pustaha*. The art of oracles is founded essentially on astrology, which will be looked at in more detail later. Batak astrology – like that of many other Indonesian peoples – shows Hindu influence, with parallels with popular south Indian astrology in particular (Parkin 1978).

Like the Indian peoples the Batak too have a calendar of twelve months, which always end with the new moon, so that the full moon falls on the fifteenth day of the month. Two days are added to these lunar periods to match the solar year, so that each month has thirty days. The Batak lunar year begins when the constellation of Orion disappears in the western sky and Scorpio appears in the east, i.e. with the new moon in May. The Batak have seven days, which, like those in the European calendar, correspond with the seven planets, though there is no division of the month into weeks. Instead the month is divided into three groups of ten days. The calendar diagrams which have survived in *pustaha* and scratched on bamboo do not present a unified picture. In some cases a thirteenth month is added to the twelve. This serves to even out the uncertainty in the numbering of the months. The calendar is not for calculating time but just to find out whether a particular day is auspicious or inauspicious for a particular action or event. Before every important undertaking the calendar is consulted – setting of on a journey, sowing and harvesting, marriage, house-building and all the other events in the social life of the Batak. In the course of the Christianization and Islamicization of the Batak the calendar, like all other oracles, has lost much of its former significance, but particularly among some of the Toba Batak, who despite their membership of the Christian Church still preserve aspects of their original religion, and among the Karo Batak who did not convert, it still plays a role. The *pustaha* are no longer used, however. It is a long time since any have been written, and the old examples are almost all in European collections. But wall calendars which show the days of the Batak calendar below the corresponding days of the European calendar, with explanations on the last page, are popular.

Turning now to the non-religious literature we must first differentiate the oral literature from written literature. As well as songs, children's songs, *pantun* (four-liners), counting-out rhymes, similes and riddles, the oral literature consists mainly of myths and legends which are covered by the term *turi-turian* (Karo and Pakpak: *turi-turin*). These *turi-turian* are a key to the understanding of Batak culture. They contain not only longpast historical events which can be very useful to the researcher, but also the cosmogony and cosmology: everything that happens in this world, life and death, the social order, and the relationship between man and the supernatural world can be explained through the wisdom preserved in the *turi-turian*. Knowledge of the *turi-turian* was an important prerequisite for a *guru* or *datu* to practise his profession (see Chapter 4). While the *turi-turian* are generally handed down orally, a legend is occasionally found written down in a *pustaha*, as in inv. no. 27210 of the Linden-Museum, which tells the story of the origin of the magic wand *(tunggal panaluan)* and which has also been published by Joustra (1904: 28ff) and Westenberg (1892: 240ff).[4]

In fact very little literature has been handed down in written form. Perhaps the most important category comprises the laments written on bamboo cylinders. The laments of the Toba and Madailing Batak are called *andung-andung*, those of the Simalungun Batak *suman-suman* and those of the Karo Batak *bilang-bilang*. Only a few examples of the *andung-andung* and *suman-suman* are found in the ethnographical collections, but there are more than a hundred *bilang-bilang*. This category of literature is largely unknown in the specialist scholarship; there are only three short essays written by missionaries about it, in which the *bilang-bilang* are described as love laments. An analysis of the many *bilang-bilang* manuscripts (Kozok 1989) has shown that in fact in only a very few instances can such laments be identified as love laments and that in most manuscripts the lament is rather that of a young man disowned by his family, who leaves his home to settle among the Malays on the East Coast or in the piedmont zone (Karo-*dusun*). The reason for his rejection by his family is often given as gambling debts which he has run up and cannot pay and which his family refuses to be liable for. Probably the motives given are invented like the rest of the song. The aim of the laments is to present his fate in as tragic terms as possible so as to arouse pity and sentimental feelings in the woman he desires and to whom he performs the song, or has it performed. The songs therefore were probably bound up with the custom of *naki-naki*, wooing. One of the Karo Batak laments from the Linden-Museum's collection (no. 3896) runs as follows: [see pp. 107–110]

Transliteration

Maka io hari kuté bilang-bilang
kin ndubé buluh minak
si mula jadi, si mula tubuh
lako ni teruh langit si la erbinangun
si la ertongkut, si man penusuk-nusuken
ni babo taneh mekapal
si man pengité-ngitén énda
lako nitabah mama anak Karo mergana
man ingan nuri-nuriken até mesui
nandé, nandéku beru Simbiring

É maka ndubé kutabah buluh minak
ni tepi-tepi Layo Pépé
katep arah kenjulu i tapin Buluh Awar
kawis dalan kahé-kahé
kemuhun dalan kolu-kolu ndubé
turang beru Simbiring

Maka kutabah pé buluh minak énda
man ingan nuri-nuriken pengindoku la mehuli
i bas buluh singawan énda
aku lampas terbaba pengindo la mehuli

Maka kuga kin ngé ndia ndubé
pemupusken nandé beru Simbiring
si sanggap mupusken dagingku enggo parang énda
si liah ngajarken dagingku parang

Maka bagé ningku
amen nidarami pé jelma
i babo taneh mekapal énda
i teruh langit meganjang
si man penusuk-nusuken énda
nandé-nandéku

Énda mambur me rupa perdalinku
nandangi taneh jahé-jahé
si la erpulo la ersisi

Anem mambur pé perdalinku
la kap erkité-kitéken utang kupasang mbelang énda
amenna muang pé anakberu-senina
erkité-kitéken aku la pantas rukur

Adi ingen pengindo kubaba pé la mehuli
é di maka anakberu-senina pé erkinigagang
anem erkité-kitéken utang kupasang énda enggo mbelang énda ngé

labo min bagi énda até cédana
silih si ngogé surat
adi labuh pé kata surat ilantas kamu
silih si ngogé surat.

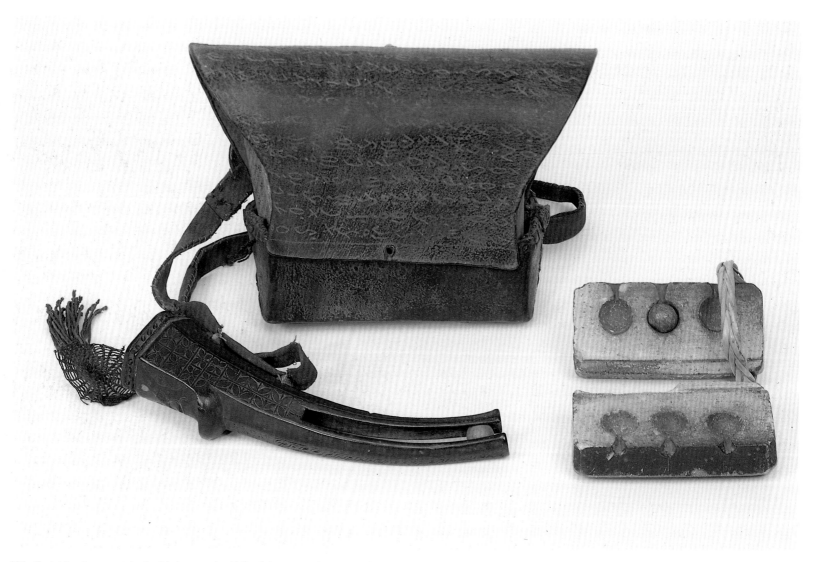

115 Cartridge bag scratched with lament (p. 106); right: a steatite mould for
casting bullets. Karo Batak

116 Inscribed shoulder blades and ribs. Amulets with texts and drawings that have magic powers. Karo and Toba Batak

Translation

This is, as has been said, a lament on oil-bamboo[5]
that once became and grew
under the pillar-less, unsupported sky
under which we must bend
on this thick earth,
on which we go on narrow bamboo gangplanks,
to be cut by the child of the Karo-Karo tribe
to serve as place, to tell of his wounded heart,
Mother, my Mother of the Sembiring clan![6]

Therefore I cut this oil-bamboo then
on the banks of the Pépé river
quickly in the direction of its upper course
at the bathing place of Buluh Awar[7]
to the right of the path downstream
to the left of the path upstream,
sisters of the Sembiring tribe.[8]

So I cut this oil-bamboo
in order to tell on this section of bamboo
of my unhappy state
from early on I had an unhappy lot.

How was it then at that time
when I was born of my mother, woman of the Sembiring tribe,
happily she gave birth to me, who am now grown up,
unhappily she brought me up.

Therefore it is so, say I,
that if one also seeks a person
on this thick earth
under this high sky,
under which we must bend,
Mother, my Mother
[... but there is nobody as unfortunate as I.][9]

So I went far away
to the land that lies downstream,
which is without islands and limitless.[10]

Even if I went far away,
it was not because of my high debts,
I was disowned by my people
because I did not consider what was seemly.[11]

Because the lot that I bear is a bad one,
therefore my people did not want to know any more of me,
not because of my high debts.

This should not sadden you, however,
friend who read this letter
even if you find it difficult, friend,
to read this letter.

Another lament clearly does have the character of a love lament
(no. 121517): [see pp. 110–111]

Transliteration

Maka io ari kuté bilang-bilang buluh lumang
lako nitabah mama si tigan mergana
man tagan perkapuren
tambahna tolé man ingan
nuri-nuriken pudun la sikap
O turang karina

Di kita enggo bagi layam-layam tangké ndoli
si naktak la kenan ulihan
si ndabuh la kenan jemputen
si mombak la kenan tangkapen
O turang, é me ajang turangndu aku
O turang karina
di mama si Tigan énda ngé mabasa
O nandé karina

Di aku enggo bagi perbunga kasumpat
tengah kerangen kesawangen
di ngembus angin i barat nari
i timur cibalna
ngembus i timur nari i barat cibalna
é me umpamana ajang mama si Tigan énda
O turang karina

Énda sada erbagé nari kupersingeti
aku terbuang anakberu-seninaku
é maka la tumbuk bulang-bulangku séngkulken
ban aku terbaba pudun la sikap
O teman senina

Di aku enggo bagi manuk sampur terang bulan bana
terlali-lali, terbanggo-banggo
lawes ku lipo ndapeti kité-kité selpat
lawes ku sunun ndapeti pintun pintu
jé melambas man ingan kabang
bagé gia di gelap wari tondel ingan kabang

110

jé terjelpa-jelpa cinep terbanggo-banggo
é me ajang turangndu kami
O turang kerina si la erndobah-ndobah

Énda sada erbagé nari man onggaren
bas aku la beluh nimbangi ukur adumku
i bas ingan pusungku naktak ndubé

É maka la né lolo la
karam séa gambir
tombang séa perahu

Apé la bagé
di gedang dalan si man dalanen
mbages kelbung man képaren
petapis urat-urat man dedehen
peséwal serpang man mentasen

É me aku ngamburken perdalin
nandangi taneh jahé-jahé
turang beru Tariganku
si padan manku.

Translation

This is, as has been said, a lament on a bamboo that stands alone[12]
cut by one of the Tarigan tribe
to become a betel-lime box[13]
and also to serve as a place
to tell of uncertain fate,
Oh sisters!

We are like knots of hair made of straw:
what falls out cannot be stuck in again
what falls down cannot be lifted up
what floats away cannot be held on to.
Oh sisters, so it is with me, your brother,
Oh sisters, this is what he of the Tarigan tribe has to bear.

Like a blossom of a wild cotton tree
in the middle of a lonely forest:
when the wind comes from the west
it blows it to the east,
when it comes from the east,
it blows it to the west.
So it is for example with him of the Tarigan tribe.
Oh Sisters!

I have a further thing to mention:
I have been disowned by my people,
therefore I do not come to put on my head cloth[14]
since I have an uncertain fate,
Oh friends and brothers!

I am like a chicken in moonlight:
helpless and dismayed
it runs to the stall, but the ladder is broken,
it runs to the basket, but the door is locked,
it has room to fly,
but because it is dark it bumps into things everwhere,
so it staggers about, confused even in sitting.
So it is with me, your brother,
Oh all my sisters!

I have another thing to say:
I cannot please my people
at the place where once my navel fell.[15]

Therefore it cannot be otherwise:
It is not a *gambir* which has sunk,
not a boat which has capsized.[16]

But why is it so?
Long is the path to follow,
deep the valleys to traverse,
matted the roots to tread,
branched the crossroads to cross.

So I have gone far away,
to a land that lies downstream
Oh my sister of the Tarigan tribe,
who is promised to me!

Apart from the laments there are no written texts which can be properly described as literature. The ethnographical collections do however contain numerous letters. Most are from *raja* making a request to the colonial administration. The *raja* also wrote letters to each other, but very few of these have found their way into the museum collections. On the other hand there are many threatening letters mostly sent to the plantation administrators in the *dusun*. Most of these *musuh berngi* (enemy in the night) or *pulas*, as these threatening letters are called come from the

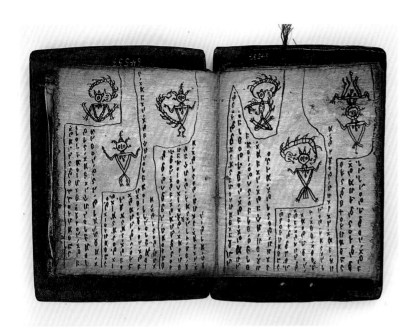

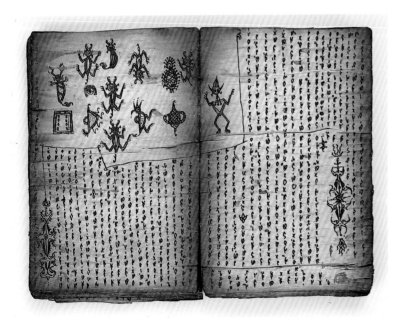

117–118 Magic book with drawings of chickens, which are the animals most frequently used for sacrifices.

119–122 Four two-page spreads with magic drawings (trees of life, representations of people and animals)

plantation district in the land of the Karo and Simalungun Batak. As a rule the writer is a Batak who was employed at a plantation to perform a particular craft activity (as we have mentioned, the Batak refused to work as coolies) and who felt cheated of his wages for the work. The *musuh berngi* belong to Batak tradition and are in a way the last resort for achieving justice. The writer of a *musuh berngi* is then an outlaw and so has to hide in the forest until his case is settled (one of his *anakberu* will represent him as long as he is unable to return to his village). These threatening letters, accompanied with models of a knife, a man trap, a spear and a flint, to add emphasis to the threat, were hung on the door of the person they were addressed to. According to custom such an "enemy in the night" had to write at least three threatening letters and repeat his demands until at last his threats to destroy the cultivated plants and burn the fruit trees (or tobacco sheds) could be put into effect.

Here is typical threatening letter of the Karo Batak (inv. no. 4147, ill. 112): [see p. 114]

Transliteration

Énda surat musuh berngi musuh suari ma ku nina
sabap upahku la nigalar Tuan, nina musuh berngi énda,
ma ku nuluhi, gatgati, kutabah bako, kusuluh bangsal,
kubunuh jelma ras Tuan pé kubunuh, karina musuhku nina aku
ni teruh langit ni babo taneh i deleng si manggun-anggun nina.

Translation

This is the letter of the enemy in the night, the enemy in the day, I say, for my wages have not been paid by the *tuan*[17], says the enemy in the night. I will burn the tobacco, chop it small, cut it down, burn the sheds, kill people. The *tuan* too I shall kill, these are all my enemies, I say, under the sky and on the earth, on the shaking mountain.[18]

Notes

[1] See M. Halberlandt 1886: 7–10; W. Marschall 1967: 559–564; P. Voorhoeve 1971: 1ff; Gonda 1973: 85; Parkin 1978: 97ff.

[2] The Pakpak script in some regions is closer to the script of the Karo than shown here. The examples reproduced here were taken from the Batak Reader by van der Tuuk (1861b), which recorded the writing in the distric of Dairi (west of Lake Toba bordering the area settled by the Toba Batak).

[3] *Aku patongun-tongunken surat sepulah siwah*

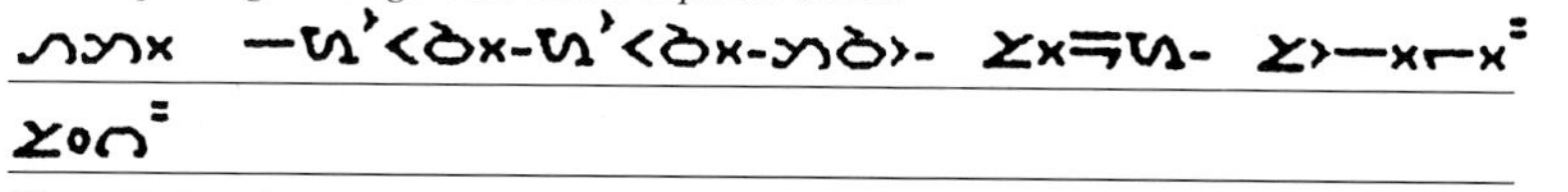

"I spell the nineteen script signs". This line is taken from a short text scratched on a piece of bamboo (Linden-Museum, Stuttgart, inv. no. 121.515) and was used by a school pupil as a writing exercise.

[4] On the oral literature of the Batak see Braasem 1951; Joustra 1901a,b 1902, 1903, 1904, 1914, 1918; Neumann 1907, 1911; Lumbantobing 1978; Pleyte 1894; Siahaan 1964; Voorhoeve 1927.

[5] A shiny yellow type of bamboo is called oil bamboo.

[6] *Nandé* (mother) may here refer to his actual mother or it be a form of address of the beloved, who according to Karo custom would be from the same family as the future husband's mother.

[7] Buluh Awar is a small village on the River Pépé in the piedmont zone (Deli-*dusun*) in the present administrative district of Deli Serdang, about 30 km south of Medan and 30 km north of Berastagi.

[8] Turang (sister) is an affectionate form of address for the girlfriend.

[9] Here I have completed the text with a usual turn of phrase as it appears in other *bilang-bilang*.

[10] The settlements on the plateau are referred to as *pulo* (islands) because they are surrounded by light forest and bamboo bush and stand out like islands in the otherwise treeless landscape. In the forested "land downstream", that is, the Deli-*dusun* the villages do not form islands of this kind.

[11] i. e. the writer has been constantly causing difficulties for his relatives, in particular for his *anakberu-senina*, so that they will at last fulfil their responsibilities towards him with a ritual (*meréken cabur pinang*).

[12] Bamboo usually grows in clumps. Occasionally, however, one also finds a few free-standing bamboo plants (*buluh lumang*). The writer is indicating that he is *anak melumang*, an orphan.

[13] Most laments are written on betel lime boxes or on tobacco boxes. These may originally have been given to the beloved as a token of a promise of marriage.

[14] The head cloth folded from a triangular cloth, symbolizes the *sangkep si telu* (the "trinity" of *anakberu*, *senina* and *kalimbubu*). The writer is here symbolizing that the corners of the cloth (i. e. the wife-givers and the wife-takers) do not come together, so he cannot marry because he has been disowned by his family.

[15] His birthplace, his native village.

[16] *gambir* (*Uncaria Gambir* Roxb.) is an important ingredient in a quid of betel. This is clearly some sort of simile, but its sense is not clear to me.

[17] Addressing Europeans.

[18] He is indicating that he has hidden himself in the forest and cannot be found.

Chapter 6 Art and Crafts

Art on buildings

The basic form of the traditional communal houses of the Toba and Karo Batak represents the cosmological ideas of their inhabitants. The houses (*rumah adat*) have three levels, corresponding to the three spheres of the cosmos. The space for animals below the living level symbolizes the underworld. The living level, raised on pillars above the underworld, is where humans dwell. Above this is the high roof, which corresponds to the abode of the gods and also sometimes of the ancestors.

Toba and Karo houses are characterized by their massiveness of construction, which is suited to the predominantly permanent nature of their settlements. The pillar house is ideally suited to life in the tropics. Unwelcome visits from strangers or animals can easily be prevented by pulling up the steps. The dirt that accumulates in the undivided interior with its open fires can be swept without too much expense through the cracks in the floorboards down into the area occupied by pigs, hens, dogs, cattle and water buffalo, an excellent use of organic waste is used. The limited ventilation provided by the small windows and doors, which can scarcely cope with the smoke from the fires, also has a positive aspect, since the smoke keeps away insects. In times of war between villages or regions the massive construction of the buildings also served as a defence against the enemy. With its doors and windows closed a *rumah adat* was almost impregnable, unless the enemy set fire to the big roof.

The construction was, however, not just a protection against hostile persons. With the help of decorations on the outside it was also possible to ward off all negative influences of *hantu* or evil *bégu*. This protection was also used against black magic directed at the inhabitants of a house by an evil-minded villager or stranger with the help of a *datu* or *guru*. The decorations on a Toba house include three-dimensional carvings of figural representations, ornaments carved in flat relief and paintings.

Compared to Toba houses the houses of the Karo are rather more sparsely decorated. On the solid wall surfaces of their exterior are lizard-shaped ornaments (*pengeret-ret*) made of *ijuk* cords. To make these patterns holes are bored in the wall at regular intervals and the cords are passed through. The patterns are supposed to keep illnesses away from the inhabitants (Sitepu 1980a: 7). The gable (*ayo-ayo rumah*) on Karo houses is woven from bamboo with a wide variety of patterns. Most are

123 Winged *singa* holding its hands protectively over a human figure. Pormonangan, Toba region, c. 1930

124–127 Traditional house paintings on houses in the Uluan district. Toba region, 1985/89

128–129 Modern paintings in the same district. 1985/89

130 Painted carvings, with electric light bulb. 1989

131 Painted carvings: the representation of a chicken (*manuk-manuk*). Huta Bolon, south-west Samosir, 1989

geometrical, but there are also figural representations. The significance of these patterns remains largely unclear. Sitepu sees them merely as decorative (op. cit.: 8ff). The ends of the roof ridges are decorated with a buffalo head, made of *ijuk* and painted with limewash, with real buffalo horns attached.

The traditional houses in the village of Lingga in the Karo highlands, which were partly restored for tourism in the 1970s with financial support from the government, have a large number of very different carved decorations on the outside of the the four planks (*dapur-dapur*, also called *melmelen*) that frame the floor. These four planks have already been mentioned for their significance in the orientaion of the house and the place where the householder lives (Chapter 3). The patterns mostly consist of various rinceau decorations with individual or interlaced leaves and flowers (ill. 33). They also served to ward off illnesses. The paints used on the incised rinceau motifs used to be made from earth or vegetable colours, but now oil paints are used. Such extensive patterns used to be applied only to the houses of distinguished and rich families.

While Karo houses have decoration on all sides of the building, the Toba houses, which stand next to each other in rows, are decorated only on two side walls and especially on the front facing the village square. The rear of the house is left completely unadorned. The long beams (*pandingdingan*) on the side walls have coloured decorative strips. Above the *pandingdingan* the side walls, never very high, are divided into compartments like coffering. These usually rectangular surfaces do not have carved decoration, but on very old houses they do contain traditional paintings (ill. 124f), which are stylistically related to the drawings in the old magic books of the magician-priests (*guru* or *datu*). The few surviving paintings executed in natural colours show mythological primeval beings and animals, e. g. hens, horses and buffalo, which had a central function in the old religion as sacrificial animals. In some paintings magician-priests are visible performing rituals. Often they are holding knives in their hands to drive away evil spirits or to sacrifice hens (*manuk-manuk*), which are also shown, for a ceremony. People are represented travelling in a boat across a lake or a river, in which various aquatic animals can sometimes be seen. The individual paintings are often surrounded with rinceau patterns, which frame the picture like stylized leaf scrolls. These leaves may be memories of old ideas of a tree of life or a world-tree, described in many Toba myths as the element linking heaven and earth. The significance of these traditional paintings is now hard to interpret, since the inhabitants of the houses are often younger than the paintings and have only limited information about when they were made and what they mean.

On the sides of more recent houses there are naturalistically drawn motifs in a very different style showing scenes from daily life and especially from the time of the Japanese occupation during the Second World War and from the War of Independence against the Dutch who returned to take possession of their colony again after the war. Battles between soldiers of the hostile sides predominate. Tanks, jeeps, fighter-bombers and antiaircraft guns are among the favourite motifs, but representations of the private life of the artists are also common. Contemporaray depictions of daily life, as well as Christian motifs such as the psalms on the outside of a shutter or the portrait of a pastor, replace the cabbalistic drawings taken from the ancient religious ideas of *guru* or *datu* lore (ill. 129).

132 A granary (*sopo*) converted into a house, with carved posts. c. 1930

However, the Toba put most of their effort into the façade, and the front wall and the gable of the houses of rich and distinguished Toba are decorated with extensive figural and ornamental decoration. While painting predominates on the side walls, the façade is covered all over with carved motifs which are also painted still in the traditional three natural colours, white, red and black. These three colours have a profound symbolism for the Toba: they represent not only the three spheres of the cosmos and the three hearthstones, but above all the three supports of the family system (*dalihan na tolu*) – the three kinship groups which are of primary importance to each individual. The three colours are also found on many objects which were in the possession of the magician-priests (*guru* or *datu*). Red is obtained from a red earth (*batu hula*), which is pounded fine with lime and a sort of resin added as a binding medium. According to Winkler (1925: 26) the blood of killed enemies was also mixed with it. Black was produced from charcoal, and lime was used for white.

The only paintings on the façade are on the lowest transverse beam (*parhongkom*) above the entrance. In the middle there is usually a sacrificial stake (*borotan*) to which a water buffalo is tethered. The stake is surrounded with people and from the side of the house there are usually other people moving in a long row on foot or on horseback to the sacrificial ceremony. The remaining surface of the facade is covered all over with rinceau and spiral patterns. At the ends of the side beams (*pandingdingan*) of many Toba houses there are large animal heads, which are of immense importance for Toba sculpture. These massive heads are called *singa* or *gajah dompak*.

The word *singa* comes from Sanskrit where it means "lion". *Gajah dompak* is a combinatation of a Sanskrit and a Toba word and means "an elephant that looks to the front". To the Batak, however, the *singa* is a mythological primeval beast of no defined zoological species, with an apotropaic function. It usually has a long tongue hanging out (often incorrectly interpreted as a trunk) which has the same effect. Its protective function can be clearly recognized in a rare type of *singa* in which a little human figure sits below the open mouth of the *singa* (ill. 123). The headdress of the *singa* has three horns, of which the middle one is the longest. This horn is often regarded as another memory of the world-tree which has already been mentioned in connection with the leaf scroll decorations on the side walls. It rises above the head of the mythological underworld beast which is imagined as the *naga*, the serpent or serpent-dragon. The side beams of the house with the *singa* heads at their front ends support the room where the people live and are thus comparable with the underworld dragon, *Naga Padoha*.

133 Women on the platform (*turé-turé*) in front of the house. Maize cobs are hung out to dry on long posts. Karo plateau, c. 1910

134 Façade or roof ridge decoration; height 56 cm. Toba Batak
135 *singa* head from the façade of a dwelling; height: 114 cm. Toba Batak
136 Façade element, width: 98 cm
137 Height: 110 cm
138 Height: 110 cm
139 Height: 100 cm
140 Height: 59 cm
141 Façade element, width; 80 cm

The *singa* as a decorative feature and magic representation is used in various versions on almost all important objects in Toba culture, whether in the field of jewellery, wood sculpture or bronze work. Indeed the *singa* is almost the symbol of Toba art. There is an enormous variation in the manner in which it is represented. Not only does the size of the *singa* heads, also called house masks, vary, but there are many local differences in style. Some *singa* show only the face of the beast, others the body and legs as well, and decorative elements on the sides which can be interpreted as ears or wings. The latter can be clearly seen in a historical photograph (ill. 123). All *singa* are covered with painted rinceaux and spiral patterns and have large, round, protruding eyes. In earlier times these were often set with little round mirrors or silver coins (Meerwaldt 1894: 525). *Singa* heads are rare on houses of less wealthy Toba, and the side beams of these houses are often just given *singa*-like heads, which are not carved separately, as is usually the case with the more elaborately carved *singa* heads (ill. 142), but hewn from the beams (*pandingdingan*).

The lowest cross board with the representation of a sacrificial procession may also be decorated with female breasts arranged in two pairs one above the other over the entrance to the house. Two lizards, also carved in high relief, approach the breasts from the sides. The lizard symbolizes the fertility god *Boraspati*, who is here represented as the guardian deity of the house *Boraspati Ni Rumah*. The female breasts and masculine lizard are clearly recognizable as fertility symbolism (Boer 1920: 13; Winkler 1925: 22). On the exterior of the doors to the rice granaries there are also carvings of the *Boraspati*, here worshipped as *Boraspati Ni Tano*, the fertility god of the fields. Pairs of breasts and lizards also used to be depicted in an identical arrangement (ill. 132).

On the wall surfaces of the house façades above the *parhongkom* with the flanking *singa* heads and the painted sacrificial procession there are usually further representations of singa heads set into the wall as carved architectural elements (ill. 143). On the parapet of the front gallery which is reached from the inside through a trap door and used as a storeroom for implements, as a place for the orchestra at ceremonies or as place for the unmarried girls to sleep, is yet another *singa*, this time flatly carved, which may also be decorated with ornaments at the sides. Above this massive and heavily decorated substructure rises the far more lightly constructed roof. The roof section of the façade is divided into two surfaces. An airy framing structure of boards with a carved pattern is set up like the wings in stage scenery in front of the inner gable wall. The main feature on this inner backdrop is a rhombus-shaped architectural element containing a large *singa* head (ill. 146 ff). The Toba call this

pandilati or *dila paung* (= tongue). The front roof ridge may also have a *singa* head or a buffalo head as decoration.

Thus the *singa* is the main decorative element on Toba houses. It is found in innumerable representations, mostly just showing the head, and is significant for two reasons. Firstly, the Toba believe that it keeps misfortune, diseases and evil influences from the house and its inhabitants, and also that it can release positive beneficial powers for the good of the inhabitants. And secondly, in the form of the *Naga Padoha* it has "supporting" functions and is closely connected with the cosmogony, which is also apparent in many allusions to the world tree and life tree in the ornament.

142 Craftsman carving a *singa* head. Toba region, c. 1920

143 Architectural decoration of the front of a house; height: 62 cm.
Toba Batak

144 Rice granary door; height: 111 cm. Karo Batak

145 Pair of step-ladders. Probably for a granary (*sopo*) or in the house as a stairway to the area in the roof. Possibly a representation of the ancestral couple (*debata idup*); height: 220 cm. Toba Batak

146–148 Diamond-shaped gable decorations; heights: 186 cm, 280 cm, 241 cm. Toba Batak

Instruments of the magician-priest

The magician-priests (*datu* or *guru*) are the exclusively male experts in religion among the Batak. In the period before the arrival of the missionaries they used their knowledge to determine much of the daily life of the community as well as the times for holding ritual ceremonies. In the traditional society the magician-priests occupied a very special place. Their extensive knowledge of the gods and spirits, of black and white magic, of sicknesses and the ways of curing them, made them influential figures in society, The relationship of people to their *guru* (I shall use the Karo term) was ambivalent: one had to consult them, and yet at the same time be wary of them. In most villages they were the only ones who could use the Batak script and so held a sort of monopoly of knowledge.

One could not become a magician-priest by one's own choice, only with the idea that even before its birth in human form the *tendi* chooses its own destiny and that this destiny cannot be influenced by any outside factors in its career. The destiny may be recognized early on, but it may gradually become apparent in the course of a person's life through particular strokes of fate and experiences. By learning from an older *guru* a "sorcerer's apprentice" can gain the knowledge needed for the exercise of his calling. As Juara Ginting has shown in his description of Pa Surdam (Chapter 4), *guru* lore is so extensive that a guru has to specialize in a particular field.

It is frequently the case that the magician-priests come from the family of the founder of the village, which further strengthens their influence on the non-religious aspects of village life. They differ from the ordinary villagers not only in their wide-ranging knowledge but also in the fact that they can make contact with the spirits of ancestors (*bégu*). And the fact that they were not merely people respected by their fellows for their powers, but also that people felt a certain reverence or even fear towards them, is also made apparent after their death. A dead *guru* was buried apart from the other graves in a squatting posture and his hands and feet were tied together to prevent his possible return.

In the course of his professional activities the *guru* could be recognized by his distinctive clothing. A historical photograph taken at the beginning of the century shows Mandailing Batak magician-priests dressed in patchwork coats (ill. 292). These coats (ill. 291) are made from corners of material sewn together in the three traditional colours: white, red and black or blue. The same combination of colours is also seen on the turbans (*tali-tali*) worn by the *guru* in ceremonies. It is possible that such headdresses and coats were also worn by the *guru* of the other Batak peoples. In the literature there is only a description of *guru* of the

149 The *raja* Isaak Lumban Gaol and the *datu* Ama Batuholing Lumban Gaol (right). Toba region, c. 1920

150 Magic wands (*tongkat malehat* and *tunggal panaluan*) of the Karo and Toba Batak

151 *tunggal panaluan* magic wand. The topmost figure represents Si Aji Donda Hatahutan; length: 187 cm. Toba Batak

152 *tunggal panaluan* magic wand; length: 169 cm. Toba Batak

153 *tongkat malehat* magic wand, wood carving on bamboo cane; length: 192 cm. Karo Batak

154 *tongkat malehat* magic wands, bronze figure (b); length: c. 140 cm. Toba Batak

155 Wands for warding off negative influences from the village and fields (*pagar*); length: 168 cm, 185 cm. Samosir, Toba Batak

Simalungun Batak who wore a comparable costume (Tichelman 1937: 628). Karo *guru* or *guru sibaso* can be recognized at ceremonies by the white cloths they place over their heads. They are supposed in the past to have worn white robes too (Neumann 1910: 4). The white colour is particularly effective in attracting spirits and the souls of ancestors. Turbans made of strips of cloth in the three colours can also be seen on the uppermost figure on the magic wands of the *guru*, and today talismans and amulets are still hung around the neck or wrist on a string made of three threads in the three colours.

The following is a description of typical instruments needed by the *guru* for his professional activity. Some of these groups of objects were collected among the Batak shortly after the onset of Christianization and since then have been kept by museums or private collectors. Unfortunately at that time little importance was attached to the complete documentation of the objects, their function and their provenance with the result that we have only very hazy ideas about the way in which many of the objects were used. The content of the many books of magic which are preserved in our museums is not only hidden from us but also from the Batak themselves, since only a very few of them are now able to read Batak script, and hardly any Batak now understand the ritual language (*poda*), which differs considerably from the everyday spoken Toba or Karo Batak. Thanks to the extensive work done by Petrus Voorhoeve and by Liberty Manik, we know the approximate contents of many of the *pustaha* now in Europe – but only those. The recipes for medicines or instructions for magic spells are still closed to us for the present.

The magic wand

The most important ritual object of a *guru* is the magic wand. The *guru* always made the wands themselves for the needs of their *marga* and often used a very special wood. Because the wands were all carved individually there is an enormous variety in the style and what is represented. Wands with a single figure in a standing or squatting posture, which occasionally are cast in bronze, are the simplest form.

These wands, called *tongkat malehat*, have shafts of a variety of materials: bamboo or different sorts of wood. The figural decoration of a *tongkat malehat* is made separately and then attached to the shaft by means of dowelling. The shafts themselves may be decorated with metal bands or with incised magic ornaments. The *tongkat malehat* is thought to be the most recent type of wand. The Simalungun Batak call it the "younger brother" of the large and heavily carved wand, the *tunggal panaluan* (Tichelman 1941: 37).

156 Figures of the ancestral couple *debata idup* (a–c); height: (a) 41 cm; alarm figure (d) which was hung up in an unknown place in the village or house. Toba Batak

157 Apotropaic figures; (a) *pagar* with container for magic ingredients; height 63 cm; (c) *pohung* to protect the harvest; height: 74 cm. Toba Batak

158 Apotropaic figure which was hung up in the house. It was formerly dressed in a waist cloth; height: 54 cm. Toba Batak

159 Apotropaic figures with *pupuk* holes in the chest, which were hung up in an unknown place in the house; (b) alarm figure; height: 54 cm. Toba Batak

The *tunggal panaluan* not only offers a greater variety in representation, but also usually demonstrates the differences in the aesthetic ideas and artistic capabilities of its makers. In contrast with the *tongkat malehat* the *tunggal panaluan* has a multiplicity of human figures arranged one on top of the other. Between the figures are carved apparently free variations of animals either attached to the sides of the wand or ridden by the humans. The representations on the wands are related to a particular myth, but it is unclear whether the myth was made to explain the wands or the wands to illustrate the myth. In many cases – though not in all – a specific number of persons can be identified on the *tunggal panaluan*. The topmost figure is usually the largest and is male. Below him is a smaller female figure either standing or sitting. The sex of the other five figures cannot usually be ascertained. Of the various traditional myths which have a clear connection with the magic wand only one will be quoted here to give the general idea. The differences between the versions is in places considerable because they have come down to us from various Batak peoples. One version from the Toba Batak runs as follows:

‚Once upon a time in the olden days there was a prince whose wife bore twins, a boy and a girl. It is misfortune enough when a twin is born, but the misfortune here was greater because the children were of different sex; for such children always want to be together. The boy and the girl, called Si Adji Donda Hatahutan and Si Tapi Na Uasan, grew up together and were always inseparable. Their parents began to fear that they might fall into incest and decided secretly to remove the girl. They thought of a ruse to do this. They sent their son to the coast to exchange a horse for other goods, and while he was on his long journey, they took the daughter to a distant village of her uncle (her mother's brother), and then went with their villagers to tell their son that his sister had died. On his return from his journey Si Adji Donda Hatahutan heard this, and at first he believed it and was deeply upset. He noticed, however, that his mother did not do as other mothers do when they lose a child and go out to the village around sunset to lament. So he began asking his fellow villagers where his sister's grave was and they told him in secret that she had not died but was living with her uncle in the distant village.

To distract himself from his grief, he said, he wanted to travel to the coast, and so he received his parents' permission. Instead he went to his uncle's village where his sister was hidden and said his father had sent him to fetch his sister back. Since the son was speaking in the name of his father the uncle could not refuse to allow them to go off together. But in the woods they fell into the evil that their parents had feared. Then they came to a

160 Figures of ancestral couple (*debata idup*); height 35–40 cm. Toba Batak

133

161 Standing female figure in dancing posture; height: 51 cm. Toba Batak

piu-piu-tangguhan tree and saw ripe fruits (*ruham*) on it. Si Tapi Radja Na Uasan felt thirsty and wished to taste the fruit. She therefore asked her brother to climb up the tree and bring some of them down. He carried out her wish, but when he was sitting up in the tree his body changed into wood and grew into the tree. His sister, who had not noticed why he had not come down again, thought that his clothes had become caught on one of the long thorns that grew from the tree's trunk, so she climbed up after him but when she reached him the same fate overtook her.

Meanwhile the parents in the village waited in vain for the return of their son. They feared that he had met with some accident at the coast. Tired of waiting, his father made ready to go in search of him, but as soon as this was made known in the village he heard from the murmuring of his subjects that the son had not gone to the coast but to his brother-in-law's village to look for the sister. When he heard this, the father hurried to his brother-in-law's village but he did not find his children there. His brother-in-law could only show him the path they had taken to return to their parents' village. The father then followed the tracks of his children into the forest and found them together on the tree.

He guessed that they had been struck by the anger of the gods and called in one of the most famous *datu* to bring the children back to life. This was the Datu Pormanuk (magician with the chicken). He came, prepared his chicken as a magic medium and climbed up the tree with it. But with the people he wanted to bring back to life he, and the chicken, lost their lives and became wood.

In horror the *raja* hurried back to fetch a *datu* of even greater reputation. Accompanied by Datu Pongpang Niobungan (lifter of the spell) he returned to the tree. This *datu* too climbed the tree and suffered the same fate.

The same thing happened to three other *datu* each of which excelled his predecessor in abilities. Datu Porhorbo Paung Na Bolon (magician with the broad-horned big buffalo), Datu Porbuea Na Bolon (magician with the big crocodile) and Datu Porulok Na Bolon (magician with the giant serpent); they were all turned into wood and grew firmly into the tree.

Thereupon the *raja* called an even greater magician, Datu Sitabo Di Babana (magician tasty in the mouth or fine speaker). He came, looked at the matter from all sides, pulled a thoughtful face and said: "Listen, my lord, ... These people cannot be brought back to life because they have been struck by the curse of the gods; but they have all died a sudden death and so from now on their image will be the strongest means of magic to put fear into enemies. My advice is this. Cut down the tree and make from its wooden wands with the image of these people: they will

162 Group of figures: pair of dancers protected by armed figures; width: 73
cm. Toba Batak

strike terror into the enemy and bring an end to long droughts." So said Datu Sitabo Di Babana. His advice was followed and ever since then such wands have been used to put fear into enemies in wartime and bring rain in times of great drought.' (Meerwaldt, in Ophuijsen 1912: 83–85).

The two topmost figures on a magic wand thus represent the twins, who through their incest had broken the most important rule in the Batak family system, clan-exogamy, and had been punished with death. The other five figures represent the magician-priests who had used their arts in vain. In the versions of the myth preserved by the Karo Batak seven dogs play an important part instead of the magician-priests and they are therefore found on most Karo Batak *tunggal panaluan* (Huyser 1927/8: 40f). As different as the various versions of the myth are the representations on the wands. In a myth handed down by the Simalungun (Tichelman 1937: 613–8), the magic wand made from the tree remains alive, or rather living. It protects the house of its owner when a fire destroys the whole village, it warns of coming hostilities and acts as a potent weapon in the fighting against the enemies. In an epidemic it informs its owner how the sickness can be driven out. As well as these abilities it was also believed that the wand could make rain and bring death. It was believed that it could ensure fertility of the fields and even of people and animals.

The magic wand is carved from the wood of the tree into which the brother and sister grew as a punishment for incest (*piu-piu tanggulan*, Cassia Javanica). The tree is a symbol of the life tree or world tree as a cosmological principle, and the wand made from its wood is an image of the tree. The powers which are attributed to it must be seen in this context. The wands which have been made from this type of wood since the mythological event are blessed and animated or given magic powers by their makers, the *guru*. The magic brew *pupuk* which is need to do this is prepared by the *guru* himself. The preparation of this substance was as far as we know very cruel, since it involved the loss of a child's life. A kidnapped child was buried in the ground so that only its head was showing. After it had promised always to support the interests of the village it was killed by having moulten lead poured into its mouth. In this way it was hoped that the child's *tendi* would be kept in its body. From the child's corpse a magic brew was prepared. In the context of this macabre procedure the magic wand was described by many missionaries and researchers in these terms:

"Thus the magic wand became a fateful weapon to kill and to murder, to cause damage and disaster, to kill their livestock and to get unpleasant persons quickly and safely out of the way" (Wirz 1929: 21).

163 Figure of a woman; height: 58 cm. Toba Batak

164 Miniature sculptures whose significance is unclear; height: 11—24 cm

165 Female figure mounted on a water buffalo vertebra. Function unclear; height: 20 cm. Toba Batak

166 *manuk-manuk*. Representations of chickens are very common with the Batak. The chicken is the most important sacrificial animal; height: 12 cm. Toba Batak

167 Apotropaic figures which were hung upside down in rows, possibly in the gable; height: c. 30 cm. Toba Batak

In such descriptions the negative evaluation of the magic wand's powers is uppermost. The *pupuk* was placed in various holes in the wand. These were bored particularly in the area of the breast, belly or liver of the topmost figure and often also in other figures. The holes were then closed with resin or a wooden plug. Now the wand was "animate" and was able to fulfil the hopes put in it. Just how powerful, but dangerous, such a wand could be is shown by the fact that it was never kept in the house but either hung below the eaves or had a little house of its own, in which the *guru* also kept his other equipment.

At the ceremonies in which the *guru* used the magic wand it was rubbed with offerings. While the *guru* dances with the wand he spits betel juice onto it and rubs it in with finely chewed rice (Tichelman 1941: 88). The blood of the sacrificed animals is dripped the magic wand (Wirz 1929: 24). To a large extent the dance of the *guru* is for the purpose of foreseeing future developments or establishing auspicious days for particular plans. These may be travel, the building of a new house or a wedding. But before an oracular ceremony can be performed a number of preparations had to be carried out. Magic signs were scratched on the open ground in the village and filled with white lime, charcoal and red pepper. The dance of a *guru* is described by Wirz (who also took the photograph on the back cover):

"Before the dance begins the cooked rice and fruits are smeared over the dark brown, smooth polished wood of the wand while spells and words of love are recited; and fragrant jasmine and areca blossoms are stuck in the hair of the topmost figure. At last the dance can begin. The drums and bronze cymbals are struck vigorously. The shaman swings the wand and waves it about in the air threateningly but soon triumphantly and conscious of victory, at the same time with small tripping steps, gracefully and elastically, pacing out the black, white and red lines of the mysterious figure.

The movements become faster and more violent, the sound of the instruments stronger and louder. Soon the dance reaches a racing tempo. A moment more and everything is in motion. Arms and legs, torso and head. The shaman runs in a circle like one possessed, he foams at the mouth. The spirit has come into him. Then suddenly he draws himself up and with a mighty swing strikes the centre of the figure with the wand.

The egg is hit. A murmur of relief and satisfaction goes through the crowd" (Wirz 1929: 24).

The trance state is achieved by the Batak not only by dancing with the magic wand. There are also many Karo Batak ceremonies, for instance for calling back a *tendi* (*raleng tendi*), in which the *guru*, the *guru sibaso* or some other participant in the ceremony goes into a trance-like state.

Medicine containers

Magician priests who possess a magic brew with special powers (*pupuk*) have various vessels which they use to keep it in. Among these are the hollow horns of water buffalo or mountain goats, the open ends of which are stopped with a wooden plug. Holes are bored in the sides to hold a wooden safety catch for fastening it. Water buffalo horns were used above all by Toba and Mandailing. These horns, called *naga marsarang*, were usually carved at the tip with squatting human figure an occasionally had incised ornament on the outside. On the interior of the horn there is often a lizard, the image of the guardian god *Boraspati*. The fastening is made of wood and has a great variety

168 Turned wooden container for holding food or medicine; height: 26 cm. Toba Batak

169–170 The *guru* traps the sickness in the sickness figure (*persilih*) which is then thrown away; height (170): 70 cm. Karo Batak

171 Protective figure *pangulubalang*; height: 25 cm. Karo Batak

172 Zoomorphic bench; height 13 cm, length: 45 cm. Toba Batak

173 Medicine container (*perminaken*); lead vessel with wooden stopper; height: 18 cm. Karo Batak

of figural decoration. Coarse and simple carvings of a single large squatting figure are sort the most commonly found in collections. But there are also some superbly carved stoppers with a powerful *singa* head sometimes with the upper part of the body. In these cases the *singa* often has several figures on its back, following in a sort of procession a *datu* who holds a bowl or similar object in his hands (ill. 175).

Among the Karo Batak the horns of the mountain goat (Capricornis sumatrensis) are the most frequently used receptacle for *pupuk*. These horns had stoppers representing an equestrian figure. A snake or lizard crawls up the rider's back. On the head of the rider a chicken is often shown as the most important sacrificial animal for the various oracles. These medicine horns (*buli-buli* or *perminakan*, *minak* = medicine) were carried by the *guru* on a cord over his shoulder or on his belt. Ceramic vessels could also be used as *pupuk* containers. The ceramics thus used, all of Chinese provenance, are small vases or shouldered pots, covered with a greenish celadon glaze or blue under-glaze painting. Vessels of this type, as well as large ceramic bowls and plates arrived at an early stage in large numbers in Sumatra. As well as horns and ceramics, bamboo boxes and lead containers were also used (ill. 173).

Instruments for fortune-telling

The identification of auspicious and inauspicious days was one of the magician-priest's principal task. Before every festival, whether a wedding, funeral or transfer of bones, before a long journey, before the beginning of sowing or harvesting, before the building of a house or a rice granary or the laying out of a new village, it was necessary to establish whether the planned time of the project was advantagious. To do this the magician-priest used various oracular instruments and his extensive knowledge of the calendar, the stars and above all the current position of *Pane Na Bolon* in the underworld. This astrological god in the form of a serpent or dragon is continually wandering. In a circular clockwise movement he moves around the centre of the world, which to the Batak always represents their own village. Every three months he pauses and founds a new village. In this way he founds four villages a year in locations corresponding to the points of the compass. When each of these villages is founded he celebrates a feast for which he requires human lives. He satisfies this need by causing unwary people to die of diseases, accidents or in war (Winkler 1956: 26ff). In order to banish these dangers to the bodies and souls of his fellow men, the *guru* must know exactly where the *Pane Na Bolon* is dwelling at any particular moment. In magic books and on bamboo boxes are representations of the *Pane* in a figure of the compass. The adjoining texts explain the

174 Medicine containers (*buli-buli*) made from the horn of the mountain
antilope; length: 20–30 cm. Karo Batak

175 Medicine horns (*naga marsarang*) made from the horn of the water
buffalo; length: 45–55 cm. Toba Batak

176 Medicine containers (*perminaken*); height (b): 27 cm. (b,c) are Toba
Batak, the rest are Karo Batak

177 Medicine container (*perminaken*); height: 15.5 cm. Karo Batak

178–179 Medicine container (*perminaken*); height: 21 cm. A small Chinese pot with lead repair and figural horn carving. Toba Batak

180 Various amulets worn about the body; left to right: (a,b,d,h,l) Karo
Batak; (c,e,f,g,m) Toba Batak

181 Three implements for squeezing limes, Toba Batak; four figures for
working black magic; height: max. 22.5 cm. Southern Batak lands

possible consequences if someone embarks on a new enterprise on particular days.

Another important instrument for the prediction of auspicious and inauspicious days are the calendars scratched on pieces of bamboo. They usually show twelve months each with 30 days. Every day has its own name. The various signs, which mostly recur in a regular pattern, indicate the particularly dangerous or auspicious days (Winkler 1913). Another oracular method is the examination of the entrails of slaughtered animals. The Linden-Museum, Stuttgart, has a very interesting wooden model of a chicken's breast (ill. 182d), on the inside of which are various dots and lines in blue which its former owner probably used in his interpretation of the breast of a sacrificed chicken. We know nothing precise about the meaning of these drawings, but I believe that their use in one of the many chicken oracles can be regarded as certain. Chickens were always suitable as oracular animals for the *guru*; they were not too expensive and, since they were consumed after use, they also supplemented the largely meatless diet.

Fortune-telling using strings was also a popular method. The *guru* first had to prepare these strings (*rambu siporhas* or *tali siporhas*) in the manner precisely laid down, with the addition of numerous ingredients. At the end the strings had a lump formed from a mixture of the ingredients and set with white glass beads and red Job's tears (ill. 182a + b). The strings were thrown by the *guru* on to a particular cloth and he could then tell the future from the way the strings fell and the arrangement of the lumps in relation to each other (Winkler 1954: 342ff). This form of oracle was used in wartime. The bands worn around the upper arm and supposed to be made from the mouths of slain enemies and enclosed in woven cords also have a similar lump which is additionally set with red seeds. They too are used as oracles in time of war. The Mandailing *guru* also interpreted his carved wooden "magic lion" (ill. 183), small wooden figures (ill. 181d–g) or inscribed buffalo ribs. Other rib oracles also give information about the health of a missing person (Winkler 1925: 190). Inscribed pieces of bamboo, which are always tied together in groups, have texts of a type connected with horoscopes (ill. 182c,e). Also the position of the feet of a sacrificial animal tied to a sacrificial stake (*borotan*) in the middle of the village, and the way it falls to the ground give important information about the future.

Aids to warding off evil influences

Another area of *guru* or *datu* lore is taken up with the innumerable ways in which one can protect oneself, one's house or the whole village against destructive influences, sickness and misfortune. It is not possible here to present all aspects of use of amulets and talismans by the Batak. The ideas connected with

182 Oracular instruments: (a,b) *rambu siporhas*, (d) chicken breast with diagrams; (c,e) oracular sticks with texts for fortune-telling; length: c. 18 cm. Toba Batak

them and the materials they are made of are too diverse. Pregnant women carried little wooden figures in their headcloths, small children had foot rings with little bells attached to protect them from the spirits of illness. Among the Karo this is still done today, even though they no longer know about the protective function of the bells (ill. 256). Hunters wore amulets which were supposed to bring them luck. The claws of bears or tigers as well as boars' teeth were filled with the necessary ingredients and carried about the person. Special medicines prepared by the *guru* were placed in finger rings either in small containers attached to the rings or in holes made in the interior or exterior (ill. 174). Magic charms made of lead in a cylindrical shape (*porsimboraan*) (ill. 180, lower right) were used to protect against poisonings, mouth ulcers, skin rashes etc. (Winkler 1925: 101f, 106). A little was scraped from the object and eaten with meals.

The *guru* was also a specialist when it came to protecting the village and the fields, and he could be asked to prepare all manner of aids. Objects in the form of a figure (*pagar*) were given a magic charge with some *pupuk* and used to protect village, house and fields against wild animals, enemies and above all against any possible black magic that enemies might use. Sculptures of wood or stone, called *pangulubalang* (first fighter), guard the entrances to the village (ill. 184). Wooden sticks with a basket-like addition woven round with cord attached to their upper end were used as a means of protection (*pohung*) for the harvest and kept garden thieves away. Magic ingredients and leaves which people believed had protective powers were placed in the basket attachment (ill. 155, 157). The figures used by the *guru* to draw sickness away from a patient have already been mentioned (in Chapter 5).

This list of the objects which a *guru* was able to make and use is by no means comprehensive but it makes clear that the knowledge of a *guru* must have been quite vast. For this enormous amount of information which he had to learn he used the magic books (*pustaha*) as notebooks for the various recipes and production methods as well as for the magic spells that he had to recite during the making and application of the medicine. The meaning and function of the many magic drawings which are found in the *pustaha* or on buffalo ribs, bamboo boxes or among the paintings on houses, or that the *guru* drew in the sandy village street in the course of the ceremonies, remain for the most part unknown to us. Unfortunately there has as yet been no detailed study of these drawings.

183 Magic lion. Oracular instrument of a magician-priest; length: 16 cm, height; 18 cm. Mandailing Batak

184 Stone figure (*pangulubalang*), set up outside a village or near the fields; height: 86 cm. Toba/Pakpak borderland

Objects in everyday use

The implements which the magician-priests make themselves for their professional use are characterized by their variety of forms and above all by the extensive figural decoration which is usually connected with old religious ideas. The implements which are used by the mass of the Batak people in their homes are in comparison much simpler and more functional. But the different materials and the many functions of these objects, which have been largely neglected in the literature, offer an extremely interesting and diverse image of everyday life in the "pre-plastic" age.

It should be remembered that the following description of these pieces is still valid today for many Batak – particularly in rural regions. Household objects used to be made by the people who used them and very rarely had additional decoration. The furnishing of a house in former times was very simple, almost Spartan. People slept on mats on the floorboards, at mealtimes they sat cross-legged and ate with the fingers of the right hand which they first washed in a water bowl made from a coconut shell. Banana leaves were used as plates and meals were served with spoons made of a bamboo shaft and coconut-shell scoop. Plain ceramic pots bought at the markets were used for cooking. Tall bamboo vessels were used to store water for drinking or washing (ill. 185). Drinking vessels were also made of bamboo and were of various forms (ill. 187). Basketwork bowls with feet with a ceramic bowl or a banana leaf for putting the food on, were used by the more well to do and their guests. To pass food to guests on bowl with a foot was a sign of great respect. These *dulang* (Karo) or *ragian* (Toba) could also be cast in metal or carved in wood, as was the case with the Toba (ill. 186). On a grater made of volcanic stone the ingredients of the meal were finely ground with a rock.

For the preparation of food there were various wooden and bamboo vessels which were hung on a cord from the roof to protect them from vermin. The Toba Batak used large storage containers for rice (*rumbi*) which were made from a single tree trunk, the production of which represented a great feat of craftsmanship (ill. 189). As well as these rice containers the Toba also used to have in their houses great long chests (*hombung*) which usually belonged to the family of the *raja* of the village. These chests were made of massive wooden boards fitted together and decorated at the front with *singa* heads, and were used by the *raja* for keeping his family heirlooms and particularly valuable textiles, or his weapons. At night time he used it as a bed (ill. 188). It was never, however, used as a coffin, as has been claimed elsewhere (Cameron 1985: 85). Some of these *hombung*

185 Bamboo vessels. (a,b) tall water containers; height: 123 cm; (c–g) storage vessels for rice (*busan*) – the lid is used as a measure; (h,i) small vessels for salt or dried fish (*abal-abal*). Karo Batak

186 (a,b) Turned wooden pots (rice measure?); height: max. 22.5 cm, (c) turned bowl with foot, (d) bowl with foot, basketwork, used as a plate for respected guests. Toba Batak

187 (a,b) Palm wine vessel (*kitang*); height: 50-53 cm; (c,d) water container for the washing of infants and for drinking water (*cimba lau*); (e, f) container for drinking water (*kuran*); height: 65 cm; (g) water vessel (*també*) for work in the field. Karo Batak

also have decorative carvings at the sides which are partly painted. Stylistic differences are particularly apparent in the animal heads which are applied to the front of the *hombung*. Especially splendid examples, like some I saw a few years ago in an antique shop in Medan, have *singa* heads up to 140 cm high. Occasionally the two *singa* heads may be of different sizes.

Cupboards, chests of draws or other chests were not used by the Batak in the past. Everything was kept in wickerwork baskets (ill. 192) or stored in bark containers which were made in various sizes (ill. 191). These were either piled against the wall at the back of the living area or moved up into the roof.

Smaller containers were also made of bamboo, calabash or coconut, some with woven cords or rattan. These were used for small valuables, such a jewellery, or spices and other food – except for rice which was kept in the *rumbi* or in the granaries. Large baskets woven from freshly felled bamboo were used at harvest time for transport to the village or to the market. Today such crude baskets are still made and used by the Karo to transport the vegetables they have harvested (ill. 201, 204).

188 Bed-chest for storing food or valuables (*hombung*); length: 190 cm. Toba Batak

189 Rice storage container (*rumbi*); diameter: 88 cm. Toba Batak

190 Women preparing bundles of fibres while one sits on a *rumbi*. Toba region, c. 1930

191 Bark containers (*kepuk*). The larger ones (height: up to 38 cm) were used for keeping clothing and jewellery. Karo Batak

192 Food containers (*gumbar*) made of bamboo; height: 12–50 cm. Karo Batak

193 Wickerwork baskets made of rattan for keeping clothing and jewellery; height (b): 26.5 cm

194 Vessels made of wickered sections of bamboo; height (c): 14.8 cm. Toba Batak

195 Containers made of wickered coconuts or half shells with wooden lids (*cajak*) (e,f) for opium, Karo Batak; (a,b,g) water or food containers; (c,d) tobacco boxes, Toba Batak; height (a): 22 cm (g): 13 cm

196 Boxes made of bamboo, wood, ivory and horn; (a) vessel for reels of
thread; (c,d,e) opium containers (*setik*); height: (a); 13.7 cm, (i): 16 cm

197 Wooden box with sliding lid for keeping valuables; length: 12 cm,
width: 5 cm. Toba Batak

198 Small containers of wood (a), bark (b,c), coconut (d–f) and horn (g);
height (a): 5.5 cm, (f): 9 cm

199 Lime containers (*tagan*) of the Karo (a,b,e,f,i,k), the Simalungun (c,d,m,n), the Toba (g,h,o), the Angkola/Mandailing (l); height (a): 15.8 cm, (i): 9.5 cm, (l) with beads: 22.5 cm

A particularly wide variety of containers is needed for the requisites of betel chewing (ill. 199). This practice used to be very widespread among the Batak. This slight stimulant is now chewed only by older people - mostly women. A piece of betel nut (the seed of the areca palm) together with some lime and *gambir*, a concentrated leaf extract, is wrapped in a leaf of the "betel pepper" (*sirih*), and then placed in the mouth and chewed. This colours the saliva red and produces the desired effect. Betel enhances the appetite and stimulates the digestion. For the Batak – as for many other south and south-east Asian peoples – the reciprocal offering of betel has important social and religious functions (Sibeth 1986: 256–264).

200 Small containers; height (d): 12.5 cm, (g) 5.7 cm

201 Basket-weaver near Raya. Karo plateau, 1989

202 Women on the way to a church festival. Hatingian, Uluan district, 1989

203 Knives for slitting leaves before basket-weaving; length: (a) 13 cm, (b) 7.5 cm

204 Transport of freshly harvested vegetables on the roof of a minibus. Berastagi, Karo plateau, 1989

205 Basketwork betel bags (*kampil*), (b,c) rice bags, Toba Batak; (e,i) southern Batak lands; the rest are Toba and Karo Batak

To store the various ingredients of a betel quid the Batak use basketwork betel bags or little baskets (ill. 205). Today plastic bags or bags woven from plastic cords predominate. The lime was kept in metal or bamboo containers. There is a lot of variety in the bamboo containers; among the Karo there is even a difference between containers for women (low) and for men (tall and thin). Bamboo vessels were decorated with finely incised ornament which show up particularly well in old lime containers because of the patina of wear. On the underside of these vessels a mirror was occasionally fixed with rattles inserted behind it (ill. 199).

Basket-work calabashes (Karo: *tabu-tabu*) were used for various purposes: as vessels for drink or rice, or for keeping home-made gunpowder used for the old muzzle-loader guns. In pre-colonial times when the carrying and use of firearms was still permitted these were kept in the houses or the assembly house. Small quantities were inserted in narrow bamboo cartridges, ten or twelve of which were carried about in a leather cartridge bag (Karo: *kampil bedil*). The smaller quantity of powder needed to ignite the gun was kept in small powder horns made of buffalo horn with carvings on the sides. The *singa* head is used as decoration on the cover of and on the sides of the powder horns. As well as the larger opening at the end which is for filling the horns, they also have a closing mechanism which makes it possible to extract a relatively small quantity of ignition powder. Ignition powder was kept in a variety of small containers (ill. 207, 208).

206 Wickered calabashes for larger quantities of gunpowder; height: (a) 29 cm, (c): 30.5 cm, (f) 18 cm

207 Small containers for keeping ignition powder; horn scoop for filling (k); height: (b): 14.5 cm, (q): 10 cm

208 Powder horns made from the horn of a water buffalo and of wood.
Toba Batak

209 Muzzle-loader guns; length: max. 139 cm. Karo Batak

210 Powder containers made of bamboo; (b) with wickerwork bullet bag;
height: 28 cm

The bullets needed for hunting and warfare were, like the gunpowder, home made. This was done with a steatite mould consisting of two parts (ill. 115). A variety of materials was used for the bullets: iron, tin, copper – whatever was available. Porcelain sherds or lumps of iron were included in the casting. Another method of producing bullets was shaping them with a hammer. The were kept in bullet containers (Karo: *paruh-paruh*, Toba: *baba ni onggang* = "beak of a hornbill"). These were made from the horn of the water buffalo by slitting the tip of the horn at the sides and shaping the front like a mouth (ill. 211). The bullets could thus be pulled from the "beak" using two fingers and at the same time it was possible to keep an eye on how much ammunition was left. To fill this bullet horn the cover was removed from the larger end or the bullets were simply pushed into the opening in the "beak". The basic shape of the bullet holder, when seen from the side, is the head of a hornbill. One can see the curved beak and the horn-like thickening on the upper side which gave the bird its name, and the eyes of the bird are represented by a hole bored in the horn. On the top of the bullet horn there is usually a large human face.

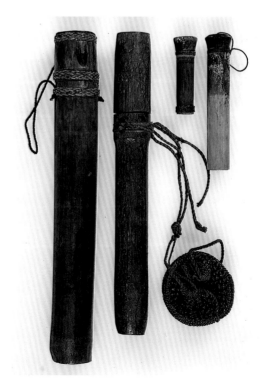

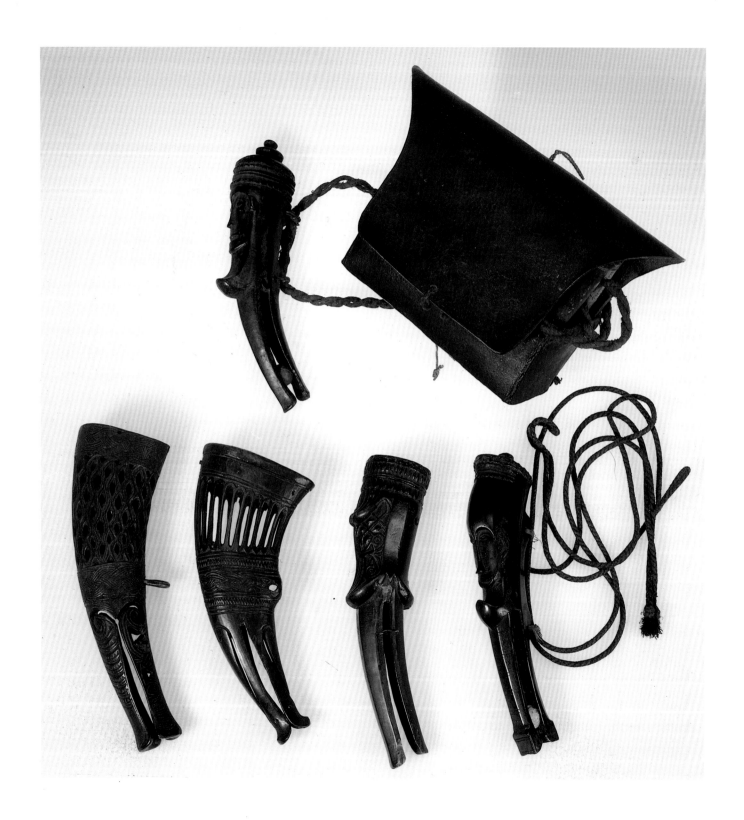

The products of the smith

Strangely enough we know practically nothing about one of the most important crafts practised by the Batak: smith's work. In the early stages of closer contact between the Europeans and the Batak after the middle of the 19th century clearly other aspects of Batak culture were regarded as more important by the European observers. When ethnographic collections began to be made in the late 1880s, people were only interested in the objects not in the various techniques of production or the status of the smith in Batak society. When after 1910 more research into this was done the brass and bronze work that had been so important among the Toba Batak had largely been forgotten. The Rheinische Missionsgesellschaft attempted to revive this craft by founding the technical and applied arts school at Laguboti at the south-east end of Lake Toba (Nieuwenhuis 1913: 29). But the working of iron and copper which was then current, and is still to some extent today, has been surprisingly little documented. The following is intended to give an overview of the products made by Batak blacksmiths, bronze workers, and silver and goldsmiths.

Blacksmith's work

The Batak blacksmiths either got their raw materials from the coast – as they still do today – or melted down damaged tools or weapons. A smith's workshop is a wooden building built on even ground with a floor of compressed earth. Its roof used to be covered with split bamboo instead of common ijuk to reduce the risk of fire (Brenner 1894: 269). The fittings of the smithy which can still occasionally be found in Batakland can be simply described. There are two vertical bamboo tubes used as piston bellows which are operated by an assistant, usually the smith's wife. She stands to the side on a platform and in each hand holds a long piston the end of which is wrapped in cloth. These pistons are moved up and down with a regular movement. The blast of air is carried through a small tube in each of the pipes to a single through which it is blown directly into the furnace. Charcoal is used as fuel. When vertical piston bellows are used the furnace is built directly on the ground, but horizontal piston bellows are also used in which case the furnace is raised to a height at which the smith can work standing up and his assistant operates the bellows in a horizontal direction.

Among the objects produced by a blacksmith are weapons and various farm implements such as hoes, weeding tools and harvesting knives. Harvesting knives are divided into the sickle-type knives used for cutting rice in bunches, and small blades with wooden handles used for cutting each stem individually (ill. 13). The blades of the spout axes (ill. 14) are

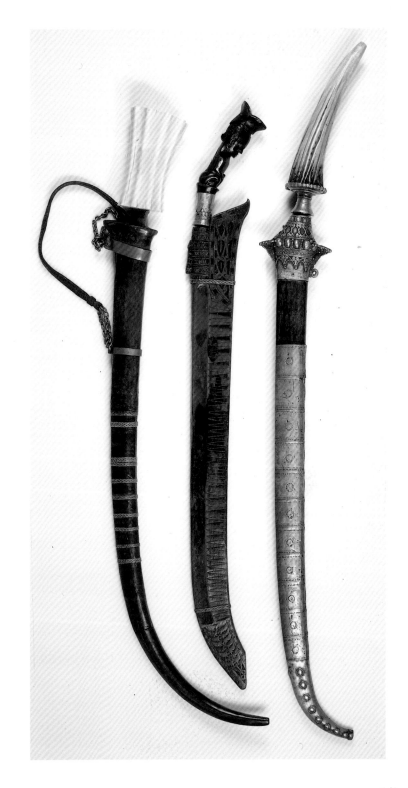

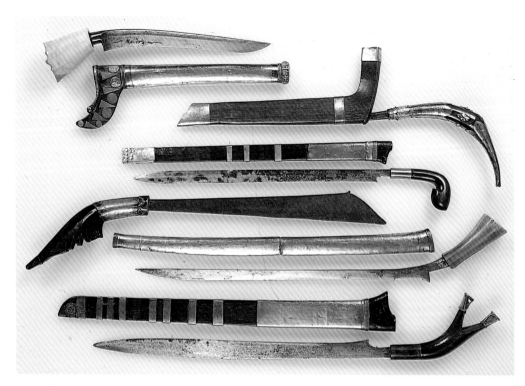

213 Various knives with ivory or wooden handles; sheaths covered with sheet silver or *suasa*; length: 31—55 cm, Karo Batak

214 Machetes and swords; length: max. 89 cm. The cross-shaped hilts of the two middle *podang* come from captured Portuguese weapons; Karo Batak. Sword with brass hilt and scabbard, Toba Batak

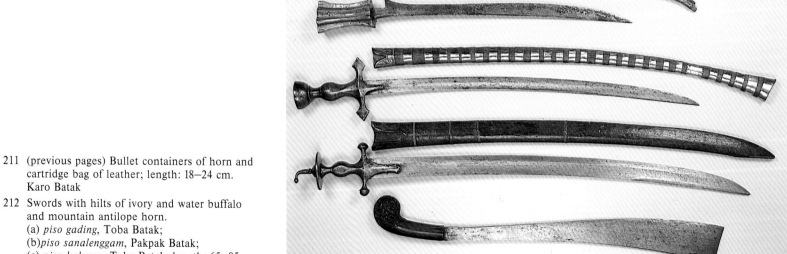

211 (previous pages) Bullet containers of horn and cartridge bag of leather; length: 18—24 cm. Karo Batak

212 Swords with hilts of ivory and water buffalo and mountain antilope horn.
(a) *piso gading*, Toba Batak;
(b) *piso sanalenggam*, Pakpak Batak;
(c) *piso halasan*, Toba Batak; length: 65—85 cm

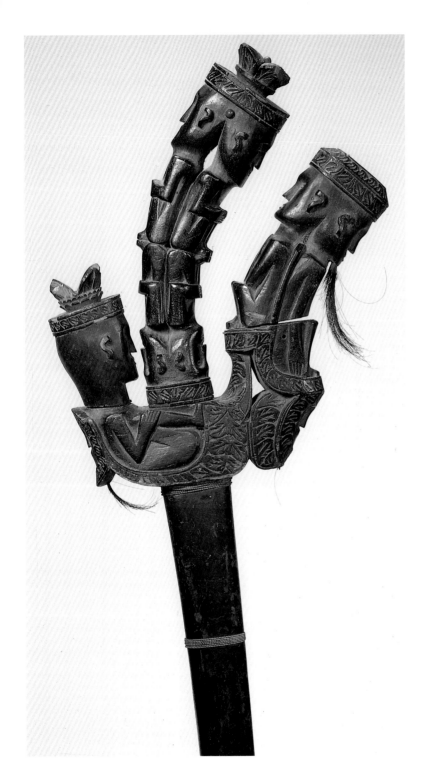

215 Sword; length: 84.5 cm. Karo Batak
216 Carver on the Karo plateau, c. 1915

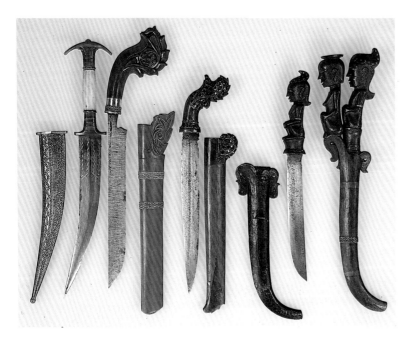

217 Knives, Toba Batak. Far left: insignia of a Karo Batak *pengulu* which comes from Aceh; length: c. 35 cm

218 Spears; length: max. 219 cm; left to right: 4 lances each, of the Karo, the Mandailing and the Toba Batak

219 Spears; left to right: 2 lances each of the Toba, the Karo and the Mandailing Batak

220 Parts of a spear sheath; length: 26 cm. Toba Batak

removable and were stored by the Karo Batak in flat wooden boxes. Today hoes, spade heads, ploughshares and various kinds of work knives as well as simple betel cutters are still made by the smiths, but competition from machine-produced goods from Indonesia, Taiwan and China has resulted in a diminution of the importance of Batak blacksmiths.

In the past the manufacture of weapons was the blacksmith's most important task. All the Batak peoples used lances and spears with a great variety of blades. These blades were produced by the blacksmith himself from steel by welding together several thin strips of steel using charcoal. The technique of *pamor* patterning as used by the Javanese and Balinese smiths, was not practised by the Batak. Some of the wooden shafts of the lances also had silver mounts, as found among the Karo and Mandailing, or decorations made by bronze workers. Occasionally red-coloured bunches of hair were attached to the shafts. Towards the end of the last century researchers were already complaining that these lances and the leather shields were almost no longer to be found

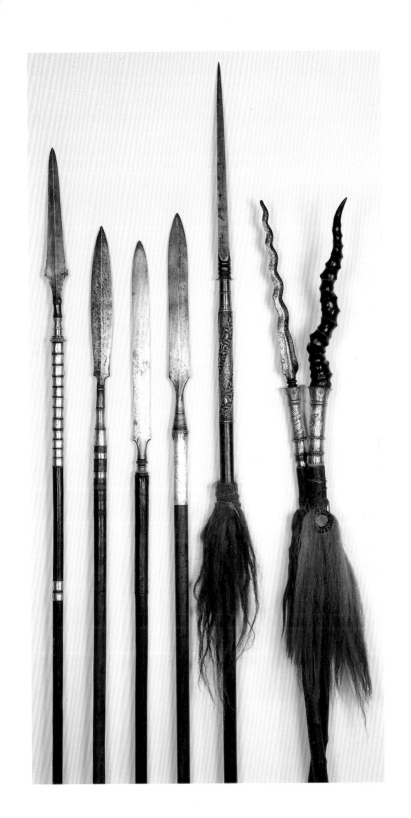

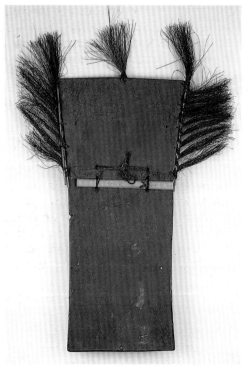

in Batakland (Brenner 1894: 334). Lances are not only used as weapons in warfare, in the case of particularly richly decorated examples they are also status symbols. In the nineteenth century firearms had made lances, spears and shields redundant as weapons of war, and the same was true of slings and blowpipes in hunting.

The production of cutting and thrusting weapons was one of the specialities of the blacksmith. The stylistic differences which made it possible in the past to identify provenance, are no longer evident, but they are described in the older literature (e.g. Volz, vol. 1, 1909: 310ff; Brenner 1894: 334). Some types of weapon were traded far beyond the borders of the region in which they were made or were carried off as booty. The swords and sabres which predominated among the Toba Batak had brass decorations on the scabbard or hilt, while the Karo weapons often had silver or *suasa* mounts. *Suasa* is an alloy of gold and copper used mainly by silver and goldsmiths for jewellery. Sword hilts were carved from wood, horn or ivory, or sometimes wrought metal (ill. 212–215).

The making of carved hilts and scabbards seems to have been the work of other craftsmen. Those hilts and upper parts of scabbards with figural decoration are often true works of art. The historical photograph of a Karo Batak hilt-maker (ill. 216) taken in about 1915 is especially interesting in this connection. He is working on the hilts of swords very similar to the sword in the Tropen Museum in Amsterdam (ill. 215). The photograph shows a specialized craftsman producing a particular type of hilt in large numbers. We do not know whether his products were restricted to a particular geographical area, whether he was working on commission for particular buyers or for a larger market.

221 Protective helmet of a warrior, woven from rattan. Toba Batak (?)

222 Leather shield (*hampang-hampang*) with *ijuk* attachments; height: 77 cm. In times of war the edge was further decorated with white feathers. War was seen as the judgment of God. If a warrior was hit or killed the war was regarded as lost and at an end. Karo Batak

223 Blacksmith forging a knife. Samosir, Lake Toba, 1985
224 Betel cutters (*kalakati penjabat*, Karo, and *sibolang pinang*, Toba):
   length (e): 16 cm; (g): 21.6 cm

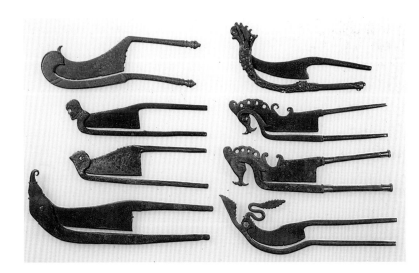

Bronze work

Work in brass or bronze was practised above all by the Toba Batak, but also to a lesser extent by the Simalungun. Brass, an alloy consisting mainly of copper and zinc, is pale yellow in colour. Bronze on the other hand is an alloy of copper and tin and depending on its copper content varies in colour from dark yellow to reddish. Through the effect of acid on the copper part of the alloy a greenish layer of oxidization (verdigris) forms on the surface. Objects made in yellow metal (brass or bronze) were produced by the Batak using the lost wax method of casting. The brass and bronze caster is a highly specialized craftsman who has to master not only the entire production process but also has to have artistic ability to create the form and decoration of his products.

The caster first makes a clay core lightened with rice straw or powdered charcoal. Around this core he builds up the outer form of the object, using wax mixed with resin. At the same time all the decorations that are to be on the object are worked in the wax and resin. This wax form is then encased in clay with a channel for pouring is left free by using a wax rod. When the clay casing is dry the wax is melted (hence the name of the process), leaving a space between the clay core and the outer which the caster now fills with the moulten metal. When this has hardened and cooled the clay casing and sometimes also the clay core are broken up – depending on the intended use of the object. Smaller objects, such as chain links, belt buckles or small figures (ill. 231, 241) are made without a core from solide wax. After casting and the breaking of the clay casing the object is worked with files, sand and polishing stones in order to make the surface smooth. In many cases the surface is also decorated with other metals as iron, liver, tin, zinc or copper are hammered into holes left in the object (ill. 236). Some pieces of jewellery cast in brass or bronze are also gilded (see below).

Among the most impressive works of the Toba Batak yellow metal casters are the tobacco pipes (*tulpang*) some of which are enormous, which were used by the Toba *raja* as a sort of status symbol. These pipes (ill. 240), which can measure up to 120 cm in length and may weigh several kilograms were carried by their owners over the shoulder on heavy brass chains. To smoke them one sat down and placed the heavy bowl of the pipe on the ground in front of one.

The chain which has two human figures with raised arms on its disc deserves particular attention (ill. 232b). It comes from Tongging on the northern shore of Lake Toba and at the beginning of the 1930s was still being worn by the *raja* there as a symbol of his status (Neumann 1939: 275).

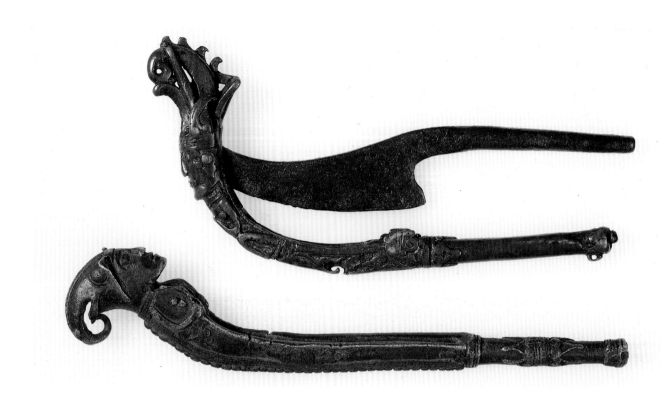

225–227 Betel cutters with figural decoration, brass; length (b): 19 cm.
Toba Batak

228 Lime containers and mortars made of brass. Toba Batak
229 Tobacco tins (*salapa*), brass, Toba Batak. Betel box, chased silver with
attached *stupa*-shaped lime container. Karo Batak

230 Fur bags (a,c) with chains and brass mounts; height: (c) 37 cm; (b)
leather bag of a *datu*. Toba Batak

231 Three supports for steel for striking fire, brass and bronze; *singa* heads as mounts for fur bags (ill. 230). Toba Batak

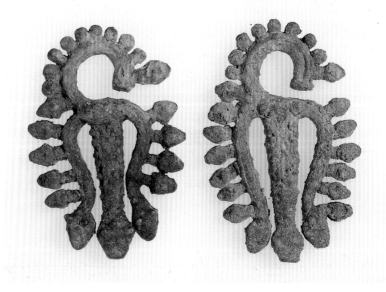

232 Massive brass chains: belt (a), insignia of a *raja* (b), woven bag (c). Toba Batak

233 Ear jewellery, brass or bronze (unearthed); stylistically these seem to be precursors of the various *duri-duri* forms; height: 6.4 cm; 6.7 cm. Toba Batak

234 Finger rings, brass, some inlaid with various materials (copper, iron). Toba Batak

235 Ear pendants (*sitepal* and *duri-duri*) were not worn as pairs. (a) silver gilt; the others of brass, some of them gilded; height (a): 5.5 cm, (v): 3.6 cm

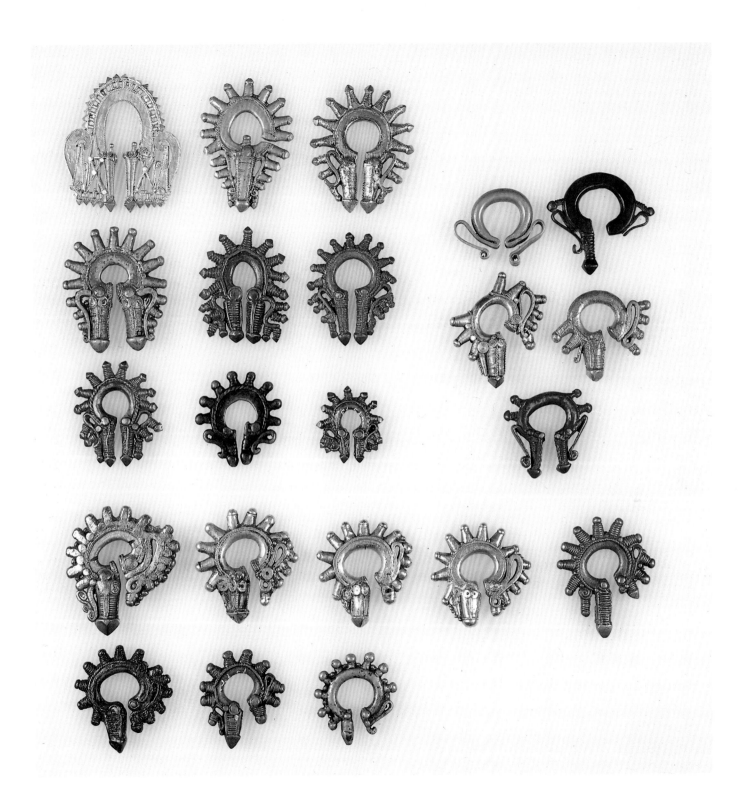

236/237 Massive arm ring with *singa* head in brass with copper, iron and tin inlays; diameter: 10.5 cm; weight: 1600 gram. Toba Batak

Brass or bronze chains were also used as handles for the large fur bags (*salipi*) used as shopping bags or as containers for tobacco or betel utensils. On the base and at the opening of the bag there are brass or bronze reinforcements at the sides. The chains are attached to the bags with brass or bronze fittings which had four eyes on the back for sewing on the bag and a *singa* head on the front (ill. 231). Swords were also attached to brass and bronze chains, and the steel used for making fire was attached to them (ill. 231). The brass and bronze casters often also produced jewellery. Arm rings, some of which were spiral shaped, usually had a *singa* head at the end (ill. 236, 237). But there were also many arm rings decorated only with geometric ornaments. A particularly splendid arm ring in the Linden-Museum collection has inlaid decorations in copper, iron and tin and weighs 1600 grams. It is a masterpiece of Batak metalwork (ill. 236, 237).

Finger rings with or without *singa* head could also be filled with medicine by the magician-priests and thus given magic powers (ill. 234).

Containers and implements for betel-chewing could also be cast in brass or bronze. These include small boxes for lime, containers of the *sirih* leaves and *gambir* or mortars for crushing the betel nut, as well as superbly worked betel cutters with figural decoration (ill. 224f). The brass and bronze casters produced figural knife handles and sword hilts and figures standing or mounted on horses which were attached to the simpler sort of magic wand (*tongkat malehat*) (ill. 154), as well as holders for combs (ill. 242) and toilet objects such as ear spoons and tweezers. Tobacco boxes of brass or bronze are often distinguished by a rich variety of floral decoration on the lids, which was either moulded in the wax or worked into the metal later.

One group of brass and bronze objects deserves particular attention. These are the representations of standing or squatting figures about 10–15 cm high, with the hands either on their knees or raised in a dancing posture (ill. 241). Someone accused of stealing livestock or some other property would pronounce an oath while holding in his hands such a figure which was called *gana sigadap*. If his statement was untrue it was believed that the perjurer would fall to the ground dead or paralysed and lie there motionless (*gadap* = fall down). Another oath (*gana siporhas*) for which these sculptures were also used was supposed to cause the perjurer to struck by lightning (*porhas*) (Warneck 1977: 86). Once a year the figure was given a food offering to keep it effective. According to Ypes (1932: 385f) such figures were owned by individuals who loaned them for the purpose of administering oaths to accused persons.

The patterns made by the brass and bronze casters in the wax-resin mixture are characterized by simplicity combined with great expressiveness. Fine rolls of wax are laid on the basic shape, either singly or twisted together, and after casting these resemble wires. A sort of fishnet pattern can be achieved by scratching the pattern on the surface of the wax. Little balls of various sizes can also be pressed onto the wax to form spiral patterns, the most common of which are double spirals. Figral decoration is restricted to representations of animals: lizards, cats and, most frequently, *singa* heads (Nieuwenhuis 1913: 33). The range of patterns is not very extensive, but the different combinations of the individual motifs give each of the brass and bronze cast objects its own expressive character.

238 Brass arm rings, some with moveable clasps. Toba Batak

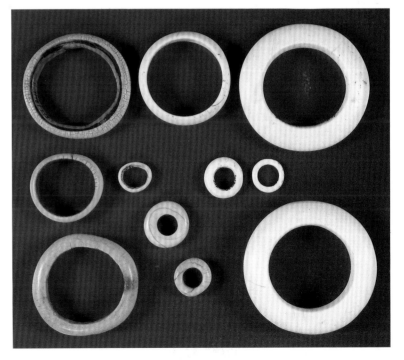

239 Arm rings and finger rings of ivory (left) and the shell of the tridacna giant mussel; max. diameter: 12 cm. Toba Batak

240 Tobacco pipes (*tulpang*), brass; (a–c) with wooden bowl; length: max.
130 cm. Toba Batak

178

241 Figures made of brass and iron; height (a): 8.8 cm, (d): 14 cm. Toba
Batak

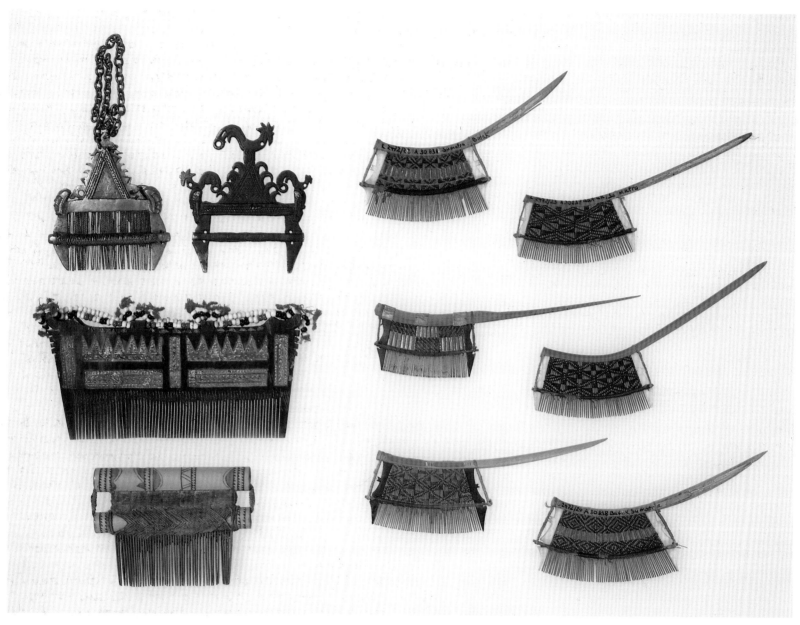

242 Combs: (a,b) brass, Toba Batak; (c,d,f,g,i,j), length: 10–12 cm. Karo Batak; (e) comb with metal decoration and beads, Mandailing Batak; (h) comb with plaited cord. Karo Batak

243 Hair ornaments. Hair pins; length: 13–15 cm; head cloth tuft; length: 30 cm. Karo Batak

244 Cosmetic implements. The chisels, file and little bone hammers were used to chisel away the front teeth. This practise vanished around the turn of the century. The chisels were kept in a wooden container (a). Karo Batak

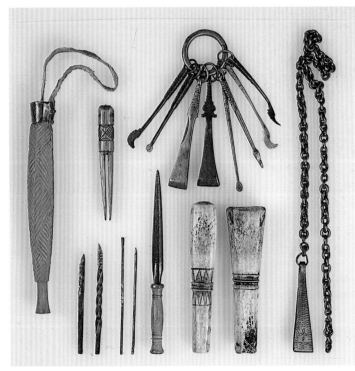

Works of goldsmiths and silversmiths

Unlike the material used by the blacksmiths and bronze-casters which came on the trade routes from the coast, a large part of the gold used by the goldsmiths in Batakland was mined in the region. Most of the silver on the other hand was obtained by melting down Spanish, Mexican and Japanese silver coins. The favoured coins for this, because of their high silver content, were the large coins known as canon dollars or Spanish mats (ill. 254). Jewellery was usually made by the silver and goldsmiths on commission. The client had to provide the raw material. Simple and cheap pieces of jewellery were also produced to be offered to sale at markets.

As well as the Batak smiths there were also many Chinese gold and silversmiths especially in the coastal regions. They produced works for the market in the tastes of the various ethnic groups which were sold in a wide variety of regions throughout Sumatra. As a result of their work and their trading activity many of the pieces of jewellery found in Batakland are also worn in other parts of Sumatra. Among these are various belts made up of rows of silver coins from the British Straits Settlements (ill. 258). The belt buckles are often decorated with fish and fabulous beasts from Chinese tradition. Belts of this type are worn by the Malay population in Aceh, Gayoland, Alasland and in the coastal region. However, most of the forms of jewellery used by the Batak can identified as specific products of Batak smiths.

Batak jewellery also has the functions of status symbol, badge of rank, indication of membership of a particular age group, amulet and talisman, and simply jewellery. It was worn equally by men and women, even children and infants were decorated with jewellery of gold, silver or the goldcopper alloy *suasa*. These pieces of jewellery, mostly intended to ward off evil, are still given by the parents (*kalimbubu*) of young Karo Batak mothers to the new born child. The foot rings with bells are called *gelang lonceng* and like the arm rings made of *suasa* are worn by the child until the next child is born (ill. 256).

Today the Karo Batak are about the only ones who still use traditional forms of jewellery. The traditional framework for a marriage has changed least among the Karo, and so even today wedding jewellery is made which bears comparison with old pieces in collections. Today occasionally cheaper materials are used, depending on financial circumstances. The wedding jewellery of a Karo couple is characterized by the multiplicity of the pieces worn. Contrary to the opinion expressed by Rodgers (1985: 321), men and women both wear heavy pectoral chains (*bura-bura*) with large crescent shaped plates attached to red cords or box-shaped chain links. The plates are decorated with

(next two pages)

245 Hair ornaments. Gilded sheet silver over a wooden core; height: 45 cm. Toba Batak

246 Necklace (*bura-bura*), silver gilt. Karo Batak

247 Necklaces. (a) *sertali rumah-rumah*, (b) *sertali layang-layang*, (c) *bura-bura*; silver gilt. Karo Batak

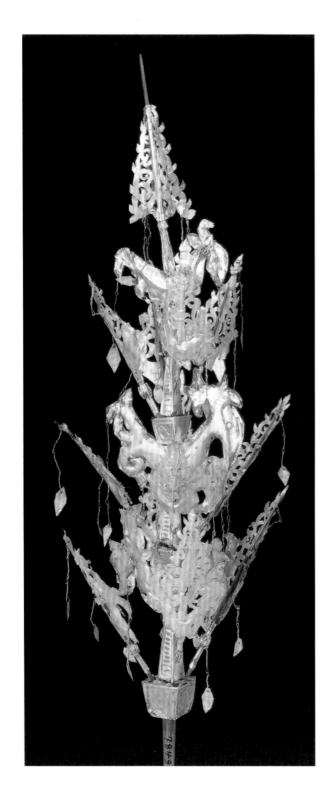

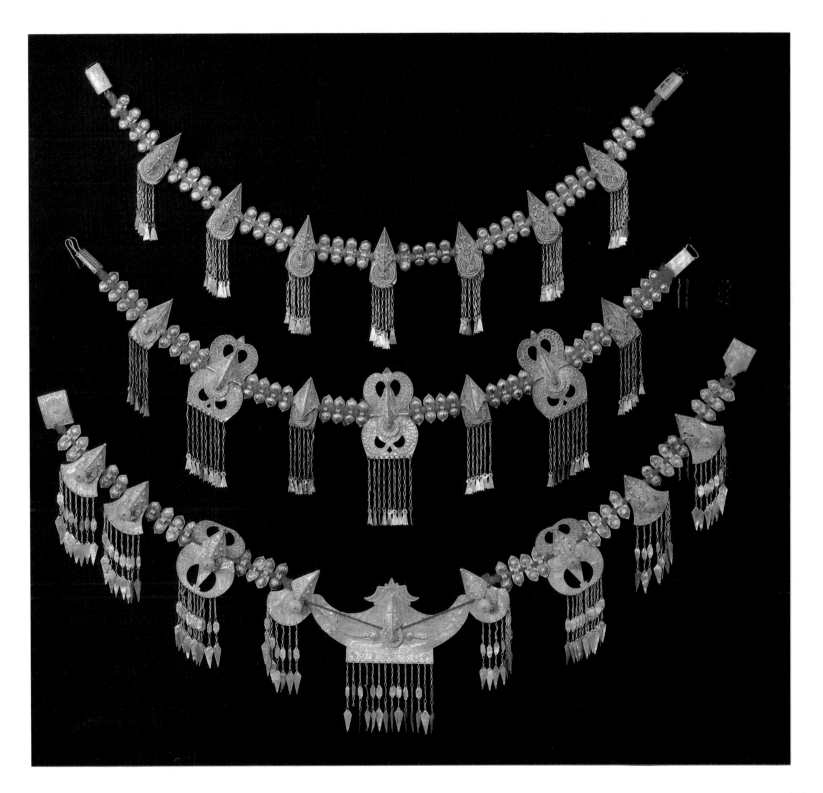

granulation and filigree work. On the necklaces (ill. 247) small "beads" (*anak bura*) decorated at the sides with hemispheres are strung together on plaited red cords. Another form of chain is seen in the second *bura-bura* (ill. 246) of which the box-shaped chain links are decorated with filigree work like the crescent plate. On the lower edge of the large plate are small rhombus-shaped metal leaves which are called *pilo-pilo* and are also attached to houses as decoration and to wards off evil or as a sign of hospitality.

Another type of chain, *sertali layang-layang*, is worn by women at a wedding as decoration on their headdresses (ill. 247, centre). On this chain the principal elements are three or five large plates in the shape of buffalo horns, between which are *anak bura* "beads" as well as other decorative elements of a shape reminiscent of house roofs and therefore called *rumah-rumah* (= like a house). On this chain too the little metal leaves (*pilo-pilo*) are attached to the larger elements. The *sertali rumah-rumah* necklace (ill. 247, top) is worn at wedding ceremonies by the bridegroom as decoration on his headdress, but at other ceremonies it is not restricted to one sex (Sitepu 1980b: 21; Rodgers 1985: 320). For earrings the women wear large pendants called *raja mehuli* or *raja mulia* (Sitepu 1980b: 22; Neumann 1957: 243). These were attached by large rings to the ear lobes.

248/250 The holder of the festival and his wife at a transfer of bones at Seribujandi. Karo plateau, 1987

249 The goldsmith Sobat Sitepu, Berastagi with a necklace (*bura-bura*). Karo plateau, 1989

251 Gold jewellery. Arm ring for men; diameter: 9 cm; finger ring (*cincin tapak gajah*); ear jewellery (a–c): *kudung-kudung*; (d) *padung curu-curu*; (f) *raja mehuli*. Karo Batak

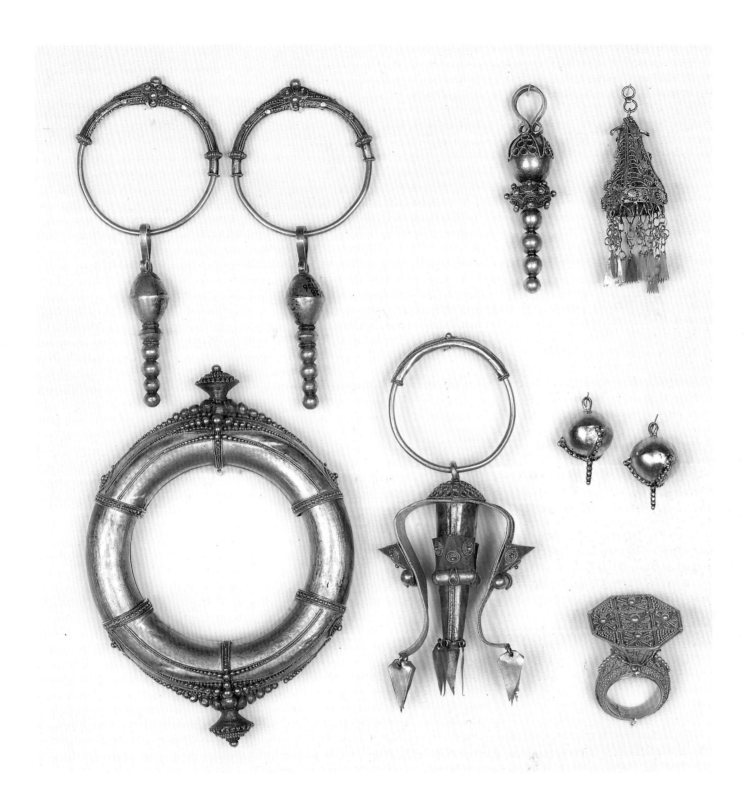

252 Silversmith drawing a thick silver wire at the *liun*. Kabanjahe, Karo plateau, c. 1910

253 Old woman with *padung-padung* decorated with stars made of *suasa*. Karo plateau, c. 1915

254 Ear pendants (*padung-padung*); height: 7.5 cm; 13 cm; 16.5 cm; bottom left: "Spanish mats", silver coins used as raw material. Karo Batak

255 Karo Batak girls. Karo plateau, c. 1910

(next two pages)

256 Arm rings made of *suasa* and silver foot rings (*gelang lonceng*), given as a present by the maternal grandparents to their first grandchild. Karo Batak

257 Finger rings, silver and brass, some with holes for holding medicine. Karo Batak

258 Belts made of silver wire and coins. (d) Necklace (*ranté*), Karo Batak; (e) forehead ornament (*sortali*); length: 52 cm. Toba Batak

259 Necklaces (a–d); (a) *kalung berahmeni* for children; (b–d) for older girls. Head ornament (e): *ranté perluasan tudung*, length: 43 cm. Karo Batak

260 Insignia (?). Necklaces with beard tweezers and silver gilt pendants; length: 150 cm, 188 cm. Toba Batak (?)

261 Glass bead necklaces; length: (a) 52.5 cm, (b) 93 cm. Southern Batak lands

262 Pectoral ornament, sheet silver chased and gilded; width: 26 cm, height: 15 cm. Toba Batak (?)

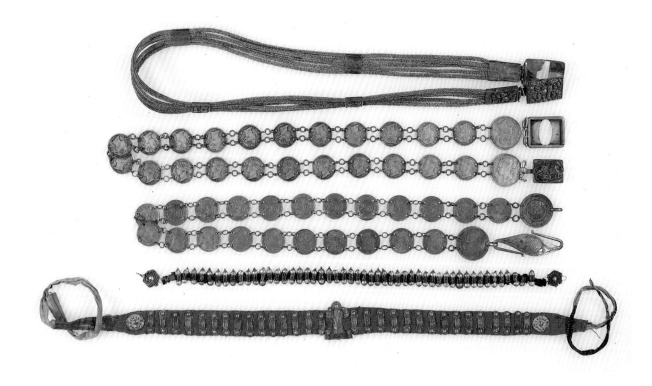

The men wear splendid decorated arm rings consisting of an inner hollow ring made of *suasa* over which two separately worked ring segments can be drawn to open and close the arm ring (ill. 251). The arm rings were also worn by rich and influential people on other official occasions. Other jewellery for men include an ornament which is stuck into the headdress with a long needle above the ear. In the past this consisted of leaves (ill. 243), but today it is made for weddings out of the same material as the chains. Depending on its financial resources a family has all the jewellery for a wedding made of silver or brass. When the blank together with it lavish decoration is ready the parts are gilded – the thickness of the gilt varied according to the size of the family's purse. In the past such extensive and expensive jewellery was restricted to rich families, but today anyone can borrow the jewellery for a wedding from a rich family for a fee, or else use the cheaper jewellery instead. There is, however, no compulsion for Karo Batak couples to wear such lavish jewellery. These chains were worn not only at weddings but at all important family ceremonies at which they served to identify the giver of the ceremony and his wife.

The best known type of Karo Batak jewellery is the women's ear pendant (*padung-padung*) which nowadays is no longer worn (ill. 253ff). It consists of very thick silver wire which is either worked from a single piece or has a removable clasp at its narrow part. The forging of these earrings, weighing up to 1500 grams, used to be completed actually in the ear of the wearer and they could therefore not be taken out. Karo women wore two of these *padung-padung* (ill. 253/5) and would attach them to their headdresses to reduce the weight on their ears. The left one pointed forwards and the right one backwards. The silversmith made these double spirals from silver coins, and to draw the 5–10 mm thick silver wire he used an instrument consisting of a large post (*liun*) which would be turned by assistants using a long pole (ill. 252). Unlike the *padung-padung* which is typical only of the Karo, the drop-shaped ear pendants, *kudung-kudung*, were traded beyond the ethnic boundary and are also found among the Simalungun (ill. 251, top left).

Karo girls wore necklaces called *cimata* consisting of silver beads and little pieces of jewellery from the great "wedding chains" arranged in various variations (ill. 259). In the past small children wore the heavy chains known as *kalung berahmeni* to protect them against illnesses. These consisted of large balls made of a sort of pitch covered with sheet silver. Various geometric patterns were worked into the surface (ill. 259). The Karo had a great variety of finger rings. Simple, undecorated rings and those consisting of several parts hooked together alternate with rings with a small hollow in which the healing or protective

ingredients prepared by the *guru* would be placed. Such rings were often used as *upah tendi*, a gift to the *tendi* (ill. 257). If a woman gave her desired daughter-in-law a necklace (*ranté*), this was almost seen as an advance deposit for the future marriage. Sewn on to the cloth band of this necklace are little flat beads similar to the *anak bura* of the large gold chains (ill. 258).

The best known type of Toba Batak jewellery are the various forms of ear pendants known as *duri-duri*. Their many variations are actually the work of brass and bronze casters, but since often enough these worked as silver and goldsmiths as well and some of the ear pendants have silver as their basic material while others are covered with a layer of gold, they are discussed here (ill. 235). The enormous bronze ear pendants shown in ill. 233 are very unusual. Their patina suggests that they must have been found in the earth and that they are considerably older than other *duri-duri*. On the basis of their shape they can be regarded as a rather clumsy precursor the later types. It is impossible to make out any patterning on the pair since they are covered in such a thick layer of oxidization.

Two very unusual necklaces (ill. 260) not mentioned in the literature consist of glass beads and semiprecious stones and a long cylinder made of sheet gold decorated with filigree and granulation. According to their collector both objects are Toba and were collected in the vicinity of Barus where they had been used as insignia of rank by the *raja*. Equally unusual is a piece of jewellery made of sheet gold and described as a bride's head decoration (ill. 245).

It consists of wooden stick on which is a sort of layered tree of life in the branches of which birds can be seen. In my view these birds seem rather to suggest south Sumatra. Another object in the same collection is a flat pectoral plate made of sheet gold with two eyes on the back for attaching to a chain or a clasp (ill. 262). Barus is also given as the provenance of this object. Since the collector, August Grubauer, otherwise has very correct information concerning the origins of his collection, I assume that these four objects must be as yet unknown forms of jewellery from a particular region affected by influences from the coastal Malays.

The current state of our knowledge indicates that Batak metalwork was far from homogeneous. The Karo Batak were well known as skilled gold and silver smiths, whereas the Toba were considered the best brass and bronze casters. Hardly any study has been made of the role of the smiths in the various Batak societies, and lack of comparative material and documentation means that the provenance of many objects must remain open or doubtful, as in the case of the last pieces mentioned.

263 Women weaving. The middle one is weaving the side strips, the woman
on the right the centre piece of an *ulos ragidup*. Toba region, c. 1920

Textiles for everyday and ceremonial use

Hand-woven cloths formed the traditional clothing of all Batak peoples before European factory-produced goods (yarns and materials) flooded the local Batak markets and supplanted the traditional everyday clothes. In the course of missionary and colonial activity – and indeed in recent decades – European patterns became socially acceptable even in the smallest villages. Today the streets are full of people in suits, dresses, blouses, shirts, skirts, jeans, T-shirts, sweat shirts and pullovers, but for ceremonies traditional cloths with their particular patterning are still of central significance.

The cloths were called *ulos* by the Toba and *uis* by the Karo. Since the production of hand-woven cloths still continues in many regions I have kept the following description in the present tense. Traditional Batak textiles are always rectangular, cotton cloths woven on an almost horizontal loom. To operate this loom (ill. 265, 266) the seated woman tightens the warp of the cloth with her body using the panel attached to her back. At the same time she braces her legs against a fixed board. Weaving is one of the many tasks of girls and women and is usually done when there is no work to be done in the fields or if they happen to have a few hours free. They get out their loom and sit down with it below or in front of their house. Before she can start weaving a woman must first prepare the warp (threads running lengthwise). In Batak cloths the warp is continuous, i.e. a long thread is looped over the warp beam and the breast beam. This means that the completed cloth has to be cut off the frame.

In the past the weaving of *ulos* was practised by all Batak peoples, but home weaving has greatly declined because of the arrival of European factory-produced cloths and has only survived in a few villages mainly in the Toba region. But the demand for *ulos* among other Batak peoples too remains as high as ever, so today Toba women weave many cloths which they sell at the markets at Kabanjahe and Pematang Siantar. They weave these cloths in the style of the Karo, Simalungun and Angkola Batak, depending on the requirements of their customers or middlemen. A Toba woman's loom (ill. 266) was recently acquired for the Linden-Museum's collection at a village on the west coast of Lake Toba. The cloth was intended to be sold at the market at Kabanjahe in the Karo uplands. The cloths made for Toba Batak customers were offered by the weavers to the many women who trade at the various markets in Toba land (ill. 270–271).

Besides the slowly vanishing craft of home weaving there also developed shortly after the turn of the century small centres of textile production on the south coast of Lake Toba in which *ulos* in the traditional style were at first produced on semi-mechanized

264 Woman preparing the warp threads before weaving. Silalahi, west shore of Lake Toba, 1989

265 Woman weaving at a loom which was acquired for the Linden-Museum Stuttgart, Silalahi, 1989

266 Loom with work started, acquired 1989. Gold threads in a woven pattern are increasingly popular for ceremonial dress. Produced for Karo Batak by Toba Batak

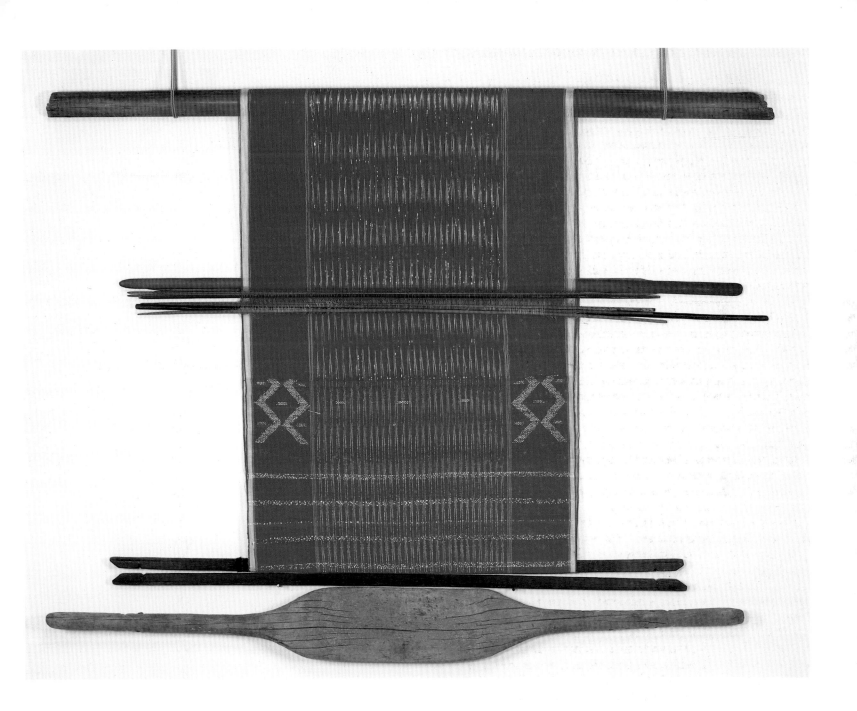

267 Woman applying rice starch to the warp threads before weaving. Toba region, c. 1930

268 Woman weaving. Silalahi, western shore of Lake Toba, 1989

treadle looms. To operate these looms the women used pedals to lift the various heddles to create the pattern. A few of these looms are still in use in small textile factories near Balige.

About sixty years ago fully mechanized looms appeared in the textile factories. Japanese, British and today Indonesian machines which can work very much more quickly than the two looms mentioned above have now almost monopolized the production of some *ulos* which are particularly in demand. In this region alone there are fourteen textile factories. Some of the machinery is now several decades old and makes a deafening din – which is not good for the health of the weavers. A lack of spare parts has stopped many looms in the factories, most of which are in family ownership.

According to information obtained in Balige 48 cloths a month are woven on a loom, and these then have to be cut and finished (ill. 272–273). Depending on the type and quality of textile the side edges of the cloths are embroidered with glass beads in white, red, orange and black. The monthly wage for a weaver is about 70,000 rupees (£ 20), with no provision for sickness or old age pension. Even considering the very low cost of living this is a real pittance, and many weavers also have to pay with their damaged hearing. Babies and small children who have to accompany their mothers to work and are either carried on their backs set to play or sleep next to the clattering looms, suffer particularly from these working conditions.

The most important traditional textile produced on these mechanized looms is the *ragi hotang* cloth. This is relatively easy to weave since it only has a weft pattern and does not consist, like other cloths, of several parts. However, the *ragi hotang* pictured here (ill. 278), a cloth with rattan pattern (*hotang* = rattan), was produced on a traditional back-girdle loom. This cloth, which today still has a central function and symbolic significance at the important family ceremonies, may possibly have received its name from the unusual plaited yarn border (*sirat*), the making of which is called *manghotang-hotang* by the Toba. A *ragi hotang* was accordingly a cloth with a plaited border. Besides the *ragi hotang* the mechanized looms are mainly used today for the production of simple *sarong* material usually with check pattern in glowing colours.

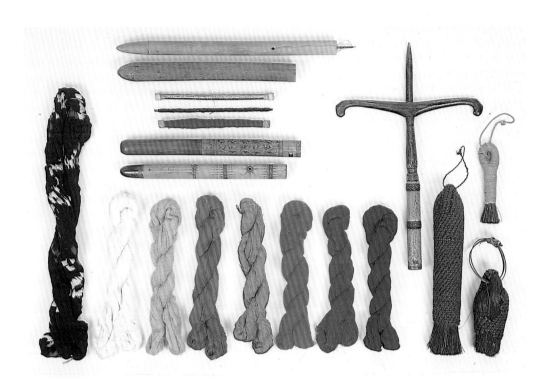

269 Materials for weaving. Skein of ikat thread and chemically dyed skeins. Shuttles (*tuldak*), a bobbin (height: 37 cm), and brushes made of *ijuk* for applying the starch to the warp threads before weaving. Toba and Karo Batak

270 Textiles for sale in a shop on Samosir. Lake Toba, 1985

271 Textile shop in the market at Panguruan. Samosir, Lake Toba, 1989

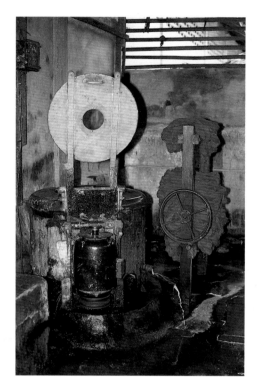

272 Room with equipment for dyeing yarn. Balige, 1985

273 Fully mechanized looms in a textile mill at Balige. 1989

Traditional textiles in everyday use

Before European clothing supplanted them woven cloths were used by all the Batak. They were worn around the waist, as shawls, as breast cloths, shoulder cloths and head cloths. In addition they were used for transporting food or small children who were always carried on the backs or hips of their mothers or older sisters. In many regions the women, like the men, used to wear only a cloth around the waist, or they covered the upper part of their body with short jackets or shirts. Among the Toba Batak these jackets were often very skilfully embroidered with glass beads (ill. 287, 288), while among the Karo they have appliqué work in glowing colours (ill. 290). The pattern of the shirt illustrated here has many parallels with patterns used in carving and tatooing by some Dayak peoples in Kalimantan. For everyday work, which means – especially for women and girls – hard work in the fields and in the house, relatively simple *ulos* are worn. These are woven from coarse yarn and have only a sparse weft or ikat pattern. The few decorated everyday cloths of the Karo Batak are as a rule very dark with indigo and dull dark red as the dominant colours. There are relatively few of them in the collections of museums because they are less spectacular than the many different Toba cloths.

For various reasons men follow the trends of the time much more quickly than their womenfolk and gave up the wearing of traditional costume with *ulos* soon after close cultural contacts had been established. This is partly because of the greater mobility of the men, who often travel to the coast to trade or earn money in some other way. In the coastal region they came into close contact with the coastal Malays and Europeans on their tobacco plantations. The ethnocentric attitude of the population there who regarded the Batak as an uncivilized mountain people must have exerted an enormous social pressure on them to conform in their outward appearance. Another reason is the relationship with the early travellers and tourists who not only brought worthless trinkets as gifts for the *raja*, but also trousers and well tailored jackets which gave their wearers an "official" appearance (ill. 7). The missionaries too played a part by putting their native pupils and assistants into clothes which in their view were not only more moral and respectable but also supposedly suitable for the tropical climate.

274–277 Traditional cloths in everyday use. Toba region, c. 1930

278 *ragi hotang*, length: 218 cm, width: 81 cm. Toba Batak

279 *ulos ragidup*, length: 192 cm, width: 114 cm. Toba Batak

The use of *ulos* in ceremonial life

In private life the most important occasions for wearing particularly valuable cloths are weddings, funeral and transfers of bones. The value of these cloths is measured not only by the higher quality of the material and the extensive decoration but also mainly by the symbolism of the patterns woven into them. At the ceremonies the cloths were not only worn but also exchanged according to established rules. The more highly ranked person gives to a subordinate person a cloth suitable for the occasion. The gifts made at a wedding are particularly rich in symbolism. The ritual presentation of an *ulos* has two purposes. It expresses wishes for the good luck and happiness of the couple, and it establishes and cements the new relationships between the kinship groups as a whole. The presentation of an *ulos ragidup* from the father of the bride to the mother of the bridegroom is an important symbolic act. The Toba Batak call all the gifts from the bride's family (*hulahula*) to the husband's family (*boru*) by the name *ulos*, while the gifts made in the opposite direction – the "bride price" – are known as *piso* (= knife). These two terms represent the exchange of male and female gifts. Precious *ulos* together with jewellery and household objects are heirlooms that women can hand down to their daughters and granddaughters.

The *ulos ragidup* (*ragi idup* = life pattern) is the most important and most symbolically charged cloth of the Toba Batak. It is also one of the largest and usually consists of several separately woven cloths sewn together (ill. 279). The two strips at the sides with two linking panels across the middle frame the central strip which consists of three parts. The middle part is of a single colour or has a striped pattern. The stripes can contain further patterns produced using the *ikat* technique.

In this process of making a pattern the warp threads in those parts are tied with threads or plant material before weaving, so that they remain undyed. The term *ikat* used for this technique comes from the Malay and is a verb meaning "to tie up, wrap round". The basic colour of a *ragidup* may be black or red. Of special significance in a *ragidup* are the two large end panels of the middle strip. These are not sewn onto the middle part, as they may appear to be at first sight, but are connected with the middle part by a very unusual method. Described in simple terms this is by linking the warp of the middle panel with the warp of the end panel and weaving them together. This method is not found elsewhere in Indonesia and is used only by the Batak (Gittinger 1975: 14). In recent cloths, however, the end panels are usually simply sewn on to save time. The not very complex pattern of the end panel of the *ulos ragidup* illustrated here indicates that it is probably not more than 25–30 years old (cf

Niessen 1981: Abb. 17), but the panels are still woven in using the traditional technique. In the past the manner in which the end panels were attached was one of the most important criteria for distinguishing an *ulos ragidup* from an *ulos pinuncaan* (often spelt *pinunsaan* or *penusaan*). In size and appearance both cloths are almost identical, and the only differences have to do with who could wear the cloths and on what occasion (Gittinger 1975: 28f, note 1).

The end panels of these two significant cloths are decorated with very delicate patterns in a large number of rows. The patterns are created from cross-threads which used to be black, reddish brown or dark brown, though one can find modern cloths with patterns woven in pink threads. The precise magical significance of the various patterns is not known (ibid.: 19ff). The two large rows of patterns framing the middle field (*badan*) are called *pinar halak* (*halak* = person) by the Toba Batak. On row is seen as male and the other as female. The pattern was regarded by the Toba as having strong magical powers and it was left to particularly knowledgeable people to interpret and check the pattern of a *ragidup* to find out whether it would bring good luck to a particular individual (ibid.: 21f).

The putting on of such a cloth during a religious ceremony activated the magical powers of the cloth for its new owner. Such cloths, known as soul cloths (*ulos ni tondi*) were popular among the Toba. The first *ulos ni tondi* given by her parents to a pregnant daughter did not have to be an *ulos ragidup*, but it did need to be sought out and examined with particular care. A cloth that did not correspond to the personality of the mother-tobe could have disastrous consequences for her child (ibid.: 22). An *ulos ni tondi* accompanied a person throughout his or her life and in times of illness it was thought to possess healing powers.

At a wedding the presentation and putting on of an *ulos* is one of the central and most significant moments. When the father of the bridegroom puts a particularly symbolic *ragidup* on the shoulders of the bride's mother the newly established family relationship is blessed by the socially superior party. The wrapping of the bride and bridegroom in a *ragi hotang* (ill. 278) by the bride's father as he pronounces the wish that they will have a happy life and a large number of children marks the actual moment when the marriage is made. The *ragi hotang* is supposed to help in the fulfilment of the wishes.

At funerals and transfers of bones the *ulos ragidup* again plays a central part. At both events a *ragidup* is used to cover the body or the exhumed bones (ill. 82). The coffin on its way to the cemetery is also covered with an *ulos*.

The Toba have a large number of other textiles, the symbolic content of which does not have the central importance it has in

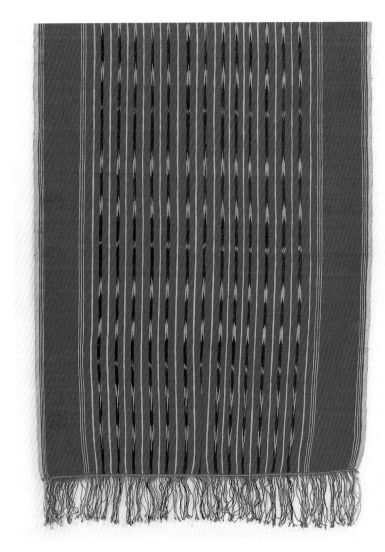

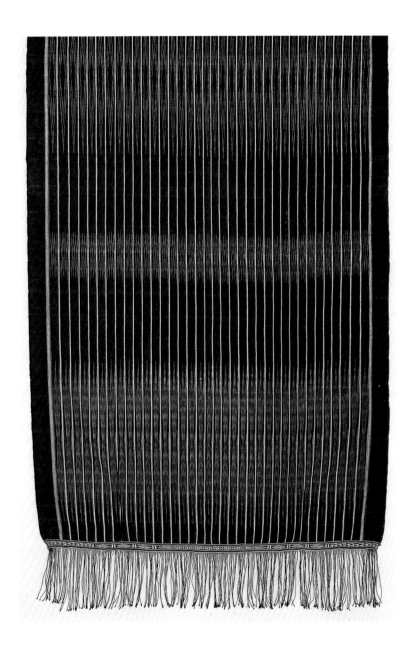

280 *ulos mangiring*, length: 171 cm, width: 58 cm. Toba Batak

281 *ulos sitoluntuho*, length: 212 cm, width: 88 cm. Toba Batak

282 *ulos ragi na marpusoran*, length: 166 cm, width; 102 cm. Toba Batak
283 *bintang maratur*, length: 218 cm, width: 80 cm. Toba Batak

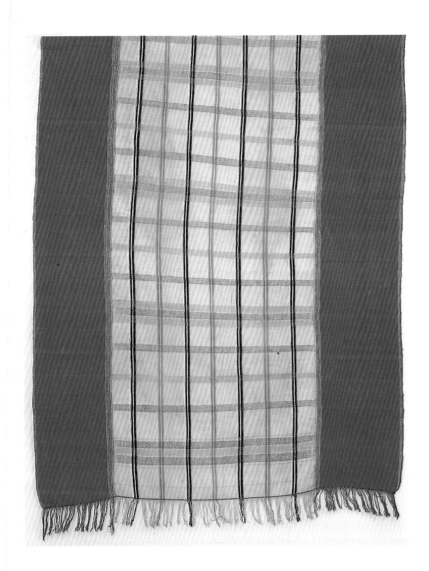
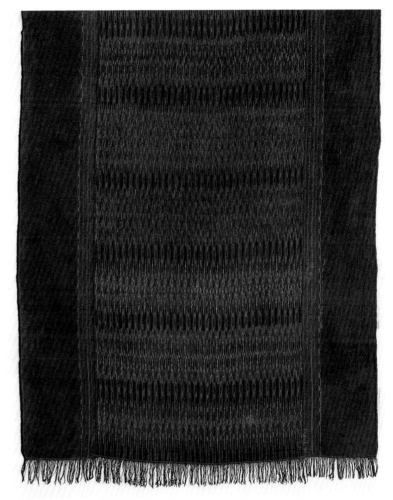

284 *uis gobar*, length: 170 cm, width: 110 cm. Karo Batak
285 *uis rojed*, length: 184 cm, width: 109 cm. Karo Batak

290 Shirt with appliqué work (*baju rompas*); height: 42 cm. Karo Batak
291 Coat of a magician-priest; length: 114 cm. Mandailing Batak
292 Mandailing Batak magician-priests in patchwork coats. c. 1900

293—296 Bride from Angkola in the traditional wedding dress. The jacket
has radiating strings of beads over a finely woven material. c. 1910

297 Dancing sashes (*simata godang*) worn at sacrificial ceremonies.
Bead-embroidered belt; length: 74 cm. Southern Bataklands

298 Detail from the pegbox of a lute (*hasapi*); total length: 71 cm. Toba
Batak

Dance and Music

(Uli Kozok)

Almost sixty years ago an article appeared in the periodical *De Indische Gids* which discussed, among other things, the music of the Batak. It ended as follows:

"It is a great shame that such [musicological] researches have been neglected hitherto, since now that the Batak lands are accessible and western influence can penetrate to an increasing extent, Batak music will soon degenerate and perhaps even vanish in the long run." (Abas 1931: 916)

Since then Batakland has experienced the Japanese occupation, the disturbances of the revolutionary period and the building of a modern national state – but Batak music still survives, and indeed is even becoming increasingly popular. The University of Medan, with help and support from the Ford Foundation, is training young music ethnologists who are advancing research into the music of the Batak, and researchers from abroad have also studied Batak music closely in recent years. In Germany records of *gondang* music of the Toba, Angkola and Mandailing and of *gendang* music of the Karo have even appeared (see discography: Kartomi 1983a,b; Simon 1984, 1987).

The music of each of the individual Batak peoples is quite independent, so it is not possible to speak of a single Batak music. Nevertheless, there are some features in common both as regards the musical instruments and the way the music is used.

The range of instruments used includes percussion, wind and plucked instruments. Percussion and wind are the more important. The complete Toba *gondang* orchestra consists of a drum set (*taganing*) consisting of five coordinated drums of various sizes with drumheads of water buffalo, cow or goat skin, the bass drum (*gordang*), similar to the *tataning* but much bigger (about 100 cm long with a diameter of about 30 cm), an oboe (*sarune*), and four gongs (*ogung*). While the Mandailing *gordang*, the Simalungun *gondang* and the Pakpak *genderang* are very similar to the Toba orchestra, the Karo *gendang* differs considerably. Its line-up is simpler consisting of a much smaller *sarune*, one *gendang* drum and a pair of drums, made up of a drum which resembles the *gendang* drum, with a second, 10-cm-long drum attached, and lastly a large and a small *gung*.

The combination of instruments mentioned forms the official *gondang* or *gendang* orchestra (for simplicity I shall use the term *gondang* for the orchestras of the Toba, Mandailing, Simalungun and Pakpak). There is also a large number of local variants and simpler line-ups. There are other musical instruments besides

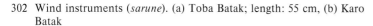

302 Wind instruments (*sarune*). (a) Toba Batak; length: 55 cm, (b) Karo Batak

303 Jew's harps made of bamboo; length: 8 cm. Karo Batak

304 Flutes. (b,c) *suling*; (d) *surdam*; (f) *baluat*, length: 27 cm; (g) *pinko-pinko*, length: 42 cm. (a,c) Toba Batak, the rest Karo Batak

305 The equipment of the *kulcapi*-player Ropong Tarigan Sibero, Berastagi: through the microphone, home-made amplifier and loud speaker the volume of the *kulcapi* is increased. On the left is a cane zither *keteng-keteng*. Karo Batak

306 The lute-player and maker of orchestral instruments Ropong Tarigan Sibero. Berastagi, Karo plateau, 1989

307 Ropong Tarigan Sibero with the *keteng-keteng*-player Pa Raden Sembiring Kembaren, who is the maker of the instrument in ill. 305. Berastagi, 1985

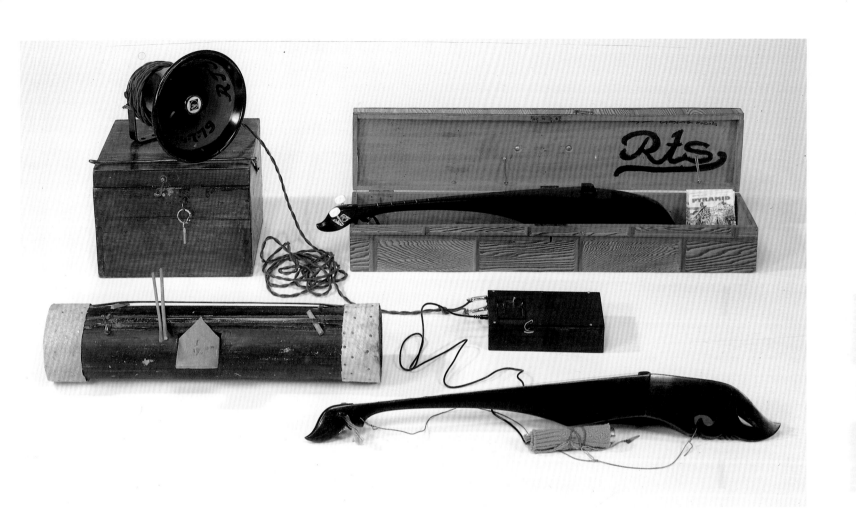

who wish to be possessed by a spirit. These dances are improvised and have an extraordinary dynamism and expressive power. The *gondang* plays a tune which begins slowly but quickens to a breath-taking speed. The dancers, who wear a white cloth over their shoulders and tied round their heads so that the spirits will see that they are ready to be possessed, gradually lose control over themselves, become ecstatic and stamp on the ground in rhythm with the music so that the house shakes. The female medium, the *guru sibaso*, takes a leading part in this and spurs her fellow dancers on. Some of the dancers reach the point where the spirit enters into their bodies, in a trance which resembles unconsciousness, they suddenly collapse and hit the back of their heads on the concrete floor. This does not bother those present, however. They immediately rush up, shake him and shout "Where are you from?" – they must avoid having an unwanted guest at the ceremony. Slowly the possessed man awakes from his trance. Despite his fall he has sustained no injury and is in no pain. If a malignant spirit has entered the ceremony the *guru sibaso* will drive it away or kill it with a knife in a dance. Those possessed behave in the manner of the spirit that has possessed them: women possessed by a male spirit speak in a deep voice, smoke and ask for palm wine; someone possessed by the spirit of a child crawls about like an infant. It also happens that people are possessed by the spirits of animals, especially snakes, but also tigers and apes, and so they crawl like a snake or clamber round the room asking for bananas. The *mayan* dance too sometimes leads to a state of trance (*mayan* is a form of the art of self defence). The dancers have a shadow fight with concentrated movements gradually increasing in speed, which, on the occasion observed by the author, degenerated into a general happy tumult.[2]

The third category of dance is the dance, generally accompanied by *gondang*, that is performed for general entertainment. This includes the dances at the *guro-guro aron* mentioned above as well as dance performances on a wide variety of occasions. As with the *adat* dances these dances are an expression of beauty and harmony, however the entertainment dances of the young people contain an erotic element, invisible to the uninitiated observer, which is expressed through certain gestures of the hand and body arousing loud laughter among the audience.

[1] The festivity has its origin in the *aron*, groups of young people who have banded together for mutual aid when working in the fields. As a rule the dancing festivities of the *aron* are held on the occasion of a harvest thanksgiving.

[2] I cannot say with certainty whether the dancers really are possessed in this dance. The *mayan* dance was performed in the course of a *perumah jinujung* ceremony which lasts about twelve hours during which many of those present repeatedly fall into trances.

Discography

Kartomi, Margaret J.
1983a   Music of the Angkola people, North Sumatra.
         Bärenreiter BM30 SL2568, Kassel [LP with commentary]
1983b   Music of the Mandailing people, North Sumatra.
         Bärenreiter BM30 SL2567, Kassel [LP with commentary]

Simon, Artur
1984   Gondang Toba, Nordsumatra. Museum Collection Berlin (West).
         Musikethnologische Abteilung: Museum für Völkerkunde Berlin
         ISBN 3 88 609 5126 [double LP with commentary]
1987   Gendang Karo, Nordsumatra. Museum Collection Berlin (West).
         Musikethnologische Abteilung: Museum für Völkerkunde Berlin
         ISBN 3 88 609 5134 [double LP with commentary]

308   *keteng-keteng*-player at the *perumah jinujung* ceremony at Berastagi. Karo plateau, 1985

Chapter 7   The Batak in the Modern Nation State

The post-war period

During the Second World War, when the Dutch were forced to yield control of their colonial empire to the Japanese, the Batak, like the other Indonesian peoples, hoped that the period of colonial exploitation and oppression would at last come to an end.

After seventy years of colonial rule the living conditions of the population of the two big provinces of East Sumatra and Tapanuli had changed radically. The traditional autonomous village communities, most of which had had economic as well as political independence, and whose contacts with the outside world had been determined by their own economic interests, had lost their independence and been integrated by the Dutch into a system of colonial dependence which they had not known hitherto. The compulsory cultivation of coffee and other agricultural products, "forced labour" and payment of taxes were used by the Dutch as a means of intensifying the economic exploitation of the region and of drawing even the most remote villages into the colonial economy. An extensive network of roads and paths, as well as a railway network was built at great expense in order to open up the countryside to transport and commerce. By 1915 a bus service had been established between Kabanjahe and Arnhemia, a settlement in the coastal region. From Arnhemia there was a direct railway connection to Medan (Lekkerkerker 1916: 69). As early as 1912 Lake Toba could be reached by car (Bodaan 1912: 273).

At the same time the old established ruling elites began to have their rights cut back by the administrative officials who had been appointed by the government, and the traditional way of life was shaken to its foundations. The greatest and most far-reaching change took place in the area of religion. Christian missionaries and Moslem scholars had driven back the traditional religion of the Batak to such an extent that by around 1930 only larger parts of the Pakpak and Karo Batak and a smaller percentage of the Simalungun Batak still held to their own religion. The majority of the Angkola and Mandailing Batak had been converted to Islam, while the Toba Batak had become Christian. Those Batak who migrated to the province of East Sumatra for economic reasons experienced strong pressure there to conform and a large percentage of them became Moslems. Some conformed to the coastal Malayan culture so completely that they are now almost indistinguishable, but to others the central elements of Batak culture have remained important.

Around 1930 the plantation region of the province of East Sumatra had a very high population density, mainly because of the work-force which had been brought in there. The people living there came from very different ethnic groups. The Javanese were numerically the dominant group (40 per cent). Then came the Malays, who had traditionally lived on the coast (23 per cent). The various Batak peoples together formed 25 per cent, of which 10 per cent were of Karo origin. In the province of Tapanuli the proportions were somewhat different. Here the colonial interests had not been so great and therefore the movements of population were of less consequence than in East Sumatra province. The Toba Batak remained the majority and in 1930 still made up over 50 per cent of the total population in the province. The Moslem Angkola and Mandailing Batak, whose settlement area formed part of the province of Tapanuli, together made up only just over 20 per cent (statistics in Langenberg 1977: 106). At that time the Chinese did not play an important part, numerically speaking, in the two provinces. Only in the region of Deli and Langkat was almost 20 per cent of the population of Chinese descent. For the development of business, however, they were already becoming an important force.

Thus, shortly before the end of the colonial period there were, broadly speaking, two very different blocks confronting each other in northern Sumatra. In one province was an internationally orientated, predominantly Moslem population used to the plantation economy, trade, craft and service industries, composed of many Indonesian ethnic groups, but predominantly Javanese and Sundanese. In the other province a dense, farming-orientated peasant population predominated, which had in large part been converted to Christianity but which was still able to preserve its ethnic identity.

In the centres of economic and political power the social structure was hierarchical. The European plantation owners and businessmen, together with the administrative officials, dominated all areas of public life, business and trade. Their executive organs were the native ruling elite who were dependent on the "white eyes", as the Batak called the Europeans. The sons of the Christianized Batak elite, who received an excellent education in the missionary and government schools, formed a thin middle stratum in the hierarchy, together with the traders of Chinese and Indian descent, and then there was a great socio-economic gulf separating these from the masses of the

309–312 Market at Berastagi. Karo plateau, 1989

313 Movie posters as seen in towns all over Indonesia. Kabanjahe, 1985

314 Jubilee festival for the 86th anniversary of the Simalungun Batak church at Berastagi. Karo plateau, 1989

315 Women at the church festival at Hatingian. Uluan district, Toba region, 1989

population (Langenberg 1977: 78). Admission to school education and western "know how" became a decisive factor in the political confrontation with the colonial system. The Christian Batak who had received a good education had a great influence on the future development. Of even greater importance, however, were those equally well educated Moslem elites in the economically and politically dominant towns. They had many contacts with republican-orientated forces on Java and introduced to northern Sumatra the ideas and hopes for an end to the colonial period and the achievement of independence.

The entry of Japan into the war and the capitulation of the Dutch colonial army (8 March 1942) was followed by the internment of the Europeans, but the period of the Japanese occupation was very far from being an improvement from the Batak point of view. Under the rigid war economy of the Japanese their hoped-for freedom became servitude. The Japanese allied themselves with the traditional native ruling elite, which had already lost much of its influence under Dutch rule and now saw the chance of regaining it (Clauss 1982: 57). But the abolition of the colonial structures and the hoped-for independence were only achieved after the Japanese capitulation (14 August 1945). The youth groups (*pemuda*) trained by the Japanese to give military support to their army were the decisive force in the Social Revolution (1946) when the traditional ruling elites were removed, e. g. in Simalungun. Some of the princes and their families were murdered, and the survivors lost all their privileges (for a detailed account of these events see Liddle 1970, Reid 1979). The *pemuda* also became an important institution in the struggle for independence.

The Dutch saw the capitulation of the Japanese as their great chance to regain their lost colonial empire and they attempted to do this from September 1945 onwards with the protection of British troops responsible for organizing the orderly withdrawal of the Japanese. The main Indonesian island, Java, the former centre of colonial power, was of course the principal focus of these events, but the plantation region of East Sumatra was also an important centre of Dutch interests because of its economic importance and the investments made there. The aim of the Dutch was to suppress the movements for independence in these regions, and independence was achieved there only after a long struggle against the Dutch who had returned.

The attempts of the Dutch to win back the whole of their former colonial empire failed because of the massive resistance of the population and the native ruling elite. The republicans under the leadership of Sukarno and Hatta were able steadily to increase the area of their power and unite the various people of Indonesia over the following years under the flag of the Republic of

Indonesia. But this came only after many years of military and political strife. The Dutch succeeded in establishing themselves again in Medan and from there to extend their area of influence by force of arms. At the beginning of 1947 almost all the plantations were under their control. But the destruction of Dutch colonial power by the Japanese had brought about a number of decisive changes on the plantations. The large plantations which were in the hands of the foreigners could only be cultivated in a very incomplete manner. The workforce who suddenly found themselves without leadership or wages, began increasingly to turn to subsistence farming on the plantation land in order to survive. Villages and even towns grew up on what had been plantations. The attempts of the former owners to stem and break up these proliferating squatter settlements so that they could get the old plantations working again started immediately after the return of the Dutch and lasted until the fifties.

In the summer of 1947 the local elites of the smaller East Coast states, under the guidance and protection of the Dutch, proclaimed an independent state of East Sumatra. In this action the Dutch had the support of the Moslem elite to whom they had given back political power, and of a large part of the Christian

Toba Batak. The large Javanese population withheld any participation in it (Langenberg 1982: 11). The Dutch were able to keep the state of East Sumatra alive for only a short time. Internal conflicts – mainly between ethnic groups – deprived the pseudo-democratic leadership of its legitimacy. In the course of the struggle for independence the Dutch were forced to withdraw early in 1950 and shortly afterwards the state of East Sumatra joined the Republic of the United Indonesian States (ibid.: 28).

The following years were marked by attempts to transform the politics of Indonesia into a parliamentary democracy on the western model. An attempted coup d'état in West Java (1956) and the efforts of West Sumatra, which rejected Javanese centralism, to break away resulted in the declaration of a state of emergency and the appointment of a military ruler. Sukarno completed the transition to "controlled democracy" which not only increased his own power but also secured that of the military over the administration and state industries. In this period all plantations were nationalized. The last of the Dutch and other Europeans were forced to leave the country and the military took over the running of the plantations. It was not until the coup of 1965 that some of these plantations were privatized again.

The political troubles of the post-war period did not leave the various Batak peoples untouched. Their homeland was now economically and politically integrated into the Indonesian state to a far greater extent than in the colonial period. Since the exclusively export-orientated plantations were of great importance as a foreign exchange earner for the new state, the inhabitants saw themselves as exposed to even greater exploitation and competition than previously. As well as the Javanese and Sundanese already living in the East Coast province, settlements were set up for migrants from Java which was said to be over-populated. But these were located only in marginal areas, at Aek Naetek, Bulungihit on the eastern shore of Lake Toba, at Secanggang, north of Medan and at Batahan, south of Natal on the border with West Sumatra (Hardjono 1977: 65) and numerically speaking were insignificant. Spontaneous migrants who made their own way to North Sumatra contributed far more to the increase in population in the trading centres and towns. One fact has not changed very much for the Sumatrans: only a very small part of the profits from the plantations and the extensive production of raw materials comes back to the local economy. The lion's share stays on Java, the seat of central government, and with the large, often international, corporations.

Education and family cohesion as the key to success

After the Javanese, Sundanese and Balinese, the Batak are the fourth largest group in Indonesia. Of the 250 or so old Indonesian peoples they are therefore numerically the strongest. Their experience of the missionary and colonial schools led the Batak to realize early on that only a good education could bring economic success, and parents have always made an effort to give their children the best education possible. Of course, even today girls are disadvantaged in this respect, but there has been a change for the better in recent years, and the proportion of girls at the various types of schools has been continually on the increase.

Not all Batak families are able to send all their children to primary school or to one of the secondary schools. In Indonesia only attendance at primary school, *sekolah dasar* (SD), is free, but the prerequisite for attending lessons is a correct school uniform consisting of red shorts or skirt, white shirt or blouse, a red tie for boys and girls and, most important, closed shoes. The parents have to see to and pay for this uniform themselves. The large number of children in Batak families (the Batak have the highest birth rate in Indonesia) means that the cost of sending them to school is sometimes too high.

At the age of twelve, after six years at primary school, the children go on to secondary school, *sekolah menengah pertama* (SMP), in which English as a foreign language is taught. The uniform here is greyish blue. After three years the children have the opportunity of attending the upper school, *sekolah menengah atas* (SMA), for a further three years. Here French and German are taught as well as English, but the time is too short for anything more than basics to be taught. As well as the SMA there is also a technical upper school, *sekolah tehnik menengah* (STM), which also lasts three years. Successful pupils at both these last schools can pass on to one of the state or private universities.

At all levels of education girls are now represented in large numbers, although the cost of direct and indirect school fees, as well as the "contributions" which sometimes bring higher marks, is relatively high. Attendance at secondary schools, which are not found in all villages, requires not only expenditure on uniforms and fees but also increased transport costs or even accommodation away from home. Nevertheless Batak parents do their best to ease their children's way in an uncertain future. Batak students study all the subjects offered by a modern university, and on graduation they usually have a good chance of finding a job suited to their qualifications. For finding a job family connections, even with distant relatives, are often very helpful.

The reciprocal obligations connected with the *adat* still have some importance even today. My main objective in this book has been to show that the Batak have by no means been absorbed in a pan-Indonesian culture but have managed to maintain their identity as an independent people to the present day. Even in the colonial period the Batak had very close relations with Europeans and other peoples. Since the turn of the century they have migrated in increasing numbers to the emerging towns and trading centres to find employment. This development is the result not only of the greater availability of information but also – and this should not be underestimated – of the rising population figures.

The Batak have always been an expansion-orientated people: according to the old myths they spread from Lake Toba over the whole of what is now Batakland. Rising population in one hamlet led to the foundation of a new hamlet nearby – if there was still sufficient land available for building. If there was no such land in the immediate vicinity then people would move to districts further away which were sparsely populated or uninhabited. In this way the various Batak peoples extended their area of settlement further and further. The individual villages were largely autonomous, and there was not necessarily any lasting connection with a particular village: at any time one could move to another village if the living conditions in the old village were no longer satisfactory. The modern age, which was about to arrive with its missionaries, colonial officials and, shortly afterwards, the first tourists, favours fast-moving and adaptable people with quick reactions and individuality of thought, and the Batak, who were compelled by necessity to be guided by their own needs, soon learned to take advantage of the changing circumstances. They developed many initiatives of their own as ways of making money, apart from traditional farming: crafts, trade and service industries boomed because of them.

But despite this very rapid and sudden change the Batak were never uprooted to any great extent. This was certainly due in part to the fact that the missionaries left some of the central parts of their culture untouched. The *gondang* orchestra was even incorporated into the church's liturgy, though certain rhythms were forbidden because they were connected with the old religion. The kinship system, one of the pillars of the Batak cultures, remained untouched, as did the system of law based on the *adat*. The sense of belonging together as a Christian ethnic minority in a predominantly Moslem environment is also an important element in retaining an ethnic identity, indeed the Church is a decisive factor in every respect here. The missionaries' technique of first winning over the *raja* of a village meant all the clan following the example of their *raja*, and the

clan therefore remained intact and was not riven by religious conflicts as happened in many other missionary areas. Above all the ceremonies which represented a renewed confirmation of existing kinship dependencies, such as weddings, funerals and the great ancestor festivals, were not prohibited by the Christian religion, some were given additional meaning and thus represented a valuable enrichment.

The Rheinische Missionsgesellschaft, which from 1860 onwards had been continually extending its influence northwards from the southern Toba territory, also laid the foundations for the conversion of the Simalungun and Pakpak Batak. However, they were less successful in these regions than in Toba country. When the German missionaries were interned by the Dutch or else forced to leave the country during the Second World War, they left a difficult inheritance for the young church communities. The individual churches soon showed that they were able to maintain churches and increase congregations without paternalistic assistance. Individual tribal churches developed, in which the members of the various Batak peoples found a home (Müller-Krüger 1968: 250ff).

The proverbial mobility of the Batak is also demonstrated by the fact that today there are many Batak living in the cities on Java and other islands. Yet in their new homeland they have not forgotten their Batak roots. Quite the contrary: it almost seems as if life in an alien environment only intensifies their sense of togetherness. In these cities there are associations based on descent. These are ethnically orientated and each is open only to members of a particular Batak people. In addition there are secondary associations for members of common *marga*. These associations arrange festivals, provide help in cases of need and also organize community service (Bruner 1972).

Any town with a certain proportion of Batak inhabitants will also certainly have a church. Even outside North Sumatra the Church has become the centre of Batak life. The feelings of the Batak for their home village, for the land of their ancestors are extremely strong, even if they live far away. The desire to be buried in the earth of their ancestors and thus come closer to their own origins or be closer to their ancestors, is for many Batak not merely romantic sentiment, it is a necessity arising from the strong sense of belonging to the *marga* and their own place in the ancestor structure. Hence it is often the city-dwelling Toba Batak who take care that their own ancestors buried in Batakland are transferred in a great solemn ceremony to as magnificent a bone house (*tugu*) as possible. By participating in such ceremonies and making a financial contribution they ensure that they are accorded respect in the village and the chances that they themselves will later be transferred to the *tugu*.

316 Hastily made souvenirs from Tobaland. (a,b) c. 1965–70; the rest
1985/89

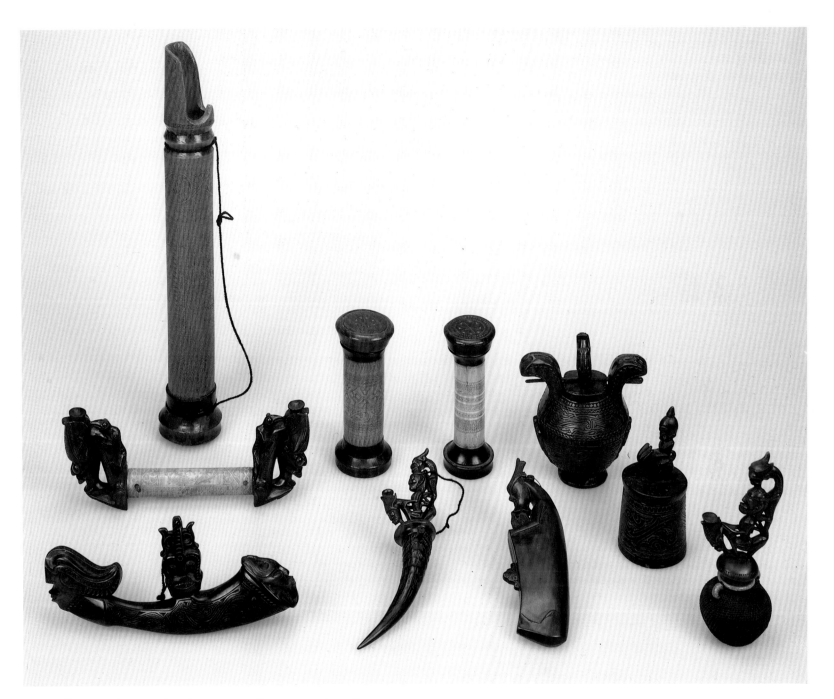

317 Craftsman-made souvenirs of superior quality are characterized by
better materials, better carving and polishing techniques and the use of
traditional forms. Parapat, 1989

These two aspects, then – the desire for a good education and the cohesion of the family system, which with its division into three interdependent kinship groups is still responsible for the clear definition of social values and norms – provide the Batak even in our fast-changing times with the sense of security and self-esteem that they need to compete with the other Indonesian peoples and preserve their cultural identity. A far greater danger for the survival of the Batak identity is the ever increasing contact with western and eastern leisure societies.

Tourism – a challenge for the culture

Scene 1:
"I would like to send all those who are afflicted by spleen, all Englishmen and non-Englishmen sated with the beauties of the Alps and Appenines, to the West Coast of Sumatra. ... There is now a fine road running for over a hundred miles through this mountainous country, which only 25 years ago was impenetrable, with a friendly staging post at the end of each day's journey where the tired rider or the female traveller borne in a litter by eight Malays can find hospitality. Rhenish wine and Champagne, English beer and seltzer, Westphalian ham and sardines are available, unless the traveller prefers the Malayan cuisine consisting of rice with curry, poultry and fish. Suffice it to say that I recommend Sumatra to all travellers, it is more beautiful than I can describe and less dangerous and more comfortable for travelling that one could believe."

Scene 2:
"Countless private cars and trucks roar through the country on the great highway from east to west. May ability win through! The tourist and the world traveller with a hunger for the tropics, who is so bright that he can make an informed judgment about the country and people from his swiftly moving car ... It is so simple: you take a few snaps with the inevitable Kodak (I feel ill when I even see that object in their hands), listen for a bit to the chatter, merrily generalize about what you happen to think you have seen on the way, and surprise us all afterwards with a penetrating newspaper article dashed off with sharpness and superiority. There are plenty of little anecdotes of how nonsensical captions are given to photographs snatched by chance and assertions are made which make a mockery of reality."

Scene 3:
"...The place of slaughter for the ritual sacrifice of the old Toba Batakers, a truly macabre place. On one of the stone seats the king took his place, around him sit his court and nobility, on the long sacrificial stone lies a human being – a slave who seemed worth transferring his strength and power to those who kill him. The old traditions describe gruesome scenes: much of the flesh was eaten raw, but not without seasoning with lemon and salt. The last 'ceremony' allegedly took place here in 1900."

Quotations such as these could be found without difficulty in their hundreds. These three excerpts from accounts of travel and life or travel guides date from very different periods. They represent three fundamentally different forms of describing a foreign country and at same time reveal the inner attitudes of the authors to the contacts they describe. The first scene emphasizes the beauty of the landscape and the comfort of the journey, with the local population mentioned only as litterbearers for a European woman. The second description is sarcastic and puts emphasis only on the tourists and their superficiality. It laments the one-sided cultural exploitation, which serves only the traveller's personal ends on his return home, but evades any close study of the culture through which he has passed. The third scene is a well-worded description in the present tense of allegedly authentic ceremonies which give the reader the impression of a truly "primitive" culture and are supposed to present a visit to this region as an adventure *par excellence*.

It is hard to believe that the three passages are separated by almost 130 years (Kessel 1854: 905; Warneck 1939: 109f; Dippe 1980: 54). The history of tourism in Batakland begins with the history of adventurous travellers whose only reason for travelling was to visit this country and fill in the white areas on the map with information they gathered in the course of their stay. In this connection I draw a certain distinction between on one side the colonial officials who travelled for the government, and the true explorers such as Junghuhn, and on the other those who travelled for pleasure and wrote accounts of their experiences in order to increase their self-esteem and their reputation as fearless adventurers.

These pleasure-travellers can be regarded as the first tourists in the region. Their journeys were not the result of any geographical, botanical, zoological or ethnological interest, nor did they have any commercial interest, or missionary zeal. To the Batak they seemed very suspicious, since the Batak did not know of such an aimless form of travelling and were not used to visits from the "white eyes".

The reclamation of the East Sumatran marshland for use as plantations (see Agthe 1979: 121–139), which was only made possible by the recruitment of thousands of coolies from China, Singapore and Java, was a murderous pioneering achievement. In this new mixture of peoples also lived many Europeans as owners or administrators of plantations, and the contacts between the local population and the "white eyes" attained new dimensions. The population was no longer confronted with just a single European, but they met them in large numbers at the new markets and towns. Moreover, the contacts were not fleeting as they had been is the early travellers; the natives realized that the life style of the "white eyes" and their material furnishings in these towns was something that was going to last. The Europeans who were used to a certain standard of living made every effort to achieve this standard even in the inhospitable East Coast region of Sumatra. So firms were established there to provide everything that a sweating European needed in the tropics.

"Not only all vegetables, vegetables with meat to go with them, sausage and potatoes cooked together, a wide variety of meat products, compotes and fruits, but also cheese, herrings, bread, puddings, cakes – everything packed in tin cans." (Carthaus 1891: 78)

Condensed milk and Dutch soups in cans were also available. At the same time the increased need for fluids was not forgotten: gin, French red wine, Rhine wine, English, Dutch, Danish and German beers were imported in large quantities (ibid.: 79f). Non-alcoholic drinks too, such as German mineral water or British Apollinaris were brought into the country "in millions of bottles" (ibid.: 177). Cinemas, night-clubs and brothels were features of the public life in Medan and Labuan Deli. A military doctor who spent twenty years in the Dutch service described the conditions:

"Labuan Dell [sic], for example, 15 years ago ... had no prostitutes and no syphilis. Since then a flourishing planters' colony full of Europeans there has even made a railway necessary, and this little insignificant port already has more than 200 priestesses of Venus vulgivaga from all the corners of the earth. The capital Medan, three miles from Labuhan Deli is now already infected ..." (Breitenstein 1899 vol. 1: 218).

318 Collapsed *lesung*. The traditional architecture is vanishing at a great rate. Seberaya, Karo plateau, 1985

319 The modern consumer society leaves behind mountains of rubbish and scrap; there seem to be no solutions to the question of how to make use or dispose of it. Lingga, Karo plateau, 1985

Some of the Europeans working on the plantations spent some of their free time outside the brothels and bars. Many set off on travels which often took them to the homelands of the still independent Karo and Simalungun Batak. From these excursions, which seldom lasted more than a few days, they occasionally brought back ethnographica, which then had only a small market value as art objects, but were put on the mantelpiece as souvenirs of a journey to the cannibals. Many collections in our museums

are derived from these sources. The names of many collectors were closely connected with the history of the plantations. Letters provide evidence of the links between the individual collectors. Well known names such as Staudinger, Meissner, Maschmeyer and Martin are always mentioned (Linden-Museum Archives).

Georg Meissner was one of the most important of these pioneers. He seems to have been the first to travel through the Karo plateau several times and gathered together a lot of ethnographica. To him, however, these were not souvenirs; he collected in accordance with the ethnographical criteria which were then current. He donated the collections he had made over twenty years to the ethnographical museums in Berlin, Dresden and Stuttgart. But he was not wholly altruistic. In the final years of the German Empire one of the important aims in life of a member of the bourgeoisie was to rise to the aristocracy by means of decorations. Gifts to ethnographical collections were one possible way of attaining this goal. For many of the other employees on the plantations this was not a goal worth aiming at. They often made a short trip into the Karo plateau, and later to Lake Toba, at the end of stay on the island, acquired a few souvenirs there and then went home.

Without anticipating too much a later work, it must recorded here that this form of souvenir trade was already widespread in 1890 and had features which many of today's tourists in the region cannot imagine.

"...The objects laid out here...which are all more or less antique, in so far as such objects are still used today, but there is nobody who could make them, as far as not bad pieces are produced for trade with European collectors. I am almost willing to believe that these newly made pieces are of Chinese provenance, for the Chinese have already sneaked in here and since they are born craftsmen and businessmen they naturally saw immediately the advantages of such a trade in fake antiques" (Martin 1891: 55).

In the first decades of the century Batakland was already opened up to tourism by the missionaries in the south and the plantation workers, adventure-tourists and businessmen in the north under the protection of the colonial government at Medan. On the Karo plateau the first guesthouses of the large plantation companies were built and by Lake Toba the first villas. Life in these tourist spots has hardly changed since. The houses of the various companies, "Deli-Rubber", "Goodyear" and "Anglo-Dutch" are furnished with toilets and bathrooms. A billiard room and cement tennis court are provided for leisure activities. The individual houses are surrounded by wide lawns which are tended by Batak employees (Kaarsberg 1923: 21). At that time many Batak were already employed in the tourist

320 Magic wands for tourists: (a) c. 1930; (b) 1975; (c) 1989, in two parts; (d) 1989, in one piece and well carved. Toba Batak

321 Carver making a miniature magic wand for the souvenir trade. Parapat, 1985

322 Goods on a souvenir stand at Tomok, Samosir. Very many Toba Batak make a living from producing and selling these products. Lake Toba, 1985

323 Colouring of newly made masks. Polishing with black or brown shoe polish is the last process in their manufacture. Parapat, Lake Toba, 1985

industry as house staff, gardeners, cooks, chamber maids and prostitutes. There were even professional tourist guides who, just as they do today seventy years later, would take "white eyes" to the *air terjun* waterfall, the Sibayak volcano, and to the Lau Debuk-debuk hot springs in the Doulu valley.

With the extension of the road network after 1915 visiting Batakland became increasingly quick and comfortable for tourists. The number of foreign travellers shot up, and there were even organized group visits available. Jan Poortenaar, a Dutch artist, who had installed himself for three months in 1927 with a

German hotelier near the Si Pisopiso waterfall on the north coast of Lake Toba, described the conditions for tourists much as they can still be experienced at the waterfall today. The tourists usually drive to the waterfall for lunch, they find themselves a meal which can be prepared quickly and should not last more than a quarter of an hour, and pass the rest of the time with a short walk to the spot with the best view of the waterfall and of Lake Toba far below. In nine out of ten cases they take a quick souvenir photograph and then go back to the restaurant. Then they climb back into the car and go on to their next stop (Poortenaar 1928: 329f). Exactly the same behaviour can be observed in many places in Batakland today.

Even the "Cultural Shows" sometimes organized today, in which the local population perform dances and similar activities for the entertainment of tourists, are not a recent invention of wily travel experts. Such performances were already being held at the house of Consul Schild at Padang in 1901. He had natives of the Mentawai Islands and Nias brought to Padang, where they would perform war-dances in his house for the amusement of his guests (Haeckel 1909: 186).

It must be clear by now that tourism came early to Batakland, and that the structures to be seen today are based on foundations laid in the last century. Tourists today move along the exactly the same well-trodden ways as generations of tourists have done before them. In this there is no distinction between independent and group tourists, even if the backpack tourists now generally stay rather longer in Batakland and occasionally even look beyond the bounds of their tourist ghetto. I shall avoid making any of the prejudiced remarks about package tourists which one finds in many of the travel books. Such comments are often based on a false interpretation of one's own behaviour as a tourist and the effect of the various forms of tourism on the local population. Because of the international economic situation it is a fact that to the natives the Europeans are always rich, no matter how much money he actually has and spends on his holiday.

If one takes the time to read the old travel accounts and compares them with the descriptions of the course of organized travel firms or the many travellers' handbooks, one can get a very good picture of what most impresses us Europeans in our contact with the Batak. One sees what features of the various Batak cultures offer the greatest effect or better attractiveness to the outside world. The cultural elements predominate in all descriptions, since they represent the Batak culture for the transient observer. Also apparent are the expectations which the tourists had already formed at home. The information about the region which the traveller accumulates from the available sources before setting off on his holiday, becomes a decisive factor in such a trip. It is the old story of prejudices which travelling does not break down, but rather confirms.

Among the cultural elements mentioned which the Europeans regard as epitomizing the Batak cultures, since the beginning of close contacts between the "white eyes" and the "black eyes", have been all those peculiarities which a visitor is aware of even during a brief stay in a village. Firstly, there are the unusual shapes of the houses. The descriptions of these houses have hardly changed over the last hundred years. Today the houses are the first things mentioned in a description of Batak villages, where they are often referred to dismissively as "dwellings" and qualified with such terms as "medieval" or even "primeval"

(e. g. Italiaander 1979: 129). The same author, who comes from ecclesiastical circles, mentions in another connection a subject which crops up hundreds of times in other publications describing the interior of a Batak house:

Scene 4:
"My accommodation in the guest house was dreadful. The bedclothes smelt musty. The walls of my bedroom were dirty and smeared all over. I washed at a cement basin which looked like a pigs trough. The toilet pan was broken and there was no toilet seat. Nowhere was there a mirror or clothes hook" (ibid.: 137)

Anyone capable of such ethnocentric comments has obviously never made any effort to understand the traditional way of life of the Batak and is only aware of his own standards.

In descriptions of villages the high defensive ramparts are usually mentioned – although these are seldom there. Villages are described as if there had been no change. The existence of modern buildings, modern infrastructure and technology is passed over in silence. The reader has an impression of primitiveness and authenticity. When mention is made of changes in the recent decades – which happens rarely enough – then the authors fall into romanticism, for which there is little justification, as they lament the decline of traditional architecture, without losing sight of the effectiveness of such a statement as advertising.

The long-gone cultural phenomena such as cannibalism or the "Megalith Culture" are particularly effective as a means of enticing visitors. The use of great stone blocks for places of assembly, for "slaughtering blocks" on which human beings were sacrificed, is described as typical of all Batak villages although this form of village layout and this arrangement of stones was only ever customary in a relatively small part of Batakland. The impression is also created that the ceremonies were taking place not all that long ago. And in these descriptions only one village is ever given as an example: Huta Siallagan part of the town of Ambarita on Samosir Island. Anyone who has spent some time in this village and observed how the tourist groups are taken round and what the visitors are told by their native guides must soon realize that this form of travel cannot lead to a greater understanding between peoples.

As we saw at the beginning of this chapter, tourists have always had the habit of bringing back souvenirs from their travels. Those acquired by early travellers have often found their way into our ethnographical museums. Almost every museum has such specimens (ill. 320). They are usually objects which enjoyed particular popularity at certain times. These include knives and swords, magic wands and other equipment of the magician-priests, and – in increasing numbers – figural wooden sculptures.

The trade in souvenirs has not basically changed in recent decades. The appearance of the individual objects has altered to suit the changing taste of the customers, and new forms have been developed. To this day, however, the works of the craftsmen and artist-craftsmen have represented a Batak culture which has ceased to exist. The objects are mostly without meaning, they are not used in religious ceremonies nor by the natives themselves.

What does tourism mean to the Batak? Does it present a positive or negative challenge? How should the effects of tourism be seen in connection with the desires and aspirations of the Batak for a better future? These complex questions cannot be adequately answered here.

Tourism in Batakland is restricted to a few small easily accessible areas in which the tourist structures have been in existence for more than a hundred years. The majority of Batak continue to live in village structures off the beaten tourist track, but they do not by any means live in isolated regions which modern developments have passed by. Radio, television and newspapers are available almost everywhere, and schools and markets are important disseminators of novelties and knowledge of new technologies.

The Batak are bound up in a dense network of commercial and cultural relationships with the other Indonesian peoples around them. Larger towns develop into multicultural communities in which the Batak live side by side with Chinese, Javanese, Minangkabau and members of other ethnic groups. They are part of a nation state which encompasses 250 different ethnic groups and which is faced with solving massive problems. They are one of Indonesia's many minorities who have to struggle to keep their ethnic identity if they do not want to disappear in a pan-Indonesian culture dominated by the Javanese and Balinese. Batak culture is often described by the latter as *kasar* (rough, unpolished). Their open and direct manner of communicating and arguing with each other is much too direct for the Javanese, who crave for harmony and who therefor often describe the Batak as uncultured (Rodgers 1986: 38).

Thus the Batak have to struggle against prejudices from a variety of directions. In this context the western tourists form a relatively unimportant minority, for they are only of economic significance to a small part of the population. But in the process of retaining their cultural identity the tourists have an effect which should not be underestimated. The consequences are double-edged. Tourist contact between the natives and the "white eyes" encourages the Batak to think about their own culture and the economic situation. Certainly many patterns of behaviour and fashions are absorbed and copied particularly by the young Batak with an unthinking belief in progress. But the interest of the tourists in the remains of their past has caused many young people to return to their old cultural values. The Batak script which used to be understood by only a few is now taught in articles in the newspapers and the popularity of the traditional music is increasing.

For an evaluation of the negative or positive effects of tourism the origin of the individual tourists is relatively unimportant. Today tourists come to Sumatra from many different countries. Besides Europeans, Americans, Australians, New Zealanders and Japanese, an increasing number of Malays and Singaporeans now travel to nearby Sumatra. Another new development with important repercussions for the future is the ever increasing number of local short-term holiday-makers, who have long outnumbered the international tourists at the tourist resorts of northern Sumatra.

324 Graves of Moslem Karo Batak. Berastagi, Karo plateau, 1989

Native tourists make use of the same infrastructures as the international visitors. They come for the same reasons and want to experience and see the same things as we do. They too have their prejudices which they find confirmed. They too buy their souvenirs and take photographs of the countryside and its people. They visit the same "traditional" villages, look at the few houses that still exist and push their way into domestic communities with the same insolence as the white tourists. Although on close examination this is alarming, to the Batak this increasing interest in them and their (old) culture signifies an intellectual reevaluation of their history and culture.

An exhibition at the ethnographical museum at Delft in 1967 was entitled "De Bataks op Weg" (The Batak on their Way). That way into the future is now less clear than ever. On one side stands the legitimate interests of a great state to bring its various cultures into conformity so that they all participate to the same degree in the national development process. On the other hand there is the danger that one of the main goals of Indonesian social politics, "unity in variety" (*bhinneka tunggal ika*) has fallen by the wayside in this process. Many of the central elements of traditional Batak cultures, such as house building and textiles, are suffering a rapid decline. The process or urbanization and the movement from the countryside to the towns cannot be stemmed, and the pressures to conform in the towns become even stronger (see the writings of Bruner). However, so long as the family system of the Batak with its many relationships of dependence and its respect for the older generation remains in its essentials, future generations will still be conscious of being Batak.

325 Advertisement for family planning. The Batak have the highest birth rate in Indonesia. "Cukup anak dua, putera-puteri sama saja" (Two children are enough, boys and girls are equal). Berastagi, Karo plateau, 1989

326 Street in Binjei, East Coast region. The increasing movement from the countryside to the towns poses almost insurmountable problems for the planning authorities in the towns and cities. 1985

327 Woman in ceremonial dress in front of a grave marked by a heap of stones (*tambak*). Samosir, Lake Toba, c. 1920

List of Illustrations

Bibliography

BKI   *Bijdragen tot de Taal-, Land- en Volkenkunde.* 's-Gravenhage

MNZG   *Mededelingen van wege het Nederlandsch Zendelinggenootschap.* Oegstgeest

NION   *Nederlandsch Indië Oud en Nieuw.* The Hague

RIMA   *Review of Indonesian and Malayan Affairs.* Sydney

TBG   *Tijdschrift voor Indische Taal , Land en Volkenkunde.* Batavia

TKNAG *Tijdschrift van het Koninklijk Aardrijkskundig Genootschap.* Amsterdam

VKI   *Verhandelingen van Koninklijk Instituut.* Leiden

ZfE   *Zeitschrift für Ethnologie.* Braunschweig

Abas, S.P.
1931   De Bataks, hun "Kannibalisme", hun Mythen en Muziek. *De Indische Gids* 53:906-16.

Agthe, J.
1979   *Arm durch Reichtum – Sumatra – Eine Insel am Äquator.* Roter Faden zur Ausstellung 5, Museum für Völkerkunde Frankfurt/Main

Anderson, J.
1971   Mission to the Eastcoast of Sumatra in 1823. London: Oxford University Press [Original ed. publ. 1826].

Bakels, J. & Boer, A.-M. (ed)
1990   *Het wapen van de bruid. Batakse weefsels.* Den Haag

Barbier, J.P.
1983   *Tobaland: the shreds of tradition.* Geneva

1984   *Indonesian Primitive Art.* Dallas: Museum of Art

Barnes, R.H.
1980   Karo Batak Terminology. *BKI* 136: 372-4

Bartlett, H.H.
1921   The Grave-Post of the Batak of Asahan. *Papers of the Michigan Academy of Science, Arts and Letters.* New York 1: 1-58

1930/31 The Labors of the Datoe. *Papers of the Michigan Academy of Science, Arts and Letters.* New York Vol.12 and 14

1934   The sacred edifices of the Batak of Sumatra. Occasional Contributions for the Museum of Anthropology. Ann Arbor

Bellwood, P.
1985   *Prehistory of the Indo-Malaysian Archipelago.* Sydney, Orlando etc.

Berg, E.J.
1920   De parhoedamdambeweging. *MNZG* 64:22-38.

Beyer, U.
1982   *... und viele wurden hinzugetan.* Mission und Gemeindewachstum in der Karo Batak-Kirche. Erlangen

Bieger, J.N.
1917   De cultuur en de Batakzending. *Rijnische Zending* vol. 48

Bodaan, L.
1912   Een reisje in het binnenland van Sumatra's Oostkust. *MNZG* 56:273-92

Boer, D.W.N. de
1914/15 De Permalimsekten van Oeloean, Toba en Habinsaran. *Tijdschrift voor het Binnenlandsch Bestuur. Batavia* 47: 378-93; 48: 184-203

1920   Het Toba-Bataksche huis. *Mededeelingen van het Bureau voor de Bestuurszaken der Buitengewesten bewerkt door het Encyclopaedisch Bureau.* Weltevreden Vol. 23

1921   Het huwelijksrecht bij de Toba-Bataks. *Koloniaal Tijdschrift.* The Hague 10: 76-97; 201-24; 354-71

1922   Een en ander over de herkomst en de uitzwerming der Bataks. *Koloniaal Tijdschrift.* The Hague 11: 86-95

Braasem, W.A.
1951   *Proza en Poezie om het heilige meer der Bataks.* Jakarta, Surabaya, Amsterdam

Breitenstein, H.
1899   *21 Jahre in Indien.* Aus dem Tagebuch eines Militärarztes. 3 vols. vol.1 Borneo; vol.2 Java; vol.3 Sumatra (1902). Leipzig

Brenner, J. Freiherr von
1894   *Besuch bei den Kannibalen Sumatras.* Erste Durchquerung der unabhängigen Batak-Lande. Würzburg

Bronson, B.
1979   The Archaeology of Sumatra and the Problem of Srivijaya. *Smith/Watson* 1979:395-405.

Bruner, E.M.
1959   Toba Batak Village. *Skinner, G.W.* 1959: 52-64

1959a   Kinship organizations among the urban Batak of Sumatra. In: *Transactions of the New York Academy of Sciences* 22, No.2 : 118-25

1961   Urbanization and Ethnic Identity in North Sumatra. *American Anthropologist* 63: 508-21

1963   Medan: The Role of Kinship in an Indonesian City. *Spoehr, A.* (ed.):Pacific Port Towns and Cities. A Symposium; 10. Pac. Sc. Congr., Honolulu (1961) :1-12

1972   Batak Ethnic Associations in three Indonesian Cities. *Southwestern Journal of Anthropology* 28: 207-29

1973   Kin and Non-Kin. *Sonthall, A* (ed.): Urban Anthropology: Crosscultural Studies of Urbanization. New York :379-92

Bruner, E.M. & Becker, J.O. (ed.)
1979   *Art, Ritual and Society in Indonesia.* Ohio University Center for International Studies; Southeast Asia Series No.53

Budaya
1987   *Budaya Indonesia. Kunst en cultuur in Indonesie.* Amsterdam: Tropenmuseum

Burton/Ward
1827   Report of a Journey into the Batak Country, in the interior of Sumatra, in the year 1824. *Transactions of the Royal Asiatic Society, London* 1:485-513

Cameron, E.L:
1985   Ancestors and living men among the Batak. *Feldman, J.* (ed.): 79-100

Carle, R. (ed.)
1987   *Cultures and Societies of North Sumatra.* Veröffentlichungen des Seminars für Indonesische und Südseesprachen der Universität Hamburg; vol.19. Berlin, Hamburg: Reimer.

1990   *Opera Batak. Das Wandertheater der Toba-Batak in Nord-Sumatra. Schauspiele zur Wahrung kultureller Identität im nationalen Kontext.* Veröffentlichungen des Seminars für indonesische und Südseesprachen der Universität Hamburg, vol. 15. Berlin/Hamburg

Carthaus, E.
1891   *Sumatra und der malaiische Archipel.* Leipzig

Cats Baron de Raet, J.A.M.
1875   Reize in de Battaklanden. *TBG* 22: 164-219

Clauss, W.
1986   *Economic and Social Change among the Simalungun Batak of North Sumatra.*
             Bielefelder Studien zur Entwicklungssoziologie 15. Saarbrücken; Fort
             Lauderdale.

Collet, O. J. A.
1925   *Terres et peuples de Sumatra.* Amsterdam

Cunningham, C. E.
1958   *The postwar migration of the Toba-Bataks to East Sumatra.* New Haven: Yale
             University

Dippe, H. W.
1980   *Indonesien: Inselwelt zwischen Asien und Australien.* Munich: Touropa
             Urlaubsberater

Djik, P. A. L. E. van
1893   Rapport betreffende de Si Baloengoensche Landschappen Tandjoeng
             Kasau, Tanah Djawa en Si Antar. *TBG* 37: 145-200

Domenig, G.
1980   *Tektonik im primitiven Dachbau. Materialien und Rekonstruktionen zum
             Phänomen der auskragenden Giebel an alten Dachformen Ostasiens,
             Südostasiens und Ozeaniens.* Zürich

Enter, J.
1933   Het wichelboek der Bataks op Sumatra. *NION* 18:103-11.

Ethnografisch Museum. Delft
1967   *De Bataks op Weg.* Tentoonstelling Oktober 1967– September 1968

Eschels-Kroon, A.
1781   *Beschreibung der Insel Sumatra, besonders in Ansehung des Handels und der
             dahin gehörigen Merkwürdigkeiten.* Hamburg

Feldman, J.
1985   *The eloquent dead. Ancestral sculpture of Indonesia and Southeast Asia.* Los
             Angeles. Museum of Cultural History

Fischer, H.
1965   *Studien über Seelenvorstellungen in Ozeanien.* Munich

Fischer, H. Th.
1940   Over de wordingsgeschiedenis van de Bataksche tooverstaf. *TBG* 80:
             585-610

Fischer, H. W.
1914   *Die Bataklãnder.* Katalog des Ethnographischen Reichsmuseums. Leiden
             vol.8. Leiden

Ginting, J. R.
1986   *Pandangan tentang gangguan jiwa dan penanggulangannya secara tradisional
             pada masyarakat Karo.*
             Unpublished examination paper. Fakultas Sastra.
             Universitas Sumatera Utara. Jurusan Antropologi. Medan.

Ginting, J. R. und Premselaar, B.
1990   De doek met de olifantstanden. Een mythe van de Karo Batak.
             Bakels/Boer 11–16

Gittinger, M. S.
1975 a   Selected Batak Textiles: Technique and Function.
             Textile Museum Journal 4, no.2:13-26

1975 b   Additional Batak Cloths That Frequently Enter Into The Gift Exchange.
             Textile Museum Journal 4, no.2:26-29

1979   *Indonesian Textiles. Irene Emery Roundtable on Museum Textiles. Proceedings.*
             Washington, D.C.: Textile Museum

Glover, I. C.
1979   The Late Prehistoric Period in Indonesia. *Smith/Watson* 1979:167-84.

Godon, A. P.
1862   De assistentresidentie Mandaheling en Ankola, op Sumatra's Westkust, van
             1847 tot 1857.
             Tijdschrift voor Nederlandsch Indië 24: 1-46

Gonda, J.
1973   *Sanskrit in Indonesia.* New Delhi (2nd ed.).

Gruyter, J. de
1941   Bataksche plastiek. *Cultureel Indië.* Leiden 3: 123-32

Haan, C. de
1875   Verslag van eene reis in de Battaklanden. *VBG* 38: 1-57

Haberland, M.
1886   Ueber die Battaschrift. *Mitteilungen der Anthropologischen Gesellschaft
             in Wien* 16 (N.F.6) S.7-10.

Haeckel, E.
1909   *Aus Insulinde. Malayische Reisebriefe.* Leipzig (2nd ed.)

Hagen, B.
1883   Beiträge zur Kenntnis der Battareligion. *TBG* 28: 498-545

1884   Die künstlichen Verunstaltungen des Körpers bei den Batta. *ZfE* 16:
             217-225

1886   Rapport über eine im Dezember 1883 unternommene wissenschaftliche
             Reise an den Toba-See. *TBG* 31: 328-82

Hall, K. R.
1976   State and Statecraft in Early Srivijaya. Hall, K. R./J. K. Whitmore (ed.)
             Explorations in Early Southeast Asian History. S. 61-105. Ann Arbor:
             Michigan Papers on South and Southeast Asia II.

Hardjono, J. M.
1977   *Transmigration in Indonesia.* Oxford

Hasibuan, J. S.
1985   *Art et culture/ Seni Budaya Batak.* Jakarta

Heine-Geldern, R.
1932   Urheimat und früheste Wanderungen der Austronesier.
             Anthropos 27. Wien. S.543-619.

Heintze, R.
1909   Über Batak-Musik. *Volz, W.* 1909: 373-81.

Helbig, K.
1934   *Tuan Gila. Ein "verrückter Herr" wandert am Äquator.* Leipzig

1935   Der Singa Mangaradja und die Sekte der Pormalim bei den Batak. *ZfE*
             67: 88-104

1938   Das südliche Batakland auf Sumatra. *Ostasiatische Rundschau.*
             Hamburg 19: 278-81; 302-5; 329-32; 491-3; 515-7; 540-2

Henny, W. A.
1869   Reis naar Si Gompoelon en Si Lindong in Maart en April 1858. Bjidrage tot
             de kennis der Battaklanden. *TBG* 17: 1-58

Heyting, Th. L.
1897   Beschrijving der Onderafdeeling Groot-Mandeling en Batang-Natal.
             TKNAG 14: 209-320

Hoevell, G. W. W. C. van
1878   Iets over't oorlogvoeren der Batta's. *Tijdschrift voor Nederlandsch Indië.*
             Zalt-Bommel etc. 7: 431-45

Holt, C.
1971   Dances of Sumatra and Nias: Notes by Claire Holt.
             Indonesia 11: 1-20; 12: 65-84.

Huender, W.
1929   Het Karo-Bataksche huis. *BKI* 85: 511-23

Huyser, J. G.
1927/28   Bataksche ruiterbeeldjes. *NION* 12: 38-63
1928/29   Indonesische muziekinstrumenten. *NION* 13: 235-47

Italiaander, R.
1979   *Die Südsee – auch eine Herausforderung. Tagebücher eines Individualisten aus Indonesien und Papua Niugini.* Düsseldorf

Janssen, C. W.
1886   *Die holländische Kolonialwirtschaft in den Battaländern.* Diss. Straßburg
1924   De Bataks als exploitanten van hun eigen gebied. *Koloniaal Tijdschrift.* The Hague 13: 353 75

Jasper, J. E. & Pirngadie, M.
1912   *De Inlandsche Kunstnijverheid. Bd.2 De Weefkunst.* 's-gravenhage

Joustra, M.
1899   Verslag van een bezoek aan het onafhankelijk Karo-Batakgebied (I). *MNZG* 43: 123-51.
1901   Naar het landschap Goenoeng-Goenoeng: 15–22 October 1900. *MNZG* 43: 123-51.
1901a   Een en ander uit de litteratuur der Karo. *MNZG* 45: 91-101.
1901b   Iets over bataksche litteratuur. *MNZG* 45: 165-85.
1902   Het Persilihi Mbelin. *MNZG* 46: 1-22.
1902   Iets over bataksche litteratuur. *MNZG* 46: 357-72.
1902a   Mededeelingen omtrent en opmerkingen naar aanleiding van het pekoelawoeh of het doodenfeest der Marga Sembiring. *TBG* 45: 541-56
1902b   Eene verklaring van den naam van het Sembiring'sche doodenfeest. *TBG* 46: 472-75
1903   Iets over bataksche litteratuur. *MNZG* 47: 140-65.
1904   *Karo-Bataksche Vertellingen.* Verhandelingen van het Bataviaasch Genootschap van Kunsten en Wetenschappen. Deel 56/1.
1907   *Literatuuroverzicht der Bataklanden.* Leiden
1910   *Batakspiegel.* Uitgaven van het Bataksch Instituut No.3. Leiden.
1914   *Toeri-Toerin Karo* (1). Leiden.
1918   *Toeri-Toerin Karo* (2). Leiden.
1926   *Batakspiegel.* Uitgaven van het Bataksch Instituut No.21 Leiden 2nd ed.

Junghuhn, F.
1847   *Die Batta-Länder auf Sumatra … 1840–1841 untersucht und beschrieben.* 2 vols., Berlin

Kaarsberg, H.
1923   *Mein Sumatrabuch.* Berlin/Leipzig

Kartomi, M. J.
1976   Gondang Music of the Mandailing People, North Sumatra. *Akten des 29. internationalen Orientalisten Kongresses.* Paris: 105-9.
1981   "Lovely when heard from afar": Mandailing ideas of musical beauty. *Kartomi, M. J.* (ed): Five Essays on the Indonesian Arts. Monash University : 1-16
1981   Dualism in Unity: the ceremonial music of the Mandailing Raja tradition. *Asian Music.* New York 12: 74-108

Kessel, O. von
1854   Erinnerungen an Sumatra. *Das Ausland.* Stuttgart 27: 905-8
1854 a   Eine Reise in die noch unabhängigen Batta-Länder von Klein-Toba auf Sumatra in 1844. *Das Ausland.* Stuttgart 27: 736-42, 760-67

Keuning, J.
1952   De Toba Bataks vroeger en nu. *Indonesië* 6: 160-82

Khan Majlis, B.
1984   *Indonesische Textilien. Wege zu Göttern und Ahnen.* Cologne: Rautenstrauch-Joest-Museum

Kielstra, E. B.
1920   *De vestiging van het nederlandsche gezag in den indischen archipel.* Haarlem.

Kipp, R. S.
1974   Karo Batak Religion and Social Structure. *Berita Kajian Sumatera – Sumatra Research Bulletin* University of Hull 3 (2): 5-11

Koentjaraningrat
1967   *Villages of Indonesia.* Ithaca: Cornell University

Korn, V. E.
1953   Batakse offerande. *BKI* 109: 32-51, 97-127

Kozok, U.
1989   *Bilang-bilang. Die Klagelieder der Karo-Batak.* Unpublished MA dissertation. Hamburg

Kroesen, J. A.
1886   Geschiedenis van Asahan. *TBG* 31: 82-139
1893   Eene reis door de Landschappen Tandjoeng Kassau, Siantar en Tanah Djawa. *TBG* 39: 229-304

Kruijt, A. C.
1906   *Het animisme in den Indischen Archipel.* 's-gravenhage

Kruijt, H. C.
1891   Bezoekreis op het Plateau van Deli (Karoland). *MNZG* 35: 309-407

Kubitschek, H. D. & Wessel, I.
1981   *Geschichte Indonesiens. Vom Altertum bis zur Gegenwart.* Berlin

Kunstmann, F.
1863   *Die Kenntnis Indiens im 15. Jahrhundert.* Munich

Langenberg, M. van
1977   North Sumatra under Dutch colonial rule: aspects of structural change. *RIMA* 11,1:74-110; 11,2: 45-86
1982   Class and ethnic conflict in Indonesia's decolonization process: a study of East Sumatra. *Indonesia* 33: 1-30

La Rue, C. de
1931   The weapons of the Asahan Bataks. *Papers of the Michigan Academy of Science, Arts and Letters.* New York 16: 73-104

Leertouwer, L.
1977   *Het beeld van de ziel bij drie Sumatraanse volken.* Diss. theol. Groningen

Lekkerkerker, C.
1916   *Land en volk van Sumatra.* Leiden

Liddle, W.
1970   *Ethnicitiy, party and national integration. An Indonesian case study.* New Haven: Yale Southeast Asian Studies 7

L[ingen], v.
1890   De nieuwe zending onder de Battaks. Overgenommen uit de Deli-Courant van 1. en 5. Februari 1890. *MNZG* 34: 210-22.

Loeb, E. M. & Heine-Geldern, R.
1935   *Sumatra.* Wiener Beiträge zur Kulturgeschichte und Linguistik vol.3

Lorm, A. J. de
1939   Bataksche maskers in de Haagsche volkenkundige verzameling. *Cultureel Indië* 1: 48-53
1940   De sigale-gale van Radja Gajoes. *Cultureel Indië* 2: 217-9
1941   Verdwijnende Bataksche cultuur. *De Natuur.* Utrecht 61: 120-4

Lorm, A. J. de & Tichelman, G. L.
1941   *Beeldende Kunst der Bataks.* Leiden

Lumbantobing, A.
1978   *Si Aji Donda Hatahutan dan Panghulubalang.* Departement Pendidikan dan Kebudayaan. Proyek Pembinaan Buku Baca dan Sastra Daerah.

McKinnon, E. E.
1987   New Light on the Indianization of the Karo Batak.
        Carle, R. (ed.) 1987: 81-110.

Manik, L.
1973   *Batak Handschriften.* Verzeichnis der orientalischen Handschriften in Deutschland. vol.28. Wiesbaden.

Manik, L.
1973/74 Eine Studienreise zur Erforschung der rituellen Gondang-Musik der Batak auf Nord-Sumatra. *Mitteilungen der Deutschen Gesellschaft für Musik des Orients.* Hamburg: 134-7.

Marschall, W.
1967   Die indonesischen Handschriften von Sumatra.
        Studium Generale 20, no. 9: 559-64.

Marsden, W.
1966   *History of Sumatra.*
        Kuala Lumpur: Oxford University Press. repr. 1975

Martin, F.
1891   Reise nach den Bataklanden und an den Tobasee. *Jahresbericht der geographischen Gesellschaft München* 14: 53-66

Meerwaldt, J. H.
1894   Aanteekeningen betreffende de Bataklanden. *TBG* 37: 513-550

1903   *Pidari of het strijd van het licht tegen de duisternis in de Bataklanden.* Utrecht

M.(eulen), D. v. D.
1925   Wij willen Batakkers blijven. *NION* 10:130-5

Middendorp, W.
1929   The administration of the outer provinces of the Netherlands Indië.
        Schrieke, B. (ed.): 54-6.

Miksic, J. N.
1979   *Archaeology, Trade and Society in Northeast Sumatra.* (Ph. D. Dissertation Cornell University) Ithaca.

Miller, C.
1778   An Account of the Island of Sumatra. *Philosophical Transactions of the Royal Society of London.* 68: 160-79

Millner, A. C. & McKinnon, E. E. & Sinar, T. L.
1978   A Note on Aru and Kota Cina. *Indonesia* 26: 1-42

Modigliani, E.
1892   *Fra i Batacchi Indipendenti.* Rome

Moor, M. de & Kal, W. H.
1983   *Indonesische Sieraden.* Amsterdam: Tropenmuseum

Moore, L.
1981   An Introduction to the Music of the Pakpak Dairi of North Sumatra.
        Indonesia Circle 24: 39-46. London.

Müller, F. W. K.
1893   *Beschreibung einer von G. Meissner zusammengestellten Batak-Sammlung.* Berlin

Müller-Krüger, Th.
1968   *Der Protestantismus in Indonesien. Geschichte und Gestalt.* Stuttgart

Münsterberger, W.
1939   *Ethnologische Studien an Indonesischen Schöpfungsmythen. Ein Beitrag zur Kultur-Analyse Südostasiens.* The Hague

Needham, R.
1978   Classification and Alliance among the Karo: an Appreciation. *BKI* 134: 116-48

Neumann, J. H.
1902a   Verslag aangande den toestand der zendingwerkzamheden en der gemeente in het ressort Sibolangit over het jaar 1901. *MNZG* 46: 63-74.

1902b   De begoe in de godsdienstige begrippen der Karo-Bataks in de Doesoen. *MNZG* 46: 23-39

1903   De Smid. *MNZG* 47: 15-20

1904 ff Een en ander aangaande de Karo-Bataks.
        MNZG: 48: 361-77; 49: 54-67; 50: 27-40, 347-364

1904   De tendi in verband met Si Dajang. *MNZG* 48: 101-45

1907   *Erbagé-bagé toeri-toerin* (1). Rotterdam.

1910   De Bataksche Goeroe. *MNZG* 54: 1-18.

1911   *Erbagé-bagé toeri-toerin* (2). Rotterdam.

1918   De parhoedamdam in Deli. *MNZG* 62: 185-90.

1920   Een mensch als "persilihi". *MNZG* 64: 260-3

1926/7 Bijdrage tot de geschiedenis de Karo-Batakstammen.
        BKI 82: 1-36; 83: 162-80

1927   Karo-Batakse offerplaatsen. *BKI* 83: 514-51

1929   De bilang-bilang. *Feestbundel Bataviaasch Genootschap voor Kunsten en Wetenschappen II*: 215-22.

1930   Poestaka Ginting. *TBG* 70: 1-51.

1933a   Bilang-bilang I. *TBG* 73: 184-215.

1933b   Aanteekeningen over de Karo-Bataks. *TBG* 79: 529-71

1939   Twee metalen voorwerpen uit de Bataklanden. *TBG* 79: 275f

1951   *Karo-Bataks – Nederlands woordenboek.* Medan

Niessen, S. A.
1981   *Batak Motieven.* Groningen: Volkenkundig Museum Gerardus van der Leeuw

1985 a Waarom het garen van de godin der Toba Batak zwart was.
        Oei, L. 1985: 137-144

1985 b *Motifs Of Life In Toba Batak Texts And Textiles.* Dordrecht (VKI 110)

Nieuwenhuis, A. W.
1913   Die Veranlagung der malaiischen Völker des ostindischen Archipels erläutert an ihren industriellen Erzeugnissen.
        Internationales Archiv für Ethnographie. Leiden 21, Suppl. :1-56

Noordman, W. E.
1935   De economische ontwikkeling der Bataklanden. *Tijd. voor Economische Geografie.* vol. 26/1: 1-9, 30-43, 54-61

Oei, L.
1985   *Indigo – Leven in een Kleur.* Amsterdam

Ophuijsen, C. A. van
1912   Der Bataksche Zauberstab. *Internationales Archiv für Ethnographie.* Leiden 20: 82-103

Otten, M.
1986   *Transmigrasi: Indonesian Resettlement Policy, 1965-1985. Myths and Realities.* Copenhagen (IWGIA Doc. 57)

Parkin, H.
1978   *Batak Fruit of Hindu Thought.* Madras

Pedersen, P. B.
1970   *Batak blood and protestant soul: the development of national Batak churches in North Sumatra.* Grand Rapids

Pelzer, K. J.
1961 Western impact on East Sumatra and North Tapanuli. The roles of the planter and the missionary. *Journal of Southeast Asian History*. Singapore 2: 66-71

1978 *Planter and Peasant, colonial policy and the agrarian struggle in East Sumatra 1863-1947.* (VKI 84). 's-Gravenhage

1985 *Toean Keboen dan petani: Politik kolonial dan perjuangan agraria.* Jakarta: Sinar Harapan.

Pfeiffer, I.
1856 *Meine zweite Weltreise. 4 Bde. Bd.2 Sumatra-Java-Celebes-Molukken.* Vienna

Plevte, C. M.
1894 *Bataksche Vertellingen.* Utrecht.

Poortenaar, J.
1928 Bespiegelingen bij de spiegelingen van het Toba-Meer. *Buiten. Geïllustreerd Weekblad aan het Buitenleven gewijd.* 22.Jg. No.27; 7.Juli : 316-8; 14.Juli : 328-30

Putro, B.
1981 *Karo: Dari Jaman ke Jaman.* Medan.

Radermacher, J. C. M.
1781 Beschrijving van het eiland Sumatra. *Verhandelingen van het Bataviaasch Genootschap voor Kunsten en Wetenschapen.* Batavia 3: 3-144

Reid, A. (ed.)
1979 *The Blood of the People – Revolution and the End of Traditional Rule in Northern Sumatra.* Kuala Lumpur/New York

1983 *Slavery, Bondage and Dependency in Southeast Asia.* New York

Ridder, J. de
1935 *De invloed van den westersche cultures op de autochtone bevolking ter Oostkust van Sumatra.* Wageningen

Rodgers-Siregar, S.
1979 Blessing Shawls: The Social Meaning Of Sipirok Batak Ulos. *Gittinger, M:* 1979: 96-114

1979 Advice to the newly weds: Sipirok Batak weeding speechs – adat or art? *Bruner/Becker* 1979: 30-61

Rodgers, S.
1985 *Power and Gold. Jewelry from Indonesia, Malaysia, and the Philippines.* Geneva

1986 Batak tape cassette kinship: constructing kinship through the Indonesian national mass media. *American Ethnologist* 13,1: 23-42

Rosenberg, H. von
1878 *Der malayische Archipel, Land und Leute in Schilderungen, gesammelt während 30jährigem Aufenthalt in den Kolonien.* Leipzig

Saragih, J. E. & Dalimunte, A. A.
o. J. *Pustaha Laklak No.252 Museum Simalungun & Pustaha Laklak Mandailing.* Proyek Pengembangan Media Kebudayaan Departement P&K. Jakarta [published 1983 or 1984].

Schadee, W. H. M.
1920 *De uitbreiding van ons gezag in de Bataklanden.* Leiden.

Schnitger, F. M.
1937 The archaeology of Hindoo Sumatra. *Internationales Archiv für Ethnographie.* Suppl. to vol.35

1964 *Forgotten Kingdoms in Sumatra.* Leiden

Schoffel, A.
1981 *Arts primitifs de L'Asie du Sud-Est.* Paris

Schreiner, L.
1970 Gondang-Musik als Überlieferungsgestalt altvölkischer Lebensordnung. *BKI* 126: 400-28.

1972 *Adat und Evangelium. Zur Bedeutung der altvölkischen Lebensordnung für Kirche und Mission unter den Batak in Nordsumatra.* (Missionswissenschaftliche Forschungen No.7) Gütersloh

Schrieke, B. (ed.)
1929 *The effect of western influence on native civilizations in the Malay Archipelago.* Batavia

Sell, H. J.
1955 *Der schlimme Tod bei den Völkern Indonesiens.* 's-Gravenhage

Sembiring, T.
1987 Lagu "Mengungsi". Sada Lagu Perjuangan Kemerdekaan I Indonesia / Song of Evacuation. A Song of Fighting for Independence in Indonesia. *Carle, R.* 1987:394-428.

Siahaan, M. A.
1964 *Umpamana ni halak Batak.* Medan (4th ed.)

Sibeth, A.
1986 *Das Sparschwein unter dem Reisfeld. Java zwischen Gestern und Heute.* Roter Faden zur Ausstellung 10, Museum für Völkerkunde Frankfurt/Main

1988 Seelenboote und bootsförmige Särge. Anmerkungen zum Totenkult der Karo-Batak in Nord-Sumatra. *Tribus.* Stuttgart 37: 119-38

Simon, A.
1982 Altreligiöse und soziale Zeremonien der Batak. *ZfE* 107: 177-206

1987 Social and Religious Functions of Batak Ceremonial Music. *Carle* 1987:337-50.

Sinaga, A. B.
1981 *The Toba-Batak High God. Transcendence and Immanence.* St. Augustin: Studia Instituti Anthropos vol. 38

Sinar, T. L.
1980 Perang besar dalam kampung kecil: Riwayat perjuangan rakyat Sunggal. *Prisma* 8. Jakarta.

Singarimbun, M.
1967 Kuta Gamber, a village of the Karo. *Koentjaraningrat* :115-28

1975 *Kinship, descent and alliance among the Karo Batak.* Los Angeles, London

Sitepu, A. G.
1980 a *Ragam Hias (Ornamen) Karo.* Seri: A. Kabanjahe

1980b *Mengenal Seni Kerajinan Tradisional.* Karo. Seri:B. Kabanjahe

Skinner, G. W. (ed.)
1959 *Local, ethnic and national loyalities in village Indonesia.* New Haven: Yale University

Slaats, H. M. C. & Portier, M. K.
1981 *Grondenrecht en zun verwerkelijking in de Karo Batakse Dorpssamenleving. Een beschrijvende studie.* Diss Nijmegen

Smith, R. B./Watson W. (ed.)
1979 *Early South East Asia.* New York

1984 Introduction [to Early South East Asia]. *Van de Velde* 1984: 79-92.

Smith Kipp, R.
1974 Karo Batak religion and social structure. *Berita Kajian Sumatra – Sumatra Research Bulletin.* University of Hull 3,2 : 4-11

1979 The Thread of three Colors: the Ideology of Kinship in Karo Batak Funerals. *Bruner/Becker* 1979: 62-95

1986 Terms of endearment: Karo Batak lovers as siblings. *American Ethnologist* 13,4: 632-45

Smith Kipp, R. & Kipp, R. D. (ed.)
1983   *Beyond Samosir: Recent Studies of the Batak Peoples of Sumatra.* Papers in International Studies; Southeast Asia Series No.62. Athens, Ohio

Soejono, R. P.
1984   Prehistoric Indonesia. *Van de Velde 1984:* 49-78.

Steedly, M. M.
1988   Severing the Bonds of Love: A Case Study in Soul Loss. *Social, Science and Medicine* 27 (8): 841-56.

Steinmann, A.
1939/40   Das kultische Schiff in Indonesien. *Jahrbuch für prähistorische und ethnographische Kunst.* 13/14: 149-205

Stöhr, W.
1965   Die Religionen der Altvölker Indonesiens und der Philippinen. *Stöhr/Zoetmulder 1965:* 1-221

1967   Inleiding. Ethnografisch Museum, Delft. *De Bataks op weg.*: 9-23

1976   *Die altindonesischen Religionen.* Handbuch der Orientalistik 3. Abt. 2.Bd. Abschnitt 2. Leiden/Cologne

Stöhr, W. & Zoetmulder, P.
1965   *Die Religionen Indonesiens.* Die Religionen der Menschheit vol. 5,1 Stuttgart etc.

Stöhr, W. & al.
1981   *Art des Indonesiens archaïques.* Geneva

Tichelman, G. L.
1937   Toenggal panaloean, de Bataksche tooverstaf. *TBG* 77: 611-34

1938   Over Bataksche Weefsels. *Natuur en Mens.* Utrecht 58,1: 64-8

1939   Van Bataksche dingen, die verdwijnen. *De Indische Gids.* Amsterdam 61: 537-43

1939   Si gale-gale, de Bataksche doodenpop. *Cultureel Indië.* 1: 106-12

1939   Bataksche maskerplastiek. *Cultureel Indië.* 1: 378-88

1941   Exegese van den Batakschen tooverstaf. *De Natuur.* Utrecht. 61: 36-42; 88-93

1942   Een Bataksch bronzen bultenaartje. *Cultureel Indië.* 4: 17-9

1942   Tooverteekens en symbolen van Indonesie. *Tichelman/de Gruyter (ed.):* 211-85

1949   *Batakse Kunst.* Amsterdam

1950   Een oud geloof. De dansende dodenpop der Bataks. *Oost en West* 43, No.21: 8-12

Tichelman, G. L. & Gruyter, W. J. de
1942   *Tooverteekens en symbolen van Indonesie.* 's-Graveland

Tideman, J.
1922   *Simeloengoen. Het Land der Timoer-Bataks.* Leiden.

1932   *De Bataklanden 1917-1931.* Uitgaven van het Bataksch Instituut No. 22. Leiden

1936   *Hindoeinvloed in noordelijk Batakland.* Uitgaven van het Bataksch Instituut No.23. Amsterdam

Tillmann, G.
1940   De motieven der Batakweefsels. *Cultureel Indië* 2: 7-15

Tobing, P. L.
1956   *The structure of the Toba Batak belief in the high god.* Diss. Amsterdam

Tuuk, H. N. van der
1861 a,b   *Bataksch Leesboek (2). Stukken in het Mandailingsch. (3) Stukken in het Dairisch.* Amsterdam.

1862   *Bataksch Leesboek (4). Taalkundig aantekeningen en bladwijzer, vertaalde stukken en inhoudsopgave tot de drie stukken van het Bataksch Leesboek.* Amsterdam.

Van de Velde, P.
1984   *Prehistoric Indonesia: A Reader.* Dordrecht (VKI 104)

Vergouwen, J. C.
1964   *The social organization and customary law of the Toba Batak of Northern Sumatra.* The Hague

Veth, P. J.
1877   Het landschap Deli op Sumatra. *TKNAG* 2: 152-70.

Viner, A. C.
1979   The Changing Batak. *Journal of the Royal Asiatic Society; Malayan Branch* 52: 84-109

Volhard, E.
1939   *Kannibalismus.* Frankfurt: Studien zur Kulturkunde 5

Voorhoeve, P.
1927   *Overzicht van de volksverhalen der Bataks.* Vlissingen Diss.phil. Leiden.

1939   Enkele Bataksche mededeelingen over de sigale-gale. *TBG* 79: 179-92

1939   Het stamhuis der Sitoemorangs van Lontoeng. *Cultureel Indië* 1: 284-91

1940   De dans met de bedjan. *BKI* 99: 339-56

1949   *Pengetahuan zaman bahari.* Pematang Siantar.

1951   Batak bark books. *Bulletin of the John Rylands Library.* Manchester 33/2: 283-98

1958   Bataske buffelwichelarij. *BKI* 114: 238-48

1961   *A catalogue of the Batak manuscripts in the Chester Beatty Library.* Dublin.

1969   Four Batak Manuscripts in Princeton. *The Princeton University Library Chronicle* 30: 158-70

1972   Catalogisering van de batakse handschriften. *Open Deventer* 4: 720-6.

1974   Some remarks on Karo literature. *Berita Kajian Sumatera – Sumatra Research Bulletin* University of Hull 3/2 : 39-42.

1975   *Catalogue of Indonesian Manuscripts. Pt. 1: Batak manuscripts in Danish collections.* Copenhagen.

1977   *Codices Batacici. Codices Manuscripti XIX.* Leiden.

1979/80   Elio Modigliani's Batak Books. *Archivio per L'Antropologia e la Etnologia.* Florence 109/110: 61-96

1985   Batak-Handschriften. Theodore G.Th. Pigeaud, *Handschriften aus Indonesien,* Verzeichnis der orientalischen Handschriften in Deutschland vol.28.2, Stuttgart

Volz, W.
1899   Zum Toba-See in Central-Sumatra. *TKNAG* 16: 415-85

1899   Hausbau und Dorfanlage bei den Battakern in Nord-Sumatra. *Globus.* 75: 318-25

1909   *Nord Sumatra. Bericht über eine im Auftrag der Humboldt-Stiftung der Königlich preussischen Akademie der Wissenschaften zu Berlin in den Jahren 1904-1906 ausgeführte Forschungsreise.* vol. 1. Die Batakländer. Berlin.

Warneck, J.
1904   Der bataksche Ahnen- und Geisterglaube. *Allgemeine Missionszeitschrift.* Berlin 31: 3-14, 65-79

1909   *Die Religion der Batak. Ein Paradigma für die animistischen Religionen des Indischen Archipels.* Leipzig

1915   Das Opfer bei den Toba-Batak. *Archiv für Religionswissenschaft.* Leipzig 18: 333-384

1922   *Die Lebenskräfte des Evangeliums: Missionserfahrungen innerhalb des animistischen Heidentums.* Berlin 6th ed.; repr. Bad Liebenzell 1986

1931   Batak-Frauen. *Welt und Wissen.* Berlin 20, no.39: 289-95

1939   *Sumatranische Plaudereien.* Berlin

1977   *Toba-Batak – Deutsches Wörterbuch.* The Hague

Wassing-Visser, R. & Klokke, M.
1984   *Sieraden en lichaamsversiering uit Indonesie.* Delft: Volkenkundig Museum Nusantara

Wegner, R.
1900   *Einzelzüge aus der Arbeit der Rheinischen Mission.* Gütersloh

Westenberg, C.W.
1904   *Nota omtrent eene militaire excursie naar de Karolanden in September 1904.* Rijksarchief The Hague.

Westenberg, C.J.
1892   Aanteekeningen omtrent de godsdienstige begrippen der Karo-Bataks. *BKI* 41: 208-53

1897   Verslag eener reis naar de onafhankelijke Bataklanden ten noorden van het Tobameer. *TKNAG* 14: 1-112

1914   Adatrechtspraak en Adatrechtpleging der Karo Batak's. *BKI* 69: 453-600.

Willer, T.
1846   Verzameling der Battahsche wetten en instellingen in Mandheling en pertibi; gevolgt van een overzigt van land en volk in die streken. *Tijdschrift voor Nederlandsch Indië* 8,2: 145-424

1849   The Batta's of Mandeling and Pertibi. *Journal of the Indian Archipelago.* 3: 366-78

Willis, J. & Diamondstein, M.
1979   *Sculpture of the Batak.* San Francisco

Winkler, J.
1913   Der Kalender der Toba-Batak auf Sumatra. *ZFE* 45: 434-47

1925   *Die Toba-Batak auf Sumatra in gesunden und kranken Tagen.* Ein Beitrag zur Kenntnis des animistischen Heidentums. Stuttgart

1954   Das Zauberbuch von Batipuh. *BKI* 110: 335-68

1956   Pane na Bolon, ein Kriegsorakel der Toba-Batak auf Sumatra. Mit einer Nachschrift von P. Voorhoeve. *BKI* 112: 25-40

Wirz, P.
1926/27   De dans met den tooverstaf. *NION* 11: 131-43

1929   Der Bataksche Zauberstab. *Atlantis* 1: 20-4

Wolfram-Seifert, U.
1982   Die Agglomeration Medan. Entwicklung, Struktur und Funktion des domierenden Oberzentrums auf Sumatra. *Mitteilungen der Geographischen Gesellschaft Hamburg* 72: 117-75

Wolters, O.W.
1967   *Early Indonesian Commerce. A Study of the Origins of Srivijaya.* Ithaca, New York.

Ydema, J.M.
1966   Aantekeningen bij het Toba-Bataks Huismasker en andere Batakse voorwerpen, hoofdzakelijk in verband met de Hagedis. *Kultuurpatronen.* Delft 8: 5-78

Ypes, W.K.H.
1907   Nota omtrent Singkel en de Pakpak landen. *TBG* 49: 355-642

1932   *Bijdrage tot de kennis van de stamverwantschap, de inheemsche rechtsgemeenschapen en het grondenrecht der Toba- en Dairi Batak.* s'Gravenhage.

1944   De Bataks en de tempelbouwvallen in Padang Lawas en Mandailing. *Cultureel Indië* 6: 135-43

Glossary

adat   Code of behaviour and law handed down by oral tradition and covering all aspects of daily and ceremonial life.

alaman   Open area in Toba villages between the houses and granaries, used as a working area or place for festivals.

anak mata   Free citizens in a Toba village, usually related to the family of the founder of the village

anakberu   Kinship group of the "wife-takers". Karo Batak.

balé   Assembly house, formerly built on posts but now a roofed concrete platform, used for special events and weddings. Karo Batak.

beberé   The mother's clan. Karo Batak.

bégu   Death soul, set free at a person's death. Karo Batak (Toba: *begu*)

bégu jabu   Spirits which dwell in the living area of an individual family and to which sacrifices are made. Karo Batak.

bicara guru   Death souls of stillborn children which could be made into guardian spirits for the family. Karo Batak.

borotan   Sacrifice post in a Toba village at which animals are sacrificed.

boru   Kinship group of the "wife-takers". Toba Batak.

buli-buli   Medicine container made from the horn of the mountain antilope with a wooden stopper in the form of a figure. Karo Batak

dalihan na tolu   The kinship system based on the three kinship groups, *dongan sabutuha*, *hulahula* and *boru*. Toba Batak.

datu   Religious specialist of the Toba Batak, see *guru*.

debata idup   Wooden sculptures of the ancestral couple kept on the *raga-raga*. Toba Batak.

dongan sabutuha   Those who come from the "same womb", i.e. one's own blood relations. Toba Batak.

dusun   Piedmont zone east of the Bukit-Barisan range. Settlement area of the Karo Batak outside the high plateau.

erpangir kulau   Ritual hair washing in honour of a *bicara guru*. Karo Batak

ersilih   Ritual for healing the sick in which a substitute figure (*persilih*) is carved. Karo Batak.

gajah dompak   Synonym for *singa*. *Gajah* is Sanskrit and means "elephant"; *dompak* means "looking forwards". Toba Batak.

gambir   (Uncaria Gambir Roxb.) Important ingredient, together with the betel leaf, betel nut and lime, in *sirih*.

guru   Religious specialist, particularly skilled in fortunetelling, healing and the use of black magic. Karo Batak.

hantu   Nature spirits which live on mountains, in ravines and similar places.

hatoban   Slaves. Slavery was abolished by a decree of the Dutch colonial government.

hombung   Chest for food and valuables, used by a *raja* as a bed. Toba Batak.

hulahula   Kinship group of the "wife-givers". Toba Batak.

ijuk   Fibre of the sugar palm used as roofing material and for ropes.

jabu   Nuclear family of the Karo Batak; also the living area of such a family in the *rumah adat*. (Toba: traditional develling house)

jambur   Granaries of the Karo Batak, used as a sleeping place by unmarried men and guests.

jinujung   Personal guardian spirits of the Karo Batak, which can dwell near the body or in the head or throat of the bearer. Karo Batak.

joro   Bone house in the style of a *rumah adat*. Toba Batak.

kalimbubu   Kinship group of the "wife-givers". Karo Batak.

karajaan   Smaller units of power below *urung* level in the Simalungun region. Ruled by a *tuan*.

kasar   Javanese: "coarse, unpolished".

kemenyan   Tree which produces benzoin resin.

kepala desa   Mayor of a village. Not elected but appointed by the administration.

kerja tahun   Harvest thanksgiving festival held by the Karo and Pakpak up to three months after the harvest, depending on the country.

kesain   Relatively autonomous part of a Karo village, which was under the leadership of a *pengulu kesain*.

kubur   A burial mound surrounded by a stones, raised up over the coffin. For distinguished people. Toba Batak.

lesung   Rice-pounding house for women in the centre of a Karo village. It was an important meeting place in the morning and evening.

mangongkal holi Ceremony at which the exhumed bones of ancestors are reburied. Toba Batak.

marga Patrilinear and exogamous family groups (clans and subclans) among the Toba Batak.

marga raja Ruling family in a particular region.

maté sada-uari The death soul of a family member who has died unexpectedly, which is then made a guardian spirit. Karo Batak.

merga Patrilinear and exogamous family groups (clans and subclans) among the Karo Batak.

musuh bergni Threatening letters of the Karo Batak, a final means of making demands, which is outside the law.

naga marsarang Vessel for magic substances made from the horn of the water buffalo. Toba Batak.

namora-mora Ruling aristocratic class among the Mandailing Batak.

nurun-nurun Ceremony at which the exhumed bones of ancestors are burned or reburied. Karo Batak.

pagar Apotropaic object in the shape of a figure of stone or wood, or of vegetable materials, to be taken or hung up in the house.

pangulubalang A spirit that had been made obedient by a datu and was effective as a front fighter in wars; it could also warn of misfortune.

para-para Four-cornered frame hanging above the fireplace, in which wood and tools are stored. Karo Batak.

parholian Stone sarcophagi hewn from a block of stone. Toba Batak.

parhudamdam Pan-Batak messianic movement which started in 1917 and spread the belief in the resurrection of the *Si Singamangaraja*.

pekualuh Festival of the dead of the Sembiring si ngombak, at which the ashes of the dead are delivered to the river on a soulboat. Karo Batak.

pelangkah Boat-shaped coffin with a hornbill head and wooden figures. Karo Batak.

pengeret-ret Lizard-shaped ornaments on the façade of Karo houses.

pengulu Title of a Karo village elder.

perbégu Traditional religion of the Karo Batak, also called *pemena*.

perminaken Medicine containers in various forms.

persilih Substitute figure carved from the trunk of a banana tree, which the *guru* can use to draw sickness away from the patient. Karo Batak.

piso Literally: knife. At a wedding all presents given to the bride's parents by the wife-takers are so called. Toba Batak.

poda Old religious priests' language in which the pustaha are written.

pohung Wooden staff with figural carvings, sometimes with containers for magic ingredients. Toba Batak.

porsili Toba Batak word for *persilih*.

pupuk Magic mixture prepared by a *guru/datu* from parts of the body of a kidnapped and murdered child.

pustaha Books written by *guru/datu* in ritual language on bast.

raga-raga House altar for the ancestral parents which was hung in the roof of the oldest house of a *marga*.

raja Village chief from the family of the founder of the village, usually elected.

raja berempat "The four *raja*". A power structure initiated by the Sultan of Aceh in the Karo and Simalungun region, where it called *raja na ompat*.

raja ihutan Leader of a village and its daughter villages. Toba Batak.

raja pamusuk Ruler's title in the southern Batak lands. Made by the Dutch into leaders of larger administrative units.

raja parbaringin A *raja* who performed important functions as a sacrificial priest at the religious festivals of the Toba Batak; he was appointed by the *Si Singamangaraja*.

raja urung Ruler of an *urung*, also called *sibayak*.

raleng tendi Karo ritual for calling back the *tendi*.

ripe Nuclear family among the Toba Batak.

rumah adat (Bahasa Indonesia) Traditional house for several families found among all the Batak peoples. Built on posts with a high saddleback roof.

rumbi Storage container for rice, carved from a single tree trunk. Toba Batak.

sada nini Karo Batak family group comprising those descended from a common grandfather.

sangkep si telu The kinship system based on three kinship groups, *senina*, *kalimbubu* and *anakberu*, which are dependent on each other. Karo Batak.

saompu Family with the descendants of a common ancestor who lived three or four generations earlier; with the *ripe* the most most important social unit among the Toba Batak.

sarang timah Apotropaic object made from the shoulder blade of ribs of a cow or buffalo and inscribed with spells to ward off evil.

si gale-gale Jointed doll used at the funeral of a dead man as a substitute for non-existent male descendants. Toba Batak.

sibaso A healer, usually female, who functions as a medium for the spirits of ancestors. Called *guru sibaso* by the Karo Batak.

sibayak Title of a "ruler" among the Karo, also called *raja urung*.

simbora Apotropaic object of lead made in human form, also called *porsimboraan*. Toba Batak.

singa Mythological animal with apotropaic function which has a central place in Toba Batak art.

sirih Leaf of the "betel pepper" in which lime, pieces of betel nut and *gambir* are wrapped, to be chewed for pleasure.

sombaon Highest level in the world of the dead. In a reburial festival lasting several months the ancestors are raised from the status of a *sumangot* to that of a *sombaon*. Toba Batak.

sopo Rice granary on six massive supports with discs at the top to keep rodents out. Toba Batak. (Among the Karo Batak: *sapo pagé*)

suasa Alloy of copper and gold used for making jewellery. Karo Batak.

suhut Group of the festival-givers, which also provides the speakers. Toba Batak.

sumangot The soul of the dead can be raised to the higher status of a *sumangot* by means of a ceremony. Toba Batak.

tabas Magic and conjuring spells used by a *guru*. Karo Batak.

tambak Tombs in forms ranging from heaps of stones to cement buildings. Older form of tomb than *tugu*. Toba Batak.

tarombo Complex genealogical family trees of the Toba Batak, going back to mythological origins.

tendi A person's life soul. It may leave the person for a time. At death the *tendi* is lost and the death soul (*tugu*) is set free. Karo Batak.

tondi Toba word for *tendi*.

tongkat malehat Magic wand with a single figure or group of figures at the upper end. Also written as *tungkat malékat* (Karo Batak).

tugu Modern tomb houses built of cement or concrete, and usually representing fantastic monuments. Toba Batak.

tunggal panaluan Magic wand with carvings of many people and animals. An important ritual instrument of a magician-priest.

turé-turé Bamboo platform in front of the two entrances to a Karo house. Used as a work area and meeting place.

turin-turian Oral literature consisting of myths and legends, and telling of cosmology, cosmogony and past events. Karo Batak.

uis Karo Batak word for traditional cotton cloths which are indispensible in ceremonial life.

ulos The term used for all the presents given by the parents of the bride to the young couple. A word meaning traditional cotton cloths. Toba Batak.

ulos ni tondi Traditional hip cloth for the soul. This cloth has to be particularly carefully chosen. It has special powers and accompanies a person throughout his life. Toba Batak.

upah tendi Gifts to the *tendi* to bind it to oneself (*upah* = reward, payment, gift). Karo Batak.